GLOBAL POLICY

Contributors

**EDWARD E. AZAR
ROLANDO E. BONACHEA
DONALD L. HAFNER
MORTON A. KAPLAN
TETSUYA KATAOKA
RICHARD L. RUBENSTEIN**

GLOBAL POLICY

CHALLENGE OF THE 80S

EDITED BY MORTON A. KAPLAN

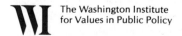

The Washington Institute
for Values in Public Policy

Printed in the United States of America

Library of Congress Catalogue Card Number: 83-050486

ISBN: 0-88702-001-1 (cloth)
0-88702-000-3 (paper)

cover design by Martin Hardy

CONTENTS

INTRODUCTION

In September 1981, the first annual meeting of the Professors World Peace Academy-USA was held in Washington, DC. The theme of the meeting was "US Foreign Policy Options in the 80s." Its purpose was to explore the world situation facing the incoming Reagan administration.

The organization has since subdivided. This project eventually came under a separate organization, the Washington Institute for Values in Public Policy. Various delays connected with these organizational problems postponed publication of the papers; they now represent less a prospectus for an incoming administration than a reflection on its first two years. Accordingly, the various chapters of the book have all been revised in the last half of 1982.

The first chapter is a global survey designed to provide a perspective for the other contributions. The second chapter on Reagan's European policy by Donald L. Hafner was not presented at the initial meeting. As the reader will see immediately, it is highly critical of the foreign policies of the Reagan administration, as are some of the other papers. Yet this criticism is conducted in the best scholarly tradition. The argument by Hafner that the most important source of disarray within NATO is "structural and therefore chronic . . . because the alliance is a coalition of unequals" is worthy of detailed attention. The lack of consistency in American policy and the erosion of American military capabilities, as he points out, are producing a major decline in American leadership. Economic difficulties exacerbate this. And since the Europeans can and do outbid us in trade with the Soviet Union, this is a source of constant friction.

The policy of detente was important to the Europeans, as Hafner notes, because it permitted them a degree of autonomy in policy. President Reagan's rhetoric, therefore, alarmed them. Moreover, President Reagan's emphasis on the Soviet Union as the cause of difficulty made him neglect European points of view. The concept of linkages and of spending the Soviet Union into defeat also gravely disturbed the Europeans. On the other hand, as Hafner points out, Reagan's actual policies were more prudent than his rhetoric.

The third chapter presents a plan for disarmament in Europe that, in my opinion, responds more pertinently to the threat of nuclear war than do the proposals for nuclear freezes or reductions. It also presents a controversial back-up plan for the period prior to adoption of an acceptable disarmament program.

Edward Azar argues that American policies in the Middle East are fragmented and that we never have had a cohesive policy for the area. Instead, bilateralism—often with respect to policies that were in conflict with one another—characterizes American diplomacy. Moreover, he says, its emphasis on military means diverts attention from those cultural, psychological, economic, and political factors that are even more important. In particular, he says, the United States seems more interested in military sales than in regional development.

Azar surveys American policy toward the Middle East in the postwar period and shows how the military emphasis usually has been a major source of the difficulties of American policy in that area. He then surveys the ethnic diversity of the Middle East as a source of conflict and the role of Moslem ideology. The factors he considers show how limited the role played by the Saudis is and how important economic development can be.

Tetsuya Kataoka's paper on Reagan's Far Eastern policy is interesting for a number of reasons. In the first place, even though he supports the American policy of a greater defensive effort by Japan, he expresses the resentment many Japanese feel toward what they see as American attempts to dictate policy in that area of the world. From my own experience in Japan, I would say this resentment is present under the surface in many Japanese minds and that it is felt more strongly by those who, in point of policy and sociological linkages, are the United States' best friends. Although he recognizes that the Soviet problem is a worldwide problem, he relates the concept of a worldwide directorate for the foreign policies of the free world to Aesop's fable about "Mice trying to put a bell on the cat's collar: it is a good idea, but there seems to be no means of getting it done." I don't even think that it is a good idea. An attempt to bring Japanese policy to bear on the Middle East or Europe, or European policy to bear on the Far East, during periods of crisis would place too great a strain on relationships and would weaken rather than strengthen the free world. Even when the United States was dominant, the Europeans were unhappy about our involvement in Korea. The Japanese would not understand involvement in European crises and perhaps not even in all Asian crises. Therefore, I agree with Kataoka, although not necessarily for the same reasons: there should be a basic division of responsibilities between the United States and its various allies, but with the qualification that the United States and Russia seem to be the only nations prepared to sustain a world role.

Finally, Kataoka concludes that the Reagan administration lacks knowledge about Asia. He is correct, but this is not unusual among American administrations. Kataoka is not too happy about the Reagan administration's downgrading of the Republic of China. He does approve of its policy toward Korea. And he does see possibly serious trouble brewing in the future for Japanese/American relations.

I contribute a short paper on the US policy toward the Republic of China, which I think is ill-advised at best. Since the position taken in this paper has been criticized as ideological by State Department bureaucrats, the reprinting of some of my comments on China published in *World Politics* in January 1965 may be useful:

At least Senator J. William Fulbright does not seem to subscribe to the emanations from some sources in Foggy Bottom that the United States and the Soviet Union will reach an accommodation that will enable them jointly to stem the aggressive designs of the Communist Chinese. Could any myth be better designed than this one to undermine American interests and values? Russia fronts on an area that is of urgent value to the United States. The skills, resources, and industry of Europe are such that the loss of the area to the Soviet Union would be a disaster. China does not front on any areas of reasonably comparable interest. Moreover, China diverts Russia from Europe. In addition, an alignment of the United States, Western Europe, and the Soviet Union against China would produce a racial confrontation that might undermine the values that characterize our institutions. Even though this notion is still not official policy, it is nonetheless deeply disturbing to hear talk of a U.S.-Russian alignment against China.

Even where Senator Fulbright speaks sensibly of the possiblity that the United States and China might eventually cooperate on some issues, he builds into this position the myth that the problems between the two nations stem from China's "implacable hostility toward the United States." Undoubtedly the Kremlin would like us to believe this, but why should we play into its hand? And where is the evidence for this hostility? Korea? We threatened legitimate Chinese national interests when we marched to the Yalu. Our disclaimers that China should not have regarded this as a threat would have been worthless even had our action in marching to the Yalu not repudiated earlier statements by the Secretary of State that our only objective in Korea was to restore the *status quo ante*. There was no excuse for this action on our part unless we intended to have a showdown with one or both of the Communist powers. Taiwan? Undoubtedly we have a moral commitment to the inhabitants of Taiwan not to surrender them to Communist tyranny. But since we cannot expect the Communists to admit that their regime is immoral, our position is weak on the basis of the more traditional criteria. India? The border region is ill-defined. Even where the Indians have a treaty claim, they undermined it themselves by the rationale of their attack on Goa. The Indians consistently refused peaceful negotiations. They engaged in deep military probes and were preparing an attack when the Chinese beat them to it. The Senator is right that we have nothing to gain now from recognition and much to lose, but why cloak this conclusion in false moralisms? It only confuses the real issue of international politics—namely, that specific interests may be incompatible. And it reinforces the myth that our problems stem from misunderstandings. They may instead stem from proper understanding.

The paper by Rolando Bonachea on "The United States and Central America: Policy Options in the 80s" grew out of the Central American Task Force of the Washington Institute that was ably led by Marcelo Alonso. I occasionally sat in on the deliberations of this task force. In general, there was agreement on the totalitarian intentions of the Nicaraguan government and of the guerrillas in El Salvador. However, there was wide and occasionally acrimonious debate on what United States policy toward the region should be. The reader will quickly see where Bonachea and I disagree with respect to policy over Cuba and Central America. It is true that one of Bonachea's reasons for taking his position relates to the disjunction between American rhetoric and a disinclination to act. Other members of the task force would disagree with both of us with respect to Nicaragua and El Salvador. Although no one in the task force supports Major d'Aubisson, several would be prepared to support the present El Salvador government without major conditions. I must admit that the success of the right-wing and centrist forces in El Salvador in an election that was advocated by the American government does place us under some moral pressure to do so. However, both Bonachea and I believe that American support must be conditional whereas other members of the task force are prepared to support what they regard as the lesser evil and to hope for the best.

The final paper by Richard L. Rubenstein, the president of the Washington Institute and a theologian by training, is on the relationship between religion and public policy. "The powerless," he says, "are always more likely to emphasize individual ethical values than those with power, because their lives are essentially private, whereas those with decision-making power must act in the public realm and must endure the risk and responsibilities of their station. Perhaps the problem of religion and politics in contemporary America can best be summed up by the fact that the majority of Americans have little understanding of the difference between the risks and responsibilities of the public and private realms."

I hope that nothing in the present volume is interpreted as displaying a special animus against the Reagan administration. I for one have been even more critical of previous administrations. And despite my distrust of former Secretary of State Haig, I have enormous respect for my former colleagues, Secretary of State George Shultz and Deputy Secretary of State Kenneth W. Dam. I wish them well.

But the best scholarship is always critical and disinterested. Those who hear only praise are being damned.

MORTON A. KAPLAN

GLOBAL POLICY: THE CHALLENGE OF THE 1980s

By

MORTON A. KAPLAN

THE GLOBAL NATURE OF POLICY

Despite the remarkable achievements of the first Truman administration—the Marshall plan and NATO in particular—American foreign policy has not been illuminated by considerations of grand strategy or by coherent global considerations. Former President Nixon and Secretary of State Kissinger are often given credit for a grand conception of strategy. Although they did articulate at a high level of abstraction the concepts of a five-power multipolarity and of linkage, these appear to be rationalizations rather than explanations of policy.

Morton A. Kaplan is Professor of Political Science and Director of the Center for Strategic and Foreign Policy Studies at the University of Chicago.

It would require considerable intellectual straining to argue that their policies were guided in any articulated fashion by such considerations.

It is much more likely that the Nixon/Kissinger policies consisted on the whole of a series of fixes that were not closely related to durable policies that supported American interests and values. Even the overdue opening to China was only superficially—rather than intimately—linked to a conception of grand strategy. It came at a time and on an occasion that was mostly of China's choosing. Although Kissinger and Nixon often talked of the importance of US reliability, they appeared to give as little thought to it when undermining the legal position of the Republic of China as did the Carter administration. Even the impact of the Shanghai communiqué upon the Vietnam negotiations was to a considerable extent the fortuitous consequence of events external to administration design; and the administration's awkward subsequent diplomacy sacrificed substance for appearance. The concluding phases of the Yom Kippur War and post-war diplomatic negotiations were conducted with more concern for the appearance of reducing the Soviet presence in the Middle East—an ephemeral victory at best that in any event was largely the product of specific Egyptian motives, including the perceived failure of the Soviet development model and Sadat's hope for massive capital access—than for bringing about a durable peace that would have served American long-term interests. In Southern Africa, administration policy changed from an untenable support for a repressive colonial regime in Rhodesia to a propagandistic and irresponsible majoritarian posture for the entire area, including the Republic of South Africa. The American strategic position was negotiated away —and in virtual disregard of the preceding Helsinki negotiations—at the Moscow summit that concluded the SALT I negotiations. The widely-held belief that these policies, and others too numerous to mention, were related to serious conceptions of global strategy attests more to administration public relations skills, press gullibility, and the low level of sophistication regarding international affairs that is endemic in the United States, than it does to serious intellectual analysis.

It would be futile, if not preposterous, to claim that a relatively short essay can present a reasonable global posture in which the relatedness of the elements to guiding global policy can be articulated, spelled out, and defended. At best, I can hope to mention some of the elements of such a posture and some of the more important reasons for them, to throw into sharper focus some of the perceived defects of past and present policy, and to point to a better framework for future policy.

STRATEGY MUST BE GLOBAL

The first point I want to make is obvious; but it is often overlooked in the formulation of policy, if not in speeches about policy. Strategy today needs to be global strategy. An arms control agreement in Europe affects the Soviet/Chinese axis because, among other things, it affects the potential distribution of military forces on that border and also the general political framework within which national and bloc policies are formulated. Obviously the different effects operate with different vectors. A suggested troop drawdown by the United States in South Korea spreads shockwaves both in Japan and Southeast Asia. American incompetence or powerlessness in Iran raises significant political and military questions in Israel, South Africa, and Saudi Arabia. The list is interminable; there is no point in proliferating it.

GLOBALISM OR REGIONALISM

Many argue—and the position has received prominence in the academic world—that regionalism is an appropriate, and even preferable, alternative to globalism: that policies must be adjusted to the individual circumstances of specific regions. That such a debate occurs at all attests to the lack of intellectual sophistication in the area of international theory. Of course, a policy that is not adjusted to regional circumstances may, and likely will, be counterproductive. Instances will be provided later in this essay. However, a policy that is adjusted to regional circumstances without consideration of, and careful attention to, the impact of that policy on other regions and on the general framework of global policy is at best unwise and at worst potentially catastrophic.

This so-called debate between globalism and regionalism treats the intimately linked aspects of the real world as exclusive alternatives. Which perspectives should be given preeminence in a particular case depends upon the case.

In strictly regional terms, the American base on Diego Garcia in the Indian Ocean was undesirable because of the intense antipathy of India and of some Middle Eastern states to an American naval presence and because of their fear that it would bring a cold war naval race into the region. Its importance in American global strategy, however, made it necessary despite the then contemporary senatorial opposition. Lack of a naval base somewhere in the area could have been compensated for only by a factor-sized, and practically infeasible, increase in naval expenditures; and the political costs of the base, despite regional opposition, were slight.

On the other hand, certain basing requests by the American military in the Middle East, although equally important from a military standpoint, may be counterproductive in regional terms. Whereas the naval base at Diego Garcia, approximately 1,300 miles south of the tip of India, had only marginal impact on Indian politics, bases in the Middle East which will be on actual national territory seriously risk producing unfavorable regime or international policy changes. Whether the more recent policy of securing facilities rather than bases entirely avoids or merely de-emphasizes these risks remains to be seen. Whether or not one agrees with these particular examples, it is important to recognize that individual issues must be examined in their concrete circumstances rather than argued according to rigid assumptions.

Declaratory Aspects of Policy

The implementation of foreign policy in the contemporary world requires support both at home and abroad—and, therefore, relevant declaratory statements—in ways that were not relevant during the heyday of the "balance of power" system. On the whole, it is more important to maintain support over time than to squeeze the last ounce of advantage out of particular policies, whether in terms of instrumental advantage or momentary increases in popular support.

The domestic public is not sophisticated; and other governments tend to see things from parochial perspectives. Therefore, it is important that most policies have some perceived consistency, at least in the large; that they be understandable; and that they be seen as relatively resistant to external pressures.

Few expect the Soviet Union to keep its troops out of action in Poland if Poland in the near future permits real opposition parties that might gain power. Therefore, neither the Poles themselves nor their non-Communist friends abroad try to push them in this direction. This is not to say that secular changes cannot occur; and if the Poles are wise in manipulating this process—or if the Soviet Union correctly estimates the true costs of intervention—the Soviet Union eventually may consider seriously alternative foreign policy postures. However, the limits of contemporary pressure are understood by the actors in that situation. This is not true of American policy, which often bends excessively to the last perceived important pressure and which usually is sold to the public on the basis of immediate benefits rather than on the basis of guiding criteria.

There are declaratory positions that are very important both for maintaining support for American policy and for insulating it from external pressure. No one in his right mind wants to risk war without testing reasonable alternatives. One of the most important declaratory tenets of American policy should be the willingness to accommodate the legitimate interests of all other states in the system.

It is important that the Soviets and the Chinese both perceive that they can reach reasonable agreements with the United States that are consonant with their great power status and the rights and interests of less powerful states. It is important that our allies in Western Europe and Japan perceive that our policies are designed to permit such agreements and, thus, to reduce the potential for conflict.

It is also important that the United States be seen to insist upon maintaining a degree of military strength that will permit it to support its allies against attack, threats of attack, and undue political pressure. And that it have the will to use that strength for those purposes. It is important that the United States be seen not merely as implementing particular policies—even those specifically advantageous for other states—but to be working toward an international order that optimizes the independent abilities of individual states to seek their own objectives. It is better to have stable and occasionally cantankerous friends than mere clients. It is important within this framework that the United States be seen as having a real interest in the protection of human rights and in their further progress over time. It is also important that American diplomacy be seen as problem-solving rather than as gamesmanlike.

Let other nations make debaters' points or try to make us look bad. That is the politics of the ephemeral. We should be seen by others as durably pursuing durable solutions to problems that confront us and other nations. Furthermore, we should minimize playing to the gallery. With all due respect for the domestic political problems that constantly confront political leaders, the attempt, for instance, to induce our allies into unenforceable sanctions against Iran lacked seriousness. There were other forms of symbolic support that we could and did get, such as the condemnation of Iran's seizure of the hostages in the United Nations and in the World Court.

As frustrating as it may have been for the public to understand that the proposed sanctions were unenforceable, the willingness of the government to lose some immediate public support by clarifying the unrealistic character of the proposed sanctions not only would have made for stronger policy on other issues, but over time even on the subject at issue. It would have increased the respect of America's allies for American statecraft and their willingness to cooperate with our policies on a wide range of issues. It also would have avoided some of the excesses of frustration public misunderstanding engenders.

The public may not be sophisticated, but national leaders should not undermine the public's ability to understand even the simpler aspects of the complicated problems of international politics. That only increases public pressures for unworkable policies that are con trary to American values and interests and that undermine long-term public support for workable policies.

EAST-WEST RELATIONS

East/West differences are certainly important, and should not be minimized in US declaratory policy. It should not be denied that on occasion specific confrontations may be desirable or even necessary. However, a general stress on confrontation is likely to be both coun-terproductive and diversionary. It, and not simply neutralist sentiment, probably accounts to some extent—although obviously not entirely —for some of the disturbing reactions in Western Europe to current US policy. Moreover, confrontation encourages reactionary forces abroad to oppose those reforms that clearly are in the American interest in the belief that the United States will be forced to support these reactionary forces merely because they are anti-Communist.

The Soviet geopolitical position in Eurasia does confront the United States with enormous difficulties and tasks. However, the general American emphasis should be on the constructive tasks of its statecraft: maintaining NATO and the treaties with Japan and Korea; working out common energy policies; moving forward on trade agreements; concerting realistic development policies; and so forth. The empha-sis should be on what we are accomplishing and not on what we are opposing. The latter emphasis diverts attention from the tasks that are of overriding importance.

The East/West conflict should be the iron fist inside the velvet glove of diplomacy. The declaratory stress—and the actual thrust—of American policy should be on the common interests we share with the Soviet Union. These are real. It should be clear that our basic objective is to create a world order within which the Soviet Union will find its own best interests served by reducing its military presence in Eastern Europe, by permitting more political freedom in those areas, and by coming to an accommodation with Communist China.

To view relations with the Soviet Union primarily from a confrontational standpoint pushes the United States toward temporary policy fixes that do not serve long-term American interests. Moreover, it assumes that aggression and expansionism necessarily are constant objectives of Soviet policy rather than objectives that can change over time, and that current Soviet policies are designed to accommodate such permanent expansionism. These are doubtful assumptions at the present time. They underestimate the American and free world potential to restructure Soviet alternatives. Furthermore, they oversimplify the ways in which the men in the Kremlin make their policy choices.

Just as the weak accommodationist policy of the Carter administration reduced the costs of Soviet expansionism, and increased its attractiveness, so emphasizing East/West conflicts reduces Soviet incentives to seek accommodation with the United States and diverts the United States from those policies that best serve its interests. The contest between the United States and the Soviet Union is a subtle and sophisticated contest of systems that cannot be placed within the simple-minded context of the raisers of alarm or of the heralds of detente. If we reduce the contest to its simplest level, we may have to solve it in those terms; and this may do enormous damage to our own institutions and to our hopes for the world.

However, it may be desirable on occasion to defeat specific Soviet objectives. For instance, we initially should have given much greater support to the Afghani insurgents. The Soviet Union did not hesitate to fight us by proxy in Vietnam. These policies, however, should be factual and without declaratory overemphasis. But then it is the small dog that barks a lot, as did the Carter administration, and as did the Reagan administration after it shot down Libyan planes in self-defense in the Gulf of Sidra. America should have emphasized the necessity to maintain its legal rights against desuetude in the Gulf and the regretful aspect of the necessary destruction of the Libyan planes.

During 1982 President Reagan somewhat de-emphasized his rhetorical conflict with the Soviet Union. However, he has not been consistent in this respect. For instance, during his address to the British Parliament in 1982 he spoke of defeating the Soviet system. This is excessive. The restrained rhetoric of his message to the new Secretary General of the Communist Party of the Soviet Union, Yuri Andropov, upon his accession to office after the death of Leonid Brezhnev in 1983, is preferable.

LINKAGE

The Reagan administration has told the Soviet Union that Afghanistan and Cambodia are tests for US-Soviet relations: that these relations will not improve unless the Soviet Union makes substantial concessions on these issues. The problem here is not that international policies are not, or should not be, linked in the real world. Of course, they are; and, on occasion, they should be linked in American policy. The problem lies in the rigidity and declaratory aspects of the policy.

Regarding the last aspect, the Russians are very nationalistic and, thus, are less likely to make concessions if issues are publicly linked. Their feelings of national pride will get in the way. Secondly, they will feel they have manifested weakness if they respond to public demands for linkage rather than to negotiations on a specific issue. And they will fear that this would reduce their influence on other issues of importance to them. Moreover, in the case of Poland, no one doubts that linkage exists and that US/USSR relations would go into a deep freeze if an invasion occurred. Thus, overt linkage is unnecessary as well as counterproductive in this case. Alternatively, we may fail to reach useful agreements in other particular cases if we are afraid of breaching our public posture on linkage.

From the American standpoint, declaratory policy on linkage is too rigid. The specific public linking of policies may be overridden by more important considerations. In this case, an agreement that makes sense in its own terms, and in relation to overall policy considerations, may appear to constitute an American retreat, with obvious consequences.

There is no harm in a declaratory policy that makes clear a relationship between American and Soviet policies in general. This is likely to be useful. But specific linkages in the usual case should be made in non-public negotiation and, even then, not in a way that is too offensive to Soviet pride; or they may well be counterproductive.

The more general concept of linkage, as earlier proposed by Kissinger, was to tie the Soviet Union into a framework of linkages with the West that would impel it to engage in more cooperative world policies. Like other general statements, this one might be correct for certain world conditions. But Kissinger's specific implementation was more likely to increase the Soviet Union's technological capabilities and, thus, its ability to take risks than it was to inhibit aggressive Soviet behavior.

In any event, the Reagan policy of linkage has been a mistake. The counterproductive ban on components for the gas pipeline from the Soviet Union to Western Europe, for instance, which subsequently was retracted, was preceded by President Reagan's attempt to sell even more grain to the Soviet Union with the weak excuse that the Soviets would pay hard currency for the grain. The fact is that the Soviet Union buys grain from us because it can do so more cheaply than it can produce it; and the released funds can be put into military areas.

THE GLOBAL BALANCE: EUROPE

Even granted that the mercator mode of projection employed in the map below makes the Soviet Union look larger than it is on a globe, it can be seen clearly that the problem posed to the West by the Soviet Union stems at least as much from its geopolitical position as it does from assumed aggressive intentions or inherent expansionism, even if the latter were present in the simple-minded sense often proposed. An outline of the state of Pennsylvania in scale virtually covers the distance between Paris and the frontier with East Germany. In an age of modern weapons and technology, that is not meaningful defensive space.

Those of us who grew up with earlier textbooks in which the kings of Europe marched back and forth across what seemed to be a great continent must face up to the fact that today Western Europe geopolitically is a skin and not a surface. In an age of fast armored tanks and modern jet aircraft, a blitzkrieg might advance that far in a few days.

The Russian acquisition of territory from Finland and Poland after World War II responded in part to how space saved Russia

Map of Eurasia

With scale map of Pennsylvania superimposed between East German border and Paris

against both Napoleon and Hitler. The present Russian predomi-
nance in Eastern Europe is related at least in part to a Russian-felt
need for space for protection. How helpless Western Europe must
feel! A cat chained next to an elephant would necessarily feel insecure even if the elephant were the most peaceful creature one could
imagine. The vulnerability of Western Europe with its skilled
population, its great industrial strength, and its massive urban areas
provides the Soviet Union with enormous political leverage that could
change the entire global balance. Indeed, it would take enormous
self-restraint on the part of the Soviet Union not to take advantage of

that leverage. And, even in the absence of Russian threats, vulnerability in West Europe may produce moves toward accommodation out of fear, an intolerable situation.

No reasonable person can doubt that the geopolitical situation of Eurasia creates a great threat to Western European and to American interests, almost regardless of Soviet intentions. In the absence of NATO, Western Europeans might "Finlandize" themselves. Even with it, fear may lead to counterproductive rationalizations in European policy. Although the hearty citizens of Finland may bridle at the talk of Finlandization and insist upon their independence, not only do they take great care not to offend the Soviet Union even in their choice of president, but they maintain their present degree of independence to some extent only because of NATO and a protective Sweden.

Moreover, if I have objected to overly simple-minded statements of Soviet aggressiveness, it is noteworthy that Cuba is not Finlandizing itself vis-à-vis the United States. Despite the best efforts of some intellectuals to argue that both the United States and the Soviet Union are interventionary states, this suggests that there are some important differences. One could hardly imagine that Finland would ship arms to anti-Soviet rebels or that its government would send out emissaries to meet with the leaders of Solidarity. But Cuba is shipping arms to El Salvador, training guerrilla officers, and even assisting a guerrilla campaign against Mexico.

While some conservatives oversimplify the issue of Soviet aggressiveness, some liberals fail to comprehend that the Soviet leadership style bears somewhat the same relationship to the American leadership style that the styles of the Rockefellers, Carnegies, and the Morgans of the nineteenth century do to the current leadership styles of the Chrysler Corporation and US Steel. They are cruder, more brutal, and in many ways more effective.

THE SOVIET PROBLEM

The European security problem might be easier to solve if the

Soviet side of the coin were not as difficult as it is in certain respects. The Russians are becoming a minority in the Soviet Union. Their population is aging. Despite the assertions of former Ambassador Thomas Watson that the Soviet Union will enter an arms race with the United States if SALT II is rejected, in the absence of an American posture that arouses Soviet patriotism, as does the current US posture, the Soviet leadership has probably pushed its working population as hard as it can without counterproductive results. Life expectancy has been declining sharply. Drunkenness and industrial sabotage are rife; and belief in the ideological system, except as a route to power and comparative advantage for the party and the managerial and technological elites, has reached its nadir. Except in Bulgaria and East Germany, what transpired in Poland likely foreshadows potential developments elsewhere in Eastern Europe sometime in the next generation.

The Soviet system is an enormously powerful military state—in which the military leadership and the political leadership, and much of the population, take great pride—sitting on top of a decaying economic system and a rotting political empire. The present Soviet leadership could not survive—and not merely in terms of political position—a major system transformation. The Soviet system is prone to continued crises.

One of the great dangers of these latter Soviet weaknesses lies in the fact that, under some conditions, particularly if the West is weak, a forced Finlandization of Western Europe for purposes of economic exploitation might seem the best way out to the Soviet leadership. Even those Europeans who might be willing to accept the risk of a poor defense posture because of the option of surrender in extremity, should consider that World War III might arise from a Soviet miscalculation in attempting to Finlandize Western Europe. Even those who then wish to surrender may find that they do not control events. The best and safest course for Europe is to create a defense force that raises the costs of a Soviet attack sufficiently to deter the Soviet Union from gambling upon the efficacy of political blackmail. Otherwise, miscalculation may produce war.

NATO strength and assurance enhance those voices in the Soviet Union that argue for constructive internal change in preference to external adventure. The danger is not that such a threat is now predictable, but that it is a genuine and not merely a phantasmagoric possibility. If it arises, it will then be too late to prepare for it. And the means for avoiding it enhance present security at a reasonable price.

The only reasonable alternative lies in some proposal for separating the NATO and Warsaw Treaty forces in Western Europe. However, this is a long-term solution that does nothing to solve the present military problem, although it may do something to convince public opinion that NATO policy is a peace policy.

CURRENT CIRCUMSTANCES AND EASTERN EUROPE

It hardly needs stating that the United States looks forward to the day when the nations of Eastern Europe are independent and democratic. Certainly, it was not possible for the United States to remain indifferent to, or silent about, the Polish crisis. And we certainly hope that sometime in the future current Polish developments will lead to the emergence of a free and democratic Poland. On the other hand, as long as military bipolarity is an essential characteristic of the contemporary world, the United States would be ill-advised to pursue measures that are directed at removing Poland from the Warsaw pact or that would increase the anti-Russian feelings of the Polish people.

It is an unhappy and dangerous fact that Russian policy is creating deep enmity in Poland toward the Soviet Union. That Russian policy has its roots in history, and particularly in that of the period since the end of World War II; in the crude Russian conceptions of *machtpolitik*; and in the dilemmas posed to the current Russian leadership by unpalatable alternatives.

The institution of a military dictatorship under General Jaruzelski that occurred after the original presentation of this paper has enormously complicated matters. The precedent of a military dictatorship must be uncomfortable for the Soviet Union, even though it could hardly have occurred in the absence of great pressure from that nation. Only the absence of any alternative except the use of Soviet troops permitted this move. And it is not a simple disaster from a Western point of view. An eventual "Bonapartist" regime in the Soviet Union may be one way out of the current mess. However, the United States can in no way condone the actions of this dictatorship without betraying the Polish people and its own values.

When General Jaruzelski set up his military dictatorship, the United States should have made it clear that the price of Western economic support for Poland—in the absence of which the Polish economy would collapse and that of the Soviet Union would be threatened —was the release of political prisoners, the elimination of apparatchiks, who were the main reason for the decline of the Polish economy both before and during the Solidarity reforms, the restoration of at least a non-revolutionary Solidarity, and a rational economic system.

Unfortunately, the United States, under the then Secretary of State Alexander Haig, indulged in talk while doing very little of substance. There was not even the threat of a grain embargo against the Soviet Union. Furthermore, the banks have been making new unpayable loans to Poland so that they can continue to receive the interest payments on the old unpayable loans. The enormous interest of both German and American bankers in current balance sheets regardless of the consequences for Poland, Western Europe, or the United States, or even the long run health of the banks, is a strong argument for nationalizing major banks or allowing some of them to fail. It gives ample testimony to Lenin's maxim that the capitalists will sell the Communists the ropes with which the former will be hung.

General Jaruzelski of late has been making a career of protesting the modest restrictions of the United States, including the removal of the most favored nation clause, while maintaining that, as a Polish patriot, he is forestalling Russian intervention. This argument is bogus. And it is strange that he denounces the United States, which wants a free Poland, while taking every effort to appear arm-in-arm with the Soviet leaders who threaten armed intervention.

It may be that the general had to install a military dictatorship in order to prevent the collapse of the Communist Party in Poland. This alone might have brought an extremely reluctant military intervention from a Soviet Union bogged down in Afghanistan and under very heavy economic burdens. However, the measures Jaruzelski took internally have far exceeded what was needed to forestall direct Soviet military intervention. Moreover, his contemporary claims to be moving toward more liberal forms of governance may be every bit as deceptive as many of his earlier claims prior to the imposition of martial law.

Therefore, the United States should impose strong sanctions against Poland until General Jaruzelski shows good faith in coming to terms with Polish opinion. His success in undermining Solidarity, which is at least partly a result of the weakness of American policies, does not mean that the United States is without any bargaining strength. Moreover, it has an interest in the state of affairs in Poland that goes back to the Yalta Pact. A solemn agreement was reached at Yalta that specified the existence of plural political organization in Poland within the framework of a Poland in which the Communist Party would play a leading role while Poland, at least within the contemporary organization of world politics, remained within the Russian military sphere. That agreement has been violated repeatedly both by Russia and by successive Polish governments. The United States has both a political and a moral right to bring pressure to bear in these circumstances. That pressure can be applied only by greater intensification of the crisis in Poland.

When the situation deteriorates sufficiently in Poland, the United States can then return to a moderate position. Although no guarantees can be given that any policy will work, the United States will hold a number of important cards. The Soviets cannot easily afford an occupation of Poland and that may be their only option unless the West comes to Poland's economic assistance. Indeed, at that time the failure to be in a position to act accordingly may assist the Russians in getting rid of Jaruzelski, whose behavior will have cost him the support of the Polish people. He will be able to regain a modicum of support only in a deal with the US.

On the other hand, if Jaruzelski accepts such a bargain, he should have Western support for austerity measures and a lengthened work week. Only such support, in addition to internal reform, can permit a restoration of the Polish economy. Even with such support, the process would be long and hard. Precisely because we will not threaten Poland's membership in the Warsaw Treaty Organization and will have supported a modest brake on political change in Poland, the Soviet Union could intervene only at a cost even they are likely to regard as excessive.

JAPAN

The Far East exemplifies the global nature of world politics. The United States cannot choose between Europe and the Far East. Because of its economic strength, if Japan is lost to the communist world, the chances of holding Europe as a barrier to communist world control would be minimal. And vice versa.

Japan is essential to the defense of the free world. However, it is counterproductive for Americans to propose a NATO/Japan/China alliance or even a NATO/Japan alliance. This would be too provocative toward the Soviet Union and would raise unnecessary and counterproductive opposition in Japan. Of course, if a Japanese government wants to commit Japan to a more positive alliance posture with the United States, that would be desirable if it is not tied to NATO and particularly to China. What is really essential, however, is to improve the defensibility of Japan. American bases in Japan and the Japanese economy, however, should be available for the defense of Korea. The present Japanese ambivalence on this issue is inexcusable.

There are many statements to the effect that even the lowly one percent of the Japanese GNP that is devoted to military expenditures makes Japan one of the strongest military powers in the world. However, the harsh facts are that the current Japanese Self-Defense

Forces cannot defend Japan even for the postulated one week that (theoretically and counterfactually) would permit American intervention. And even this weak capability depends upon the Soviet Union's being kind enough to attack where the Japanese have chosen to defend in Hokkaido.

The Japanese Self-Defense Forces are inadequate to their tasks and will remain so even if the current plan for the build-up is continued to term. Furthermore, the weaponry that we are attempting to get the Japanese to buy and the missions we are trying to encourage them to perform are misguided. Japan is an exceptionally elongated island chain. Its coastline is immense. And the most crucial phase of any amphibious attack is the first twenty-four hours.

What the Japanese require, in addition to the current defense forces, is a large and trained citizen militia with quick access to dumps of anti-tank and anti-air weapons that are placed along the periphery of the island chain. Japanese armored vehicles must be very light so that they can be quickly transported by a large number of modestly-sized transport planes. There must be a large number of them and they must be emplaced near transport. Japan's naval mission must not be to defend the sea lanes in Southeast Asia—where Japanese naval forces would be politically counterproductive—but to penalize amphibious invasion forces. In this respect, very large numbers of relatively small hunter and killer surface and subsurface craft are required.

If the Japanese were to overcome their nuclear antipathy—and this should be a purely Japanese decision—then the neutron bomb would be an exceptionally useful defensive weapon that would serve no possible offensive purposes for Japan. If the Japanese do not wish to go this far, then perhaps the United States should consider maintaining stockpiles of neutron bombs offshore that quickly could be transferred to the Japanese upon their request at the onset of an attack, or threat of attack, upon Japan.

Certainly the United States should not attempt to influence a nuclear debate in Japan, for this would be counterproductive. But that does not mean we cannot think about what is required. Moreover, those who argue that any Japanese use of nuclear weapons, even if restricted to neutron bombs in Japanese territory, would lead to Soviet counteruse should consider that successful conventional defense might produce the same result. If the Soviet Union were that determined to commit successful aggression, then it might do anything. The Soviet Union in fact only wants to frighten Japan; and it may succeed in doing so unless the Japanese develop a credible military posture. If they do so, the Soviet Union will accommodate to this fact and will have more respect for Japan.

In any event, as in the case of Europe, the primary object of the suggested measures is to affect Soviet decision-making before a decision to attack or to threaten attack. Good defensive strength is related to resolution and political strength. Deterrence is not likely to be high unless there is an effective war-fighting capability. It is very unlikely that the Soviets would launch an offensive that would be costly. And if an offensive move by the Soviets is unlikely, then the Soviet threat position and the Soviet ability to undermine Japanese resolution are also effectively reduced.

The threat of war, whether explicit or implicit, is the most likely Soviet tactic for attempting to force political and economic change. By diminishing the credibility of Soviet threat tactics both in the Far East and Europe, one enhances deterrence in major ways. A refusal to have strong defense enhances the alternatives of surrender or war. And, during a crisis, which is enhanced by weakness, the choice from among these alternatives may escape rational control.

KOREA

The neutron bomb would be even more useful in Korea than in Europe because of the narrowness of the attack channels at the DMZ. Moreover, any significant increase in the credibility of the defense of South Korea is likely to have favorable political consequences inside South Korea. Although it is very difficult to prove the case, one cannot help noting that President Park began his repressive measures after Secretary of Defense Laird started talking about a Korean troop drawdown and that matters got much worse after President Carter enunciated a similar policy. In any event, for a divided nation that faces a heavily-armed and manic enemy to the North and whose number one goal is rapid economic development that permits both effective defense and a citizen body that is not restive, the political situation inside South Korea, although far short of perfection, does create the conditions for substantial future improvements in both political and economic terms.

The best medicine would be the creation of a stable detente in the entire Far East and between North and South Korea. However, although it is desirable to work towards this, the immediate prospects seem very slim, particularly given the current posture of North Korea. The United States should not negotiate with North Korea over the head of its ally. That could prove destabilizing in the specific area and, by further tarnishing the image of American reliability, would be counterproductive in all of Asia.

China

The Chinese issue has been consistently misunderstood in the United States. It was certainly desirable to have an American embassy in Peking. However, despite Russian fears, this would not affect in any major way American global military strategy vis-à-vis the Soviet Union. The very existence of a China bordering on the Soviet Union and fearing Soviet encroachment—while the Soviet Union has vague and irrational but real fears of a "yellow menace"—serves to complicate Soviet ventures or threats directed against Western Europe or Japan. The United States does not need, and China cannot offer, more than this.

As long as China continues to view Russia as the greater enemy and the more immediate threat, there is no likelihood that the prior judgment will be invalidated unless the United States becomes so weak that China is left with no choice but to accommodate to Soviet pressure. On the contrary, if there were any likelihood of China's moving closer to the Soviet Union, it would have been enhanced by the normalization of US/China relations. China no longer needs to withhold moving toward a middle position in order to achieve normalization. Perhaps, however, the Taiwan Relations Act has been influential in inhibiting such a Chinese move. Since these words were originally written, the Peoples' Republic has made some tepid moves toward a middle position between the United States and the Soviet Union. It should not have come as a surprise, nor should it have been viewed with alarm as it was in certain circles. In any event, both domestic and international considerations move the Peoples' Republic in this direction; and no American policy will prevent it.

The argument, if there is an argument in China over relations with the Soviet Union, likely consists in the evaluation of the strength of the Soviet threat and of the gains to be obtained from the United States either in military or economic terms. Although it is not really arguable that the consequences of this Chinese evaluation process would make no difference under any circumstances in the effectiveness of the American strategic position, its potential significance is much exaggerated. Furthermore, American interests would be better served by some reduction in hostility between China and the Soviet Union. There is no need for even a quasi-alliance with China against the Soviet Union or such great frictions between those two nations that the probability of armed conflict is enhanced. Such a policy would be neither moral nor prudent.

Moreover, if the Soviet Union were ever to withdraw from Southeast Asia, it is highly likely that China's beneficent posture toward the ASEAN (Association of South East Asian Nations) powers would decline and that it would once again give substantial assistance to subversive groups. Although this prediction might be affected marginally by China's relations with the United States, I think that the degree of effect can easily be overstated.

In short the American posture towards China should be influenced more by the type of world system the United States is trying to produce than by considering China as a quasi-ally in a contest with the Soviet Union. Although either of the alternative positions taken to an extreme would overlook some matters of importance, nonetheless, as a first approximation, this view is the correct one.

The loss of the Iranian monitoring sites made it important from the security standpoint to establish new monitoring sites if possible. Although the availability of Chinese territory and Chinese willingness to permit site installation validated the potential risks of too great an appearance of Chinese/American partnership against the Soviet Union, it was not necessary to make a blatant public announcement of this fact, particularly while the former American Secretary of State was in China. To the already suspicious Russians, a public announcement emphasized the quasi-alliance characteristic of the arrangement over its instrumental security aspects.

Although it can be argued that the current American policy on arms sales and technology transfers to China is sufficiently cautious if the policy is analyzed in its concrete details, the announcement of the policy coincident with former Secretary of State Haig's visit to China and with concerted publicity on the monitoring sites seemed to place a different light upon the policy and to make it potentially destabilizing not merely with respect to the Far East but with respect to Eastern Europe as well. If it appears to diminish the prospects of agreements or accommodations between the Soviet Union and the United States, that might be weighed, although marginally at most, in the Soviet balance, if a Soviet decision to intervene in Poland comes into serious consideration.

THE MIDDLE EAST: ISRAEL

Regarding the Israeli/Arab dispute, it would be absurd to deny that severe injustices were done to Palestinian Arab lives and expectations when the state of Israel was created. On the other hand, it would be equally absurd to deny that the creation of Israel was a necessity. More than a millennium of anti-Semitism and the holocaust had produced a situation such that there was no acceptable alternative to a Jewish state in which the Jews of Europe could control their own destinies and provide a place of refuge to Jews, who might be subject to persecution. The Jewish historical connection, never entirely broken in fact, and live memories made Palestine the only acceptable site. Historical circumstances made it the only feasible site. Any discussion of this problem that centers attention on abstract principles does too much violence to concrete realities to be worthy of serious discussion.

Until the Yom Kippur War, and perhaps beyond it, the core of the problem lay in the refusal of the Arab states to accept the existence of Israel. There are distinct signs that this situation may be changing. However, one should not overstresss the present willingness of Arab states, important as that is, to seek moderate solutions. The Israelis would be quite right to point out how favorably disposed to Israel Iran was under the Shah and how sharply that changed under the Ayatollah Khomeini, the rise of Moslem fundamentalism elsewhere in the Arab world, and the intransigent character of the second-line military leaders in the PLO.

On the other hand, politics always operates at the margin. Present opportunities should not be missed, for they may not recur. As the technology of warfare advances, the present military occupation by Israel will have less and less value even in purely military terms. Moreover, although peace provides no guarantee that the Arabs will not unite against Israel in the future, it raises the threshhold which must be crossed for that unity to occur. A peace that adequately provides for Israeli security and that also meets the conditions for legitimacy will raise that threshhold high enough to make such a result unlikely. This is more important to Israel than the West Bank. And it alone provides a potential dignified solution for the Palestinian Arabs. Furthermore, current Israeli policy calls into serious question the democratic character, Jewish nature, and long-term security of Israel.

In view of the history of the case and of deep emotional feelings that united Arabs against Israelis no matter how much they may be disunited on other grounds, Israel cannot ignore potentially dangerous scenarios for a West Bank state. On the other hand, Israel will remain desperately insecure in the absence of peace; and there can be no peace in the area that does not meet at least some minimal standards for legitimacy. These include the right of the Palestinian Arabs to have a state of their own that encompasses the West Bank and negotiations toward that end with the recognized representatives of the Palestinian Arabs: the Palestinian Liberation Organization. Only such a process will relieve the other Arab states of their oft-resented and burdensome obligations to the Palestinian Arabs.

Since these words were originally written, the Israeli invasion of Lebanon has taken place. The Israeli military victory has solved some political problems and created others. The Palestinian forces in the south of Lebanon were hated by their neighbors for good reasons, constituted a threat to an eventual peace settlement, and included heavily-armed individuals, many of whom were controlled by foreign intelligence agencies and others of whom displayed brutal patterns of behavior that could not be accommodated within a peaceable community.

If this victory had been accompanied by a generous political opening to the Palestinians, it might well have been an act of genius. However, as part of an attempt to impose peace settlements on Israel's neighbors while turning the West Bank into sovereign Israeli territory, the policy is doomed to eventual failure. It will create a legacy of hatred that will lead to the overthrow of the Arab governments that permitted it and that will inspire further attacks upon the state of Israel when these states have at least semi-competent leaderships.

The failure to solve this problem creates pervasive insecurity for Israel and perpetual instability for the Middle East, even though this is not the only factor that does so. It is far more important from the standpoint of American diplomacy in the area to solve this problem even perhaps at the price of the neutralization of Israel and Palestine/Transjordan from bloc rivalries than it is to incorporate Israel into the American strategic posture. Continuation of the present impasse may throw the entire Middle East into turmoil and create a threat to NATO's viability.

The heavy stress on East/West conflict by the administration strengthens the forces of immoderation in this area and makes it much more difficult to produce the peace that is essential to American interests. Rather than minimizing the strength of the rejectionist component of the Palestinian front or the potentiality of the Soviet Union for creating trouble in the area, if it wishes to do so, American policy under several administrations consistently has maximized the potential for instability and disruption.

THE ARAB MIDDLE EAST

With respect to American policy in the rest of the Middle East, I should like to suggest that it is mistaken on both political and military grounds. The Saudis are not attempting to restrain the price of oil as a favor to the United States. Unlike the other Arab oil-producing states, Saudi reserves will last for at least the first quarter of the next century. The later the West is driven toward alternative sources of energy, the better it is for the Saudis.

The Saudis fear the Soviet Union for obvious dynastic reasons. They dislike the Palestinian Liberation Organization but provide financial support to it because they obviously fear the political consequences of doing otherwise. This is one possible indication that the Saudi regime has serious problems. Whether the Saudi regime —which is forced to import a continuous stream of both able technicians and managers to run its modernization program—is able to maintain itself through these changes is a question that requires serious analysis.

There is no need to make a country-by-country analysis. The United States is identifying itself too closely with regimes that may be transitory. It is seeking military bases, which may be useful if they can ever be employed, but that are politically counterproductive. The United States may be forced into more serious policy vacillations by its present policies than was the Soviet Union in the Somali/Ethiopian embroglio.

Unlike the Soviet Union, the United States cannot provide an ideology that legitimizes a one-party dictatorship and thus creates close regime ties. Its policy provides an insufficient prospect for supporting the development of that long-term stability, which, through enhancement of the national, and even nationalistic, interests of the states in the area, supports American interests best.

It is often said that politics is the art of the possible. It is a mistake, however, to confuse the temporary with the possible. The United States appears to be juggling temporary decisions. One of the advantages of being a superpower is to be able to afford the luxury of sustaining temporary policy costs in pursuit of important intermediate- and long-range objectives. There is no sign of this in American policy. We have tactics but no strategy. The military tail is important, but it must not be permitted to wag the political dog. And there is no sign that we have a coherent policy toward the region.

Africa

Contrary to what Andrew Young believed, it is not of overriding importance to earn the good will of the Organization of African Unity. Its member states will not play any significant role in the global situation, although their cooperation with respect to the transformation of southern Africa may be of marginal benefit. Nor is Nigeria likely to be able to use its oil to penalize the West if it dislikes American policies.

It is important that American policies be reasonable, perceived of as in the long-term American interest, congruent with American values, and not unsympathetic to black African interests, as distinguished from rhetoric. We have an interest in the African nations. But it is a general moral interest and also a specific interest that arises from the feelings of American black citizens.

The key issues in Africa are those of the southern part of the continent. This area is of immense importance to Europe and Japan because of its mineral wealth. It also has strategic importance. However, as Assistant Secretary of State for African Affairs Chester Crocker clearly recognizes, the United States can neither condone nor support the current situations in either Namibia or the Republic of South Africa without doing enormous damage to our values as a nation and, because of possible disunity at home, to our interests as well.

There are leaders of goodwill in that part of the world who are trying to solve their problems in ways that are consistent with the political rights and dignity of all the groups in the area. It is important that the United States show that it supports groups that propose responsible change. Sufficient pressure to change must also be applied to make it clear that our relations with the governments of the area must always be limited as long as present conditions persist.

Moreover, it is important to recognize that the great lever of change in southern Africa is economic development. In addition to providing an enormous incentive to change, economic development is necessary to prevent extreme hardship and even starvation among the rapidly growing black population of the Republic of South Africa.

In these respects, it is essential to reject the irresponsible advice of the World Council of Churches, which is seeking to prevent continued investment in South Africa. That is the worst advice that could be offered. Here, again, despite the best efforts of the assistant secretary, the Department of State's emphasis on East/West conflict strengthens the *Verkramt* group in South Africa by making it appear that for strategic reasons the United States has no option except to support South Africa.

Liberal forces in South Africa see Prime Minister Botha's plan for a three-tiered assembly as a plot to form a permanent coalition with the colored and Indians against the blacks. The conservative paper *Die Afrikaner* sees it as a plot to form a South African empire including Zimbabwe, Namibia, Mozambique, and Angola in each of which the whites would be a small and protected minority. Thus, they see the three-tiered assembly as a first step toward the destruction of the white community. My own belief is that Botha is trying to move in neither of these directions, although it is possible that the political processes may drive him to one of them. It will take the most constructive internal statesmanship and enormous help, as well as some pressure from without, to avoid terrible results that no decent person could support.

CENTRAL AMERICA

Central America recently has become a focus of American attention. Cubans and even East Germans are in Nicaragua, and the influx of foreign weaponry, including both heavy and sophisticated weaponry, is huge. The Soviet military shipments directly to Cuba exceed those of the missile-crisis days. Although some voices, including Mexico's, are arguing that the Sandinistas in Nicaragua really will permit pluralism and that the revolutionaries in El Salvador are also committed to a pluralistic solution, there seems to be a convincing mass of evidence to the contrary. The Sandinistas are committed Marxists/ Leninists and the official government newspaper has praised the imposition of military dictatorship in Poland and Soviet repression in Afghanistan.

There are important tactical reasons for the tentative moderation of the Sandinistas in Nicaragua, including the possibility of economic and political support from Western Europe and Mexico and forefending serious American countermoves. The bulk of the evidence would suggest that the current moderation of the Sandinistas is no more principled than was the "New Democracy" of Mao Tsetung in its day. And Castro, before he gained power in Cuba, had solemnly promised to restore the democratic constitution that Battista had consigned to the garbage heap.

There is no reason to object to American support for guerrilla groups opposed to the present dictatorship in Nicaragua. Somoza fell because of a national uprising and the withdrawal of American support. The present dictatorship was imposed on the Nicaraguan people by armed force supplied from without, and it subverted their democratic revolution, contrary to its own promises to the Organization of American States. The totalitarian ideology of the Nicaraguan directorate led such revolutionary heroes as Eden Pastora to revolt against it. Turnabout is fair play, even apart from our support for pluralistic values.

However, even those who wish to see some political compromise between the Sandinista totalitarians and other forces in Nicaragua should understand that only military pressure and a threat to the regime, not accommodation, will permit this. George Crile, a correspondent for CBS, has decried this pressure because there is so much internal opposition to the Sandinista regime that, in his opinion, the guerrillas are becoming effective. He, therefore, foresees a bloodbath because, he says, there are at least 50,000 armed leftist fanatics in Nicaragua who will fight to the death in support of a Marxist dictatorship. This is the weakest possible excuse for failing to support democratic forces in that area of the world. However, it is entirely possible that we are making the task of forcing reform on Nicaragua more difficult by giving most of our support to forces some of whose leaders were connected with Somoza. Much more support should go to Eden Pastora and the Chamorro brothers.

The situation in El Salvador has been mishandled. When the Reagan administration first came into office, Secretary of State Haig put the emphasis on military assistance, although former President José Napolean Duarté wanted the emphasis on economic assistance. Duarté was correct. We established again the unfortunate principle that anti-Communism is a sufficient credit card for the receipt of American assistance. This provided part of the background within which reactionary forces and regional army warlords resisted liberalizing pressures from the colonels who headed the former junta. This permitted a reactionary such as Major d'Aubisson to capture a large share of the vote from a war-weary population by promising to suppress the guerrillas.

We have witnessed the unholy spectacle of civilian courts under threat refusing to try the officers who killed Americans working on the land reform program while Major d'Aubisson publicly refers to these officers as his friends, thus letting all know that force will be used to prevent an imposition of penalties. Major d'Aubisson is an albatross around the neck of the government of El Salvador. No self-respecting American government can continue to provide substantial support to it while he occupies any role in its affairs.

Many believe that former vice-president elect Guillermo Ungo and the coalition of forces he heads in Mexico City are democratic. The problem is that Mr. Ungo has no control over the guerrillas in the field. As one of the leaders of one of the largest European Communist parties told me privately, the largest guerrilla forces are led by "crazies." These men are committed totalitarians from whom nothing can be expected. And no American policy should be advanced that permits these particular guerrilla leaders to negotiate their way into governmental posts.

The door should be open to negotiations on the conditions of the electoral process with those revolutionary leaders in Mexico City who wish to participate in future elections. It is not clear that they still represent any substantial political forces in that country. Nonetheless, they still carry considerable weight with the social democratic parties of Western Europe. They should be permitted back into the country under conditions in which they can organize and campaign without fear. Even the "crazies" should be given this opportunity if they are willing to call off their guerrilla war.

It is also unclear that the liberals in El Salvador understand economics, that the land reform imposed was the proper land reform, that adequate compensation was paid, or that an infrastructure was created that would have permitted the land reform to succeed in economic terms. However, individuals must have a stake in the future of their country. Thus, some sort of serious reform seems to be a *sine qua non* for eventual political stabilization in El Salvador.

However, the United States should be very pragmatic about this. The essential thing is a program that provides individuals with hope and gains their support. We should listen more and impose less in pressing for reform as a condition of American aid.

Before the coup that brought President Montt into office in Guatemala, it was my view that under no circumstances should the US assist the government of Guatemala despite the character of the guerrilla movement against it and the potential threat to Mexico. If the reports of the massacres of innocent Indians are correct, despite the improvement in the cities under President Montt, this advice should be repeated. However, some academics from Guatemala have assured me that the newspaper reports were inaccurate and have invited me to visit the country to see for myself. Perhaps they are right.

The United States rarely has a consistent policy. The Carter administration was not wrong to throw Somoza out of Nicaragua. On the contrary, it was delinquent in not taking action until much too late in the game. And when it did move, it moved without any plan or policy, and ensured that the Sandinistas would take over.

Vietnam, contrary to received opinion, is another case in point. In Washington during the early days of the Kennedy administration I advised my friends in the administration that there were two feasible courses that could be pursued in Vietnam. One would be to get out while the commitment was small. Although this was not the preferable alternative, it was a feasible one; and I advised them to accept it if they would not accept the other feasible alternative.

The preferable alternative would have been to maintain a threat against the North, even perhaps cutting it at the 18th parallel. This part of the operation would have involved American infantry, air and naval power. Inside South Vietnam, there would have had to have been considerable governmental reform, a nation-building operation, and massive police action.

There was a third course of action, and I advised the administration against it. I told them that they were headed in the direction of step-by-step escalations that would lead them into a deadly morass. Nobody in the administration seemed eager for this advice; and, a few years later, a then-assistant secretary of state advised me to return to the university and to deal with the academic subjects I understood because they had already won the guerrilla war. He became a dove.

The United States had much more to work with in Vietnam than it has in Central America. In the first place, the Vietnamese population is much more skilled and sophisticated than the Central American population. Second, despite all the faults of the successive South

Vietnamese governments, the Vietnamese had far better administrative staffs and military leadership than the governments of El Salvador or Guatemala. In the third place, the United States was neither hated nor detested in Vietnam: a consequence that would not occur until, under Nixon and Kissinger, we betrayed the South Vietnamese by deserting them after an ineptly fought war that had in fact been won, although at an inexcusably high price in terms of United States dollars, but more importantly in terms of its brutal effects in the Vietnamese countryside.

The first thing for the United States government to understand in Central America is that the American bona fides is not perceived and perhaps does not exist. Rarely has the United States assisted a Latin people to overthrow a repressive regime and to restore a democratic order as in the case of the Dominican Republic. And in that instance the subsequent activities of the Johnson administration removed— unfairly perhaps in light of the actual policies that were followed—any credit that the United States might have received.

Step one of any American plan must be to build support from at least some Latin American and Caribbean countries. Costa Rica, Venezuela, and more doubtfully Mexico, which seems more interested in gaining the good will of its leftist enemies than in reforming its plutocratic regime, come to mind. The second thing to understand is that we cannot exclude any party from dialogue. When the Marshall Plan was put together, the American team knew full well that it would never get through Congress if the Soviet Union participated. Yet they also knew that if the plan were not open to the Soviet Union, French and Italian participation would be impossible. During the European conference where the Marshall Plan was negotiated, the Soviet Union was allowed to exclude itself by its unreasonable behavior.

In El Salvador the United States undermined the legitimacy of its position through its support for elections prior to negotiations over the conditions for campaigning. Moreover, this assured substantial returns for the most regressive and repressive forces in the country.

Admittedly, recent American governments have shown such incompetence in negotiations with communists that perhaps there is some merit in their fear of negotiations. On the other hand, they have not shown much competence in organizing counterguerrilla wars.

Within the Central American context it is a mistake to treat each situation only when a crisis occurs. One aspect of a correct American policy must be to give support now to Costa Rica and Honduras. If the United States waits until they are under serious attack, then it will fight one losing battle after another, and under the worst conditions. A second aspect of a policy must be to isolate the regime in Haiti before there is a communist problem there. This would make it clear that our motivation is not merely anti-communist. Certainly the situation in human terms is worse in Haiti than in Cuba. The only saving grace of the Haitian regime is that it will not last forever, whereas the Cuban regime may last indefinitely, even though its maximal leader and former supporter of Hitler, Fidel Castro, is so unpopular that his private guards must point machine guns at prison guards when he visits the Isle of Pines, for instance. Perhaps, also, we should organize and support a coup against those who took over Suriname.

The United States must show that it has a deep concern for human conditions and that it is not merely on an anti-communist campaign. The communists did not need a disinformation campaign when they had former Secretary of State Haig working for them.

If negotiations over the conditions for elections permit a reasonable solution to the problem in El Salvador, then that is the correct route to go. If, on the other hand, the negotiations reveal intransigence on the part of the Marxist-Leninists or a desire to enter the government or to control the countryside before elections, then a longer range strategy is required. In this respect, I find rather ludicrous the observation made by some commentators that coalition governments that included communists seem to work in France. The communists do not control the armed forces in France, or the Ministry of the Interior, and they do not have a stockpile of weapons. Where is the instance of a coalition that did not undermine democracy when the communists controlled such assets? Surely only very special conditions would permit such a coalition to work.

If a longer-run strategy is required, then it must be understood by Congress and the American people that the United States is committed to assist in a nation-building program that may take fifteen to twenty years to carry out. In this respect, it is not good enough merely to train officers of the El Salvador army in Fort Benning in battle tactics. They need to be trained in a political program too so that they understand how to work with the peasants. They must learn how to assist in building institutions locally that secure the support of the peasantry and that give the peasantry a vested interest in a non-communist regime.

Terror will not work. Authoritarian or despotic regimes can use terror effectively if they do not face a locally-based totalitarian guerrilla movement. Their use of terror becomes counterproductive when they face such opponents. On the other hand, totalitarian regimes, within limits, can use terror effectively because they have a far more effective control system than authoritarian regimes and because they can drain off more of the political counter-elite into the control apparatus. There is more room for an upward mobility in totalitarian systems than in authoritarian, oligarchic, or despotic systems, which make little room for advancement. Hence, more military support is no answer unless it is accompanied by a political program that does not rely on terror.

Having sponsored an election that was reasonably democratic under the circumstances, and which brought the present hodgepodge of political forces into power in El Salvador, the United States is in a poor position entirely to withdraw its support from a regime that appears incapable of solving its problems. However, if within the next year the regime is still beset by a major guerrilla war, the United States should give the government of El Salvador a short list of conditions necessary for American assistance. It is their privilege to reject these conditions. In this event, it is better to allow El Salvador to be beaten without American assistance. That will likely happen anyway. And at least there may be the bonus of demonstrating to other regimes, such as the Guatemalan regime, that the United States will not support them merely because they are anti-communist.

If the strategy is accepted by the El Salvador government, then long-term support—perhaps including even some military support—will be required. However, it will not be massive. The actual details of the nation-building program should be worked out coordinately in cooperation with the democratic Central American governments. The United States cannot impose a plan. Moreover, an attempt to dictate its terms will not only run up against aspects of Latin culture but will have the same destabilizing consequences as the American welfare system has had on its unfortunate clients.

If and when such a program of nation-building is adopted, it should be publicized. There should be yearly progress evaluations, and these should be honest and serious. The various publics should be made aware both of actual progress and of plans for the future. The heart of the program will be political. Economics will be the second sheaf. The military aspect is merely the third and least important layer.

The United States with its liberal entry rules has provided a haven for many of the worst elements from the unfortunate countries of Central America. They are not really anti-Communist. They are quite prepared to risk the loss of their home countries rather than to surrender their despotic privileges. In the warm haven of Miami, they are plotting and financing the assassination of moderates. As we know that this is going on, it should not be too difficult for the FBI to obtain the evidence and for the United States to extradite the guilty parties to their home countries for trial and punishment. It is a disgrace that nothing substantial has been done to date in this respect.

Contrary to the urging of Mexico and some influential figures in the American Congress, there is no good reason for the United States to come to terms with communist Cuba. It seems strange that some of those who argue that we should have nothing to do with repressive regimes in Latin America wish to accommodate the cruelest dictator of them all. Some argue on pragmatic grounds that an agreement with Cuba will lead to a diminution in its support for terrorism in

Latin America and its intervention in Africa. Perhaps this may be so in the short run. But any concessions the United States makes will have been relatively permanent, while the concessions made by Cuba, particularly with respect to its support for terrorists, are likely to be temporary at best. Because its support for terrorism will be clandestine, the evidence presented by our intelligence agencies will always be subject to considerable doubt. Even now many doubt communist intervention in Central America despite the impressive evidence of a Cuban and East German presence in Nicaragua. Former Secretary of State Alexander Haig did not help matters with his attempt to "prove" such intervention by arguments that obviously lacked the hard quality he attributed to them. But that is precisely the problem: in the absence of defections—usually long after the event—and hard documentary evidence, which is often doubted anyway, it is not possible to prove this case to the doubting Thomases who abound in the United States.

Whereas the United States must have relations with the Soviet Union and China for obvious reasons, there is no need to come to terms with an ugly brute such as Castro who is our avowed enemy. Cuba imposes an immense financial burden on the Soviet Union now. There is no reason for the United States to lighten that burden. Furthermore, Cuba is a potential hostage. Well before candidate Reagan made the suggestion, I advocated publicly the idea of a naval and air blockade of Cuba on the heels of the Soviet invasion of Afghanistan. If the United States is prepared to make a move of this kind, the Soviet Union must consider the consequences of its next outrageous activity. If it goes ahead anyway—for instance, an invasion of Poland—Castro can be allowed to hang dry while the Soviet Union is shown to be impotent in this area. Moreover, such a blockade, despite resentment and riots at home and in Latin America, would have important demonstration effects. The one condition that would gainsay this posture would be a Cuban decision to restore political democracy.

It should be clear that the United States acts out of confidence and not merely defensively; that it is not afraid to isolate states such as Cuba, and that it is not compelled to support client states that are unwilling to make those serious efforts that alone would make American intervention defensible in terms of American values.

Functional Issues: Economic Cooperation

The brevity of discussion is not an indication of unimportance but rather the fact that the complexities of these issues are so great that in a short discussion only a few of the obvious points can be mentioned. It is increasingly clear that the world is becoming much smaller and much more interdependent. We are not too far from the time in which ecological decisions need to be carried through on a transnational basis.

However, we are full into the period in which economically complementary decisions are required. We are just beginning to build the institutions, and on a rather haphazard basis, within which economic policies regarding levels of production, levels of interest rates and inflation, and orderly marketing may be negotiated and implemented.

The need for at least quasi-institutional arrangements is clear. Many European nations, for instance, protested that high interest rates in the United States produced inflation in their countries. Clearly, policies on these issues are no longer defensible on a purely national basis. Furthermore, the development of transnational economic arangements, particularly among the twenty-six nations of the OECD, will constitute a framework of cooperation that eventually will be even more important than the systems of alliances. Indeed, in that hope for a future period in which the alliances can be dissolved, these institutions will provide the framework of transnational cooperation needed to solve major problems among the nations of the world and to produce a world with more humane values.

RESOURCE DEVELOPMENT

One issue that has received insufficient attention centers on alternative resource development. Obviously, alternative resource development will involve huge expenditures and can be justified only by the increasing costs of current resources. However, as long as resource prices are determined by cartels, as in the case of OPEC, these investments could, and likely would, be destroyed by cartel price-cutting. Thus, obviously, once alternative resource developments are agreed to, there must also be an agreement on a transnational basis to buy these products, even if price-cutting by the cartel occurs.

DEVELOPING NATIONS

The problems of the developing world are of great importance and should be viewed with compassion by the rest of the world. However, I wish to dissociate myself from the positions taken in the discussions in UNCTAD, those taken in the Brandt report, and the dependency-producing activities of the World Bank under Robert McNamara. Development that is not primarily a matter of external assistance is an essential component of an effective development strategy. Investment certainly is necessary, but South Korea, Taiwan, Hong Kong, and Singapore give ample proof that capital funds are available if they can be employed profitably. Nor is it true that external investment necessarily leads to the malstructuring of local economies. Both South Korea and Taiwan, for instance, even though their domestic markets are far more limited than those of Japan, provide evidence that local states can control their own direction of development. In fact, Taiwan recently has invested heavily in the United States. These countries have found the route to national independence, or at least to as much of it as is possible for a small nation in the modern world. And this will permit the restoration of national pride.

Nor are resources essential to development. The states named above as examples of successful development are singularly resource poor. There is almost an inverse relationship between the availability of local resources and successful development. Good government, sound economic policies, good educational systems, relatively honest and efficient local entrepreneurs, and achievement orientation are required.

If we fail to recognize these facts, and instead subscribe to the myths of the Brandt report, we will finance local elites at the expense of their nations, proliferate the number of large hidden Swiss bank accounts, destroy capital, and produce explosive frustrated expectations. The Brandt report myths reinforce dependence and inhibit those independent self-help efforts that alone permit constructive change. The Brandts and the McNamaras help to reinforce that psychology of dependence that makes constructive change impossible.

THE MILITARY

I have spoken previously of the need for a strong American military posture. This problem does not respond to dollar solutions any more than education does. The Pentagon is a colossus in which the principals get in each other's way. Even a random reduction of its size by at least fifty percent would have enormous value in improving American military policy. The system of the Joint Chiefs of Staff stresses service attachment; and the budget is a compromise among competing elites. Each of the services protects its own vested interests in weapons and often of the wrong kind.

A single service should be formed with something like a general staff system, in which the members of the general staff would have experience in all branches. The members of the general staff should be trained to think in terms of missions and strategy. And the choices of weapon systems should be related to these missions and strategies. Instead, there is a bureaucratic system that sent troops into Vietnam with backpacks designed to withstand a thermal burst and boots that caused foot rot.

This entire topic needs thorough study. A few members of the Senate Armed Services Committee—Sam Nunn, a conservative, and Gary Hart, a liberal, in particular—are attempting to make intelligent inroads into this problem. However, they have neither the time nor the staff to do a systematic job.

We must think through arms control problems in more serious ways than in the past. SALT has been a disaster because it has been negotiated by people who do not sufficiently understand what the Soviets mean by a treaty. However, the chief difficulty with arms control negotiations to date is that we are playing an abstract and foolish numbers game rather than relating agreements to the geopolitical conditions of the areas to which they apply in terms of defensive ability.

DEFENSE AND DETERRENCE

The object of changes in the military is to secure a defense posture for the United States and the free world that is adequate to protect its interests and, thus, that can deter attack or the threat of attack on the United States and its allies. The matter is urgent because the United States has allowed the Soviet Union to develop a conventional preponderance in Europe; parity, if not actual superiority, in the area of strategic nuclear weapons; and a naval force that is capable of denying command of the seas to the United States. The United States is an island nation and needs command of the seas to support the independence and viability of its allies.

If these matters were solely military, the free world would be hard pressed indeed. However, in addition to a variety of factors that make the Soviet Union disinclined to take high risks, there is another factor that the Soviets call the correlation of forces that works to American advantage. The Soviet Union is not a nation; it is an empire, and not merely with respect to its bloc structure, but with respect to its internal structure as well. The dominance and control exercised by the Slavic portions of the Soviet Union do not make for comfortable relations with the other parts of the internal empire; and, except for Bulgaria and East Germany, relations with the populations of the bloc nations range from modest to great hostility. In addition, one billion Chinese border on Soviet territory; and the Soviets have an almost paranoidal fear of them.

Even if worst came to worst, and the Soviet Union were to make a relatively successful first strike against the United States, the United States would be in a position to concentrate its counterattack upon the Slavic portions of the Soviet empire and their only true ally, the National Socialists of East Germany. The Slav portions of the empire, which, after all, include its leadership, would likely never recover from this; and Chinese spillover likely would dominate them.

On the other hand, even a relatively devastated United States would receive assistance from Canada. Although Mexico—in such a scenario —might try to occupy some southwestern portions of the United States, and might do so successfully for a period of years, the Mexicans, unlike the Chinese, demonstrate no long-range capability for political or economic managment. They would probably alienate even the Mexican/American community within a generation. Moreover, should the Mexicans develop a deeply-rooted and efficient democracy, we could easily live in peace with an expanded Mexico.

Thus, horrible though this outcome would be, the United States would have the prospect of regenerating its polity. This basic asymmetry in the correlation of forces that does favor the United States—if we recognize it and if the Soviets know that we do—can have a strong deterrent effect upon the Soviet Union.

Certainly, we do not desire such an outcome; no sane person would. But the Soviet Union has even more to fear than we do. Moreover, our basic policies will not be hostile toward the true security and the political and economic interests of the Soviet peoples; and we will try to find ways for their constructive participation in world affairs in a manner consonant with their great power status. This will help to produce alternative lines of policy that lead us away from potential catastrophe. But these efforts will be made from a position of political and social strength.

The value of military force, except instrumentally for defense, is seriously overestimated by the Soviet leaders—even though they do think in terms of the correlation of forces—just as it is underestimated by the Japanese leadership. However relevant military force may have been as a component of policy in the early twentieth century, the primary instruments for the pursuit of policy lie within the political and social structures of nations, in their collaboration with each other, and also in their moral strength.

The contemporary tragedy of the Soviet Union lies in its inability to permit that degree of political autonomy among its member republics and within the bloc that would make autonomous collaboration desirable and fruitful and the Soviet Union a stronger and more powerful, but also more benign, entity. The present stagnation of the Soviet economy, and the untoward impact upon the health of its population, result from the crude forms of political and economic control that it has adopted. These are intimately tied to the untoward military expenditures that are forced on the suffering Soviet peoples by contemporary Soviet policy.

The interests of the United States and of the free world are not opposed to the true interests of the Soviet peoples, but only to some of the interests of its present archaic structure. Thus, despite the threat position we are obliged to maintain until the situation is normalized, our object is not to defeat the Soviet Union but, on the contrary, to pursue policies that persuade it to adapt in ways that in fact will do more to satisfy the needs and aspirations of its peoples and to enhance its potentially important role in the world than do its contemporary policies.

BILINGUAL EDUCATION AND NATIONALISM

The United States might do well to pay close attention to Soviet nationality problems as well as to those in Canada, Belgium, and elsewhere. However well-intentioned may be the efforts to promote bilingual education in the United States, including in the armed forces, this may promote an unfortunate nationality problem in this country. English cannot be taught adequately through the medium of a foreign tongue. Those not fully fluent in the standard language, who do not associate with and dress like those in the mainstream, and whose interests differ significantly from those in the mainstream, will find it very difficult to rise within the system. However much prejudice may play a role in making it difficult for members of official minority groups to rise within the system, self-defining cultural characteristics probably play much more of a role.

It is a distinct mistake to view the American culture as a WASP culture, as a form of cultural imperialism over blacks and Hispanics. White Anglo-Saxon Americans are a minority themselves and, on the average, make less money per family and have a lower educational level than do black West Indians. Only a minority of Americans come from family backgrounds in which English was the native language. Jazz and popular music do not have primarily European backgrounds while most classical music is not of English origin.

The American culture is precisely that: an American culture. American blacks who go to Africa and Puerto Ricans who return to that commonwealth quickly learn that they are at least hybrids. Those who are to participate fully in the American culture must be adequately adapted to it. This does not mean there cannot be localized folk traditions that add richness to life or that the ancestral language should not be spoken or understood. But it must be made difficult for immigrant communities that are not in the current mainstream to insulate themselves from that mainstream. They should become proficient in the appropriate language skills and the cultural characteristics that will permit them to move with ease through the dominant institutions and the highest jobs and offices of this country.

Both legislation and court decisions on this subject are subversive of the unity of this country and injurious to those minorities they are intended to assist. Furthermore, there is an underlying paternalism and aura of contempt for these minorities in the assumption that they cannot successfully make the same adjustment that other minorities did.

More Americans should know foreign languages; and certainly Spanish is a language that many more non-Hispanic Americans should know. However, it should be a second language for Americans, not a first.

HUMAN RIGHTS

There is no point to appointing an assistant secretary of state for human rights. If those who formulate policy do not understand human rights, then a special office will do no good. It may make some sense to have officers to call special attention to special issues such as economic issues. But if our leaders are not alert to general and non-technical matters such as moral issues, a special office will do no good. Consideration of the impact on human rights of foreign policy is not an extraneous consideration but a prime consideration that is the province of the president and the secretary of state. Furthermore, I do not think it advisable to make a yearly formal survey of human rights unless its object is to irritate other nations while accomplishing nothing of a positive character.

There is some virtue in making the point that, on the average, authoritarian regimes do less damage and are probably more transient than totalitarian regimes. It also makes some sense to point out that a corrupt authoritarian regime is easier to live under than an incorrupt one. However, this point having been made, there is no reason to make too much of it. Overstressing it can do as much harm as the bumptious attitude of the Carter administration toward human rights.

On the other hand, some have made too little of it. One argument that was made on the pages of the New York *Times* during the period in which this essay was first presented was that Poland, a totalitarian state, was moving toward democracy. Perhaps this will still happen. But, if so, it is like the exception that proves the rule because its conditions are so different that the argument is not worth much. Poland has had *habeus corpus* since the fourteenth century and, as a Polish communist recently pointed out, there was more press freedom under Pilsudski's dictatorship than under communist rule. The church is powerful. There is a long history of resistance to Russia. And many other special conditions helped to produce the Polish spring. Where is the modification of Romania's totalitarian state or that of Cuba?

Others have argued in the pages of the New York *Times* that at least totalitarian states solve the problem of hunger and that only intellectuals are interested in the freedoms permitted by authoritarian states. They said this about China also; and we now learn from the Chinese leaders themselves that it was a myth that they had solved the problem of hunger. What are the examples and what are the conditions that make comparison appropriate? Surely no totalitarian state has done as well as the non-totalitarian Republic of China in respect to satisfying material needs.

But, even if the argument concerning hunger were correct, are intellectual freedoms really of concern only to intellectuals? I do not wish to understate the tragedy of hunger. But, then, neither do I view people as cattle, who will produce more milk if well fed and forced to listen to soothing music. There is something strange, disturbing, and ultimately immoral about such arguments.

Attacks on human rights in even friendly authoritarian states should be of concern to us. Even so, often we cannot afford to speak clearly. There are enormous restrictions on human rights in the Soviet Union; and yet it would be a mistake for the United States government to make too many hortatory comments about this.

These are complex problems. There are no simple solutions to them and any generalization is likely to obscure more than it clarifies. The important thing is that we care about human rights and that our care be viewed as an important component of the general strategy of policy, rather than of each of its particular implementations. In any political situation—and this applies even when congressmen and senators get elected in the United States—one will find oneself working with uncomfortable allies and remaining quiet about things that one would like to protest. Our goals and values ought to be clearly stated and our foreign policy related to them. But we must be mindful of the real choices that confront us and ought not to forsake the good in quixotic pursuit of the best. On the other hand, it was ridiculous for Vice President George Bush in 1982 to praise the Philippines as an example of democracy.

We cannot produce a perfect world, or improve this one by simplistic prescriptions. The important point is that our policies have a global and systematic rationale and that this rationale have as an important component the idea of building a world in which human rights are safe. Then, at least, perhaps we will not damage human rights inadvertently as we did when we shipped Eastern Europeans carelessly to Stalin's slave camps after World War II, when we withheld from a non-totalitarian Vietnamese government the sinews of war with which to defend itself, or when we rationalized the damage we did to the Republic of China and the people under its aegis at the time of normalization with the Peoples' Republic. That we will never damage the cause of human rights in the pursuit of other important objectives is too much to hope for. Sometimes after moving two steps forward, one must move one step backward. The direction of effort, however, is of paramount importance. The most important element in recognizing moral issues may lie in caring. Many moral mistakes the US has made would not have been made had we cared more.

Even when, on balance, we think government policies are mistaken, they should be made within a framework that we can look to with pride. The American revolution generated the best human values of any revolution, although sometimes we stumbled on the path. It speaks to universal hopes and needs. Its spirit should infuse our national policies, both domestic and foreign: not in hate, fear, or suspicion; but with hope, belief, dedication, emphasis, and openness.

RONALD REAGAN'S EUROPEAN POLICY

By
DONALD L. HAFNER

During his campaign, candidate Reagan spoke infrequently of the European alliance. When he did, his message was a spare extract from his palliative for domestic politics: the alliance needs leadership.

> Our European allies, looking nervously at the growing menace from the East, turn to us for leadership and fail to find it.
>
> We need a rebirth of the American tradition of leadership. . . . The United States of America is unique in world history because it has a genius for leadership.[1]

Certainly it is true that three decades after the alliance was founded, the United States remains the dominant and indispensible member. By its actions or failure to act, the US sets the context within which the European allies must find their place. The allies require a strong and steady center of gravity from which to take bearings for their own policies.

Donald L. Hafner is Associate Professor of Political Science at Boston College.

What the alliance does not need and will not tolerate, however, is a sentimental brand of American leadership based upon an image of an expectant Europe, alarmed by its own disarray, eager for new challenges, and desperately awaiting American commands. Europe's current "disarray" is an aggravated but adaptive response to its dependent and exposed position in international affairs. It would persist in the best of times, and these are not the best of times. Wrong-headed American policies which attempt to impose new burdens or a unanimity of view upon the Europeans risk driving them to ever more ingenious criticisms of American leadership and to rationalizations for diminished efforts that could irreparably weaken the alliance. The coming decade is a time requiring a clear sense of purpose and constancy in American policy, but also grace, caution, and restraint. The Europeans might well question whether Ronald Reagan is well-fitted to show such leadership.

The most important source of "disarray" within the Alliance is structural and therefore chronic: the alliance is a coalition of unequals. The common wisdom has it that America's European policy must adjust to the resurgent strength of Europe. Yet in fact, "Europe" remains no more than a regional power—or even less. Though its aggregate capabilities are impressive, Europe cannot move as an aggregate because it lacks a unified political voice, and no single member of "Europe" can command the weight of the whole on behalf of its interests.

A nuclear defense of Europe, independent of the US, is conceivably within reach if the Europeans could agree upon a division of labor among national military forces. The annual military expenditures of Germany, Britain, and France are each substantially greater than US annual spending on strategic nuclear forces. But as Britain learned in the Falklands crisis, designing national forces to fit a specialized niche in collective defenses is very risky, so long as allies retain the sovereign right to withhold the complementary forces under their command. And by deliberate choice, Europe has retreated further and further over the past decade from the full political unification that a common defense policy would require.

The European allies are "powerful" at the margins, however, where their lesser capabilities can tip a balance, especially when the superpowers overreach themselves. The Europeans have no capacity to force a settlement in the Middle East, to change Soviet policies in Poland, or to end turmoil in Central America. But they are quite capable of granting diplomatic recognition to the PLO, defying US trade sanctions against the Eastern bloc, or shipping arms to anti-US factions in Latin America, thus complicating or frustrating US policy. Europe's share of world trade is four times as large as the US; Europe accounts for 20% of the world's arms exports, and in constant dollar terms, its volume of arms sales now matches the level reached by the US in the early 1970s; Europe's trade with the Soviet bloc is three times as large as that of the US. So Europe has the power of the spoiler. Yet its fundamental security remains tied to a strategic nuclear guarantee that the US cannot convincingly and irrevocably promise and that Europe cannot independently invoke. Far from escaping from an unnatural dependence upon a distant ally, Europe appears condemned to it.

The potential risks in this unequal relationship are enormous, for each ally stands exposed to the foolishness, laxity, or narrow self-interest of the others. In any association where shared risks are not matched by shared authority to avert them, there will be a natural tendency toward fragmentation.

What makes the 1980s a potentially volatile decade is that chronic tendencies toward fragmentation have been buttressed by legitimate doubts about the long-term willingness and capability of the US to exercise a global role as the alliance leader. Much of the fashionable criticism about confusion and inconsistency in American foreign policy is not to be taken too seriously. Constancy is vital for US policy, but there is not a single member in this alliance of democracies that has not had to foster confusion here or perpetrate an inconsistency there in response to domestic political needs. Nonetheless, two facts alone would be sufficient to raise questions about the US capacity for alliance leadership. One is the sheer turmoil in the office of the presidency during the past decade. It is not prudent, but successive presidents nevertheless pride themselves on executing dramatic reversals of foreign policy. Exactly how and why the allies are supposed to zig and zag upon command from the American electorate, especially when American voters seldom vote foreign policy and even less alliance policy, is infrequently considered. Yet the allies have had to accomodate the policy changes of four presidents and seven secretaries of state in the past ten years. There are few European states with comparable records of turmoil, and they do not aspire to be alliance leaders.

The second indictment of US leadership is the erosion of American military capabilities. Much can be said about the diminished utility of military force in the contemporary period. Few of those arguments would justify the relative quantitative and qualitative decline of US strategic and conventional capabilities vital to NATO defense. Save for strategic nuclear forces (which supposedly have been subject to the greatest discount in utility), US military forces in virtually every category were less numerous in 1980 than in 1964, a trend that could be justified only counterfactually by declining hazards in the contemporary world, shrinking Soviet forces, or American technological wizardry. During the 1970s, US military spending fell as a portion of GNP to the lowest level since 1950. None of the European allies allowed its effort to erode to a comparable degree. An argument is sometimes given that aggregate NATO efforts remain high. Yet here again, each ally has authority to command only its own defense policies. When the American effort fails, no single ally can count upon "the aggregate" to pick up the burden. To offset the decline in US military spending through the 1970s, it would have taken annual real-growth military spending increases of 20% by the richest ally, West Germany, if acting alone—or increases of 7% each by West Germany, France and Britain acting together. As it was, these three managed a combined average annual real growth of 2.5%, contrasted with the average annual US decline of 3.5%. Within the alliance, there is no substitute for US leadership or US spending.

Whether the impairments in American leadership were a temporary aberration or a long-term trend did not matter immediately to the European allies. The sensible response in either case was to buy time and reduce risks, to act independently of US policy, and if necessary to seek accommodation rather than confrontation in defense of national interests. Until and unless the US exhibits greater constancy in leadership, this approach will continue to make sense through the 1980s.

Economic problems of varying severity will add to Europe's crankiness and fragmentation in the coming decade. Europe's current economic malaise will ease with the US recovery, but the rebound will not be smooth or steady. At the first hint of overheating and inflation, the US revival will undoubtedly falter as investors wait to see whether government, labor, and corporate discipline will hold. If such bounces catch the European recoveries out of phase, it may mean slower, shallower revival for the allies and longer opportunity to nurse genuine (or contrived) grievances about American economic policies. Moreover, structural problems of overcapacity and loss of competitiveness in key European industries, such as steel, autos, chemicals, and shipbuilding, will not disappear simply with economic recovery. In the best of times, the alliance members must engage in sharp competition for foreign markets in order to foot energy import bills: competition made sharper by shrinking markets in third world countries hard hit by oil price increases, adverse shifts in the terms of trade, and rising debt service burdens. As chronic unemployment, rising entitlement payments, and festering political discontent make the scramble for world trade ever more desperate, the Europeans will not be in fine humor for talking calmly about new security burdens or re-allocations of defense costs. Europe has the power to act as "spoiler" through its trade policies, including East-West trade and weapons sales to the Third World; economic pressures will heighten the incentives.

Most important, the Europeans will not defend their policies during this period on candid grounds of political and economic expediency. Instead, policies will be fitted into broader conceptual frameworks regarding alliance interests and East-West relations which will present necessity as a virtue. The core feature will be to divert inter-bloc relations from Europe's weaknesses to its strengths. In a bipolar world where military force still matters, East-West confrontations emphasize the dominant position of the United States, and necessarily constrain the allies' autonomy while heightening risks and dependence. To command influence and minimize risks, the allies must exploit a different idiom, the language of adjustment and reconciliation of interests. For the Europeans, this is necessary in any case as a preemptive tactic against domestic left-wing critics. Moreover, while there were impairments in US resolve and capablities during the past decade, "to court confrontation in these circumstances was to invite debacle."[2]

Naturally the idiom of detente had enormous attraction for the Europeans, just as the language of Gaullism and *Ostpolitik* had. Policies of adjustment and reconciliation would be a menace to Western security if the Soviet state by its nature were unrelentingly imperial and immune to transformation. The allies required a better vision of the future; detente promised to

> explore incentives to give the Soviets a stake in cooperation even while . . . seeking to make expansionism too dangerous. Over time, as other factors came into play, a stable peace might be founded on . . . Soviet conviction and not only on necessity.[3]

The principal incentives to be offered—political accords and trade ties—played to European strengths. While the Europeans could never best the US in offering the Soviets acknowledged status as a global power, they could compete and even outdo the US in trade offers. Eighty percent of the West's trade with the Soviet bloc was cornered by the Europeans.

The Europeans, however, hold distinctive views about the use of these acquired levers on Soviet behavior. The fact that $50 billion in trade, $70 billion in outstanding loans, and over 300,000 jobs in West Europe are tied to economic exchanges with the Soviet bloc obviously counts for something in times of recession. It is difficult to weave a web of obligations and dependencies around the Soviets without incurring some mutual vulnerabilities, and the Europeans did no better in anticipating or averting reverse leverage than the US has. But casting the matter simply in these terms implies that European behavior might change once economic recovery begins. That would ignore the deeper causes which preceded and will persist after the current economic slump. The paradox of leverage here is that the time to use it is during East-West confrontations over important interests. Yet it is precisely when US-Soviet relations break down that the Europeans are most threatened with diminished autonomy and heightened risks over which they have little control. If contacts are completely terminated between East and West, Europeans argue, an essential motive for moderation in Soviet behavior would be taken away and those immoderate impulses within the Soviet Union would be strengthened. "Thus we must carefully see to it that longer term chances for cooperation are not spoiled by the necessary short-term confrontation or even tests of strength."[4] The Europeans see themselves playing such a role when they resist "linkage," exercise restraint in applying levers, and sustain contacts with the East as US-Soviet relations deteriorate. And arguably, in acting in this way, Europe is not being selfish or foolish but is pursuing a vision:

> Can one imagine an ambition more ennobling and at the same time more necessary than seeking to reconcile East and West in order to assure the survival of humanity, which is threatened by scarcities of every sort and even by war? Is it too much to dream that Europe might play a part in this effort at reconciliation?[5]

The dynamics of detente that supposedly will moderate Soviet behavior are also pertinent to Europe's other security concerns in the Third World and most importantly in the Persian Gulf. Europe, for practical and historical reasons, may be barred from being more than a "regional" military power, but its economic reach is global and so is its power to confer political status by association. The Europeans can hold more of the strings that control their fate in the Gulf if the themes of detente—emphasizing interwoven political and economic benefits and obligations—can be used to discount the over-weening presence of the superpowers in that region. (The Europeans may also appreciate what their own mad scramble for arms sales in the Third World will mean for future European or American attempts at military intervention, a lesson that the British have already learned in the Falklands affair.)

In sum, the disagreements which emerged between the US and its allies in the events of Iran, Afghanistan, and Poland were not a temporary aberration. The basic cause of tension is systemic. Detente was not a temporary policy experiment for the Europeans but the culmination of decades of effort to carve out a realm of autonomy within an unnatural dependency upon the US. In a deeper sense, Europe's "disarray" represents an advance toward precisely what the US said it wanted, the restoration of Europe, if not to its former glory then at least to some of its former liberty. It also represents a formidable challenge to the US to do what it has not been compelled to do in the past—to learn how to lead when it no longer can simply command.

Under these circumstances, the election of Ronald Reagan in 1980 understandably disturbed European opinion. American journalists evaluating the new president would write that his opinions in politics were closely tied to his personal experiences. Yet no president in the postwar period would arrive at the Oval Office with so little personal experience in international affairs—not even Jimmy Carter. Reagan's acceptance speech at the Republican convention contained a ringing call for the US to reassert its leadership. But Reagan's vision of that leadership, those around him would say, "was to return the republic to the status quo of an earlier day. In foreign and national security policy, that earlier day might be fixed at 1955."[6] "His is a kind of 1952 world."[7] For Europeans who recall the 1950s as a period of anxiety, utter dependency, and occasional humiliation under US leadership, such a vision of a restored future lacked sensitivity. It also bespoke ignorance of the complex and irretrievable historical conditions that permitted American global dominance in that decade. Yet for Reagan, the cause of America's decline and the loss of allied deference was simple and self-inflicted: it was the decline of US military strength and the will to use it.

Europe was not, of course, the center of Reagan's vision at all. Ronald Reagan did not then and does not now truly have a European policy; he has a Soviet policy, and a role assigned to Europe within it as an auxillary to the US. It is a bare sketch of a policy, with the same assumption about the ability of restored American strength, particularly military power, to transform all before it. The world remains tractable before American strength because Soviet meddling, invited by US weakness, is at the core of the world's upheavals.

> Let us not delude ourselves, the Soviet Union underlies all the unrest that is going on. If they weren't engaged in this game of dominoes, there wouldn't be any hot spots in the world.
>
> ... all over the world, we can see that in the face of declining American power, the Soviets and their friends are advancing.[8]

In explaining precisely how the restoration of American power would make the Soviets more tractable, Reagan offered two reasons, with slightly different implications regarding the nature of the Soviet threat. One was the standard Munich analogy.

> ...World War II came about because nations were weak, not strong, in the face of aggression. Those same lessons of the past surely apply today ... weakness can be provocative simply because it is tempting to a nation whose imperialist ambitions are vitually unlimited.[9]

By itself, this view left little room for accommodation of interests with the Soviets or hope for transformation in basic relations. The policy implication was pure confrontation. But there was also a more baroque Reagan view of a Soviet Union armed to the teeth yet on the brink of economic collapse.

> ... [H]ere is the most planned, controlled economy in the world

and it can't feed its people if it is unable to buy from capitalist countries the food that they need to eat. . . . I want them to know that there is a line beyond which the free world cannot be pushed, and . . . that those things that they need from the free world—*must have*—they're going to have a better opportunity to get them if they give up the pattern, the imperialism that they've been following —and I think that should lead to a better world and a better understanding between us.[10]

In Reagan's view, the rigidity of Soviet centralized control and Soviet "spiritual exhaustion" were partial causes of the coming collapse; the burdens of arms competition and imperialism were also responsible. The Western response must go to root causes. Trade with the Soviets should be restricted so that they are forced to cope with their own economic shortcomings and addiction to military spending. And the rebuilding of American military strength would add to the economic pressures of continued arms competition. The Soviets could then be drawn into general restraint in international behavior, and into arms control negotiations, by the enticements of Western trade and relief from the domestic economic (and presumably political) problems that would follow. The key, of course, is the challenge posed by Western rearmament. Unless US military forces are restored, there will be little incentive for Soviet moderation, and hence little justification to engage the Soviets in negotiations.

Only a tin ear could miss the theme of "linkages" here which had soured European relations with Kissinger and later produced the breach with Carter over Afghanistan. Kissinger in fact became a major foreign policy adviser to Reagan during the presidential campaign, but such views were a natural extension of Reagan's own ideas regarding domestic politics. This should have been warning to those who supposed that Reagan would be deflected from his views by any adviser serving as "vicar" of foreign policy.

The linchpin in this construction was the assumption that prevailing levels of Soviet military spending, and neglect of consumer demands, must inevitably produce collapse, and soon "a sad and bizarre chapter in human history whose last pages are even now being written."[11] Reagan's vision of a better world depended upon imminent Soviet collapse.[12] Without that assumption, there was little reason to suppose that a temporary policy of rearming and postponing negotiations would not become permanent confrontation as the Soviets hunkered down for the long haul. This assumption ought to have been in doubt already, since the Soviets had obviously been willing to forego the benefits of detente, including trade and arms negotiations, to invade Afghanistan and impose martial law on Poland. But for a candidate who, with conviction and ease, could attribute the loss of initiative, the crisis of the family, the spiritual decline of the republic, and the ruin of the US economy all to excessive governmental interference in American life, a belief in the imminent collapse of Soviet centralism could be taken *a priori*.[13]

The tension between Reagan's views and those of Europe regarding the Soviets spread outward to encompass international politics generally. The Europeans have sought to ease tensions in the Middle East and reduce Soviet opportunities for mischief by endorsing "the legitimate rights of the Palestinian people," including "its right of self-determination,"[14] and by showing sensitivity to regional conflicts. Candidate Reagan dismissed the Palestinian case as a refugee problem, endorsed Israel's settlements on the West Bank, praised Israel as "the only stable democracy we can rely on in a spot where Armageddon may come," and seemed oblivious to the depth or focus of conflicts in the region when he proposed a joint Arab-Israeli alliance against the Soviet Union. Where the Europeans defined their relationships with the Third World in terms of the trade preferences and mutual obligations of the Lomé Convention, the early Reagan administration declared its belief in "the magic of the marketplace" as the salvation of the Third World and cut foreign economic and financial aid to 0.14% of the US GNP.

In substance and in style, the gap between the Europeans and the Reagan presidency was seemingly immense. Those who thought that Reagan the pragmatist would emerge when confronted by reality could point to early evidence, especially the reversal of position on

arms control negotiations in the face of allied reaction and the growing anti-nuclear movement, or the administration's decision not to
undercut the unratified SALT II accord. But what did it hold for
the future if the administration's foreign policy in every case would
require a titanic effort to hammer Reagan's natural inclinations into
conformity with hard reality? How could such begrudging concessions constitute "leadership"?

More reflective consideration, however, suggests that while Reagan
does not have a European policy as such, his programs in many
respects are neatly fitted to the problems of the alliance. Reagan is
simply wrong, of course, in supposing that the US can resurrect the
military preeminence over the Soviet Union it enjoyed in the 1950s,
and wrong in supposing that restored military strength itself will
reestablish an American position of dominance within the alliance.
Nevertheless, Reagan is quite right that US neglect of the military
balance during the past decade unavoidably raised doubts about US
reliability as an alliance leader committed to its global role. Europeans who carefully examined American military budgets in the 1970s
would have noticed not just the general decline but also an ominous
trend of decreasing military investment (i.e., spending on weapons
procurement, military construction, and research and development).
Investment as a portion of the Department of Defense budget dropped
from 47% in 1964 to 35% in the late 1970s. The Department of
Defense was mortgaging future security to cover personnel costs and
daily operations and maintenance. President Carter had tried to reverse this trend, and also negotiated the Long-Term Defense Program with NATO in 1978, committing all members to 3% annual
real-growth in military spending. But the Carter achievements were
diluted by a stagnating economy, so that the US met the 3% target
figure for NATO-related spending only by reducing in other military areas. Overall Department of Defense budget real growth (TOA)
was 4.7% in FY (fiscal year) 1977, -0.3% in 1978, -0.7% in 1979,
and +2.5% in 1980, an erratic performance that hardly confirmed
American durabilty.

Reagan's own achievement has been to raise Department of Defense budget real growth to 10.9% in FY 1981, 12.7% in 1982, and 13.2% for 1983. In the process, the portion allocated to investment has been restored to 47% of the Department of Defense budget. As an expression of national resolve, these increases are significant, but equally so is the sensible (even subtle) allocation of funds among competing security needs. The quantitative disparity between US and Soviet strategic nuclear forces played prominently in Reagan's campaign rhetoric, and the alleged "window of vulnerability" of US ICBMs was his key indictment against SALT II and arms control generally. Although investment in strategic nuclear forces is certainly necessary, it is also the case that the Europeans—for whom the demise of US strategic "superiority" was supposedly most consequential—were quite prepared to live within the terms of SALT II and were less in awe of the alleged vulnerability of the Minuteman force. Nuclear war was the most extreme danger facing Europe, but other threats to European interests were more probable—especially in the Middle East, where Western military forces were stretched thin. So it is noteworthy that despite campaign rhetoric, Reagan's approach to the rebuilding of strategic nuclear forces has been quite restrained. Spending on strategic programs, as a percentage of the Department of Defense budget, was slated to rise from the 7-8% of the 1970s to about 12% by 1984—a sizable increase but far lower than, e.g., the 17% devoted to strategic forces during the building programs of the mid-1960s.

Moreover, a careful student of the Reagan strategic programs outlined in October 1981 would discover that the Reagan administration had decided to live with the "window of vulnerability" rather than divert funds from other military needs. Ostensibly, MX was to be the response to ICBM vulnerability. Yet in a surprisingly candid way, the administration made public its doubts that MX was survivable against Soviet attack without ABM protection of a sort banned by treaty and then volunteered that available ABM technology did not offer enough prospect of success to warrant abrogating the ABM Treaty. Of course, MX was continued, partly on its merits as a strategic system with distinctive uses and partly because the Europe-

ans warned that scheduled Pershing II and cruise missile deployments in Europe could not be tolerated if the US failed to maintain
its own land-based missile forces. But clearly the survivable counter-
force weapon of the Reagan program was Trident II, which would
not be deployed until December 1989.

Devising strategy and forces for protecting Alliance interests in
the Persian Gulf is the most delicate task the allies face in the coming decade—far more delicate and consequential, one suspects, than
dealing with strategic and theater nuclear forces deployments. Again,
it is a sign of Reagan's prudence that the major funding for military
rebuilding in the Reagan budgets is, properly, on conventional forces,
with major emphasis upon improving power-projection capabilities
through build-ups in the Navy, air- and sea-mobility forces, and the
Rapid Deployment Force. (Of the \$38.1 billion increase in spend-
ing for FY 1982, 58% went to conventional forces; for FY 1983,
the figure is 42%.)[15] In this respect, the Reagan administration has
shown more sense than its critics; the real dangers of nuclear war
come not from Reagan's nuclear programs (or rhetoric), but from a
neglect of conventional forces that invites tests of strength where the
use of nuclear weapons would quickly be our only recourse.

A major point of tension between the US and its allies will be
reliance upon military, as opposed to diplomatic, approaches in protecting interests in the Gulf region. In good measure, the dichotomy
between military and diplomatic options is overstated. It is true that
the most probable form of turmoil in the Gulf (including the most
probable form of Soviet meddling) is domestic political uprising,
and military intervention in such cases may prove difficult and counterproductive in the long term. It is also the case, however, that if the
alliance is to have any hope of shaping events in the region through
diplomacy, it must be prepared to throw meaningful weight into
local balances. Otherwise its "diplomacy" will be reduced to those
occasions when competing factions have already exhausted themselves
in conflict and merely seek a clever go-between to draft and shuttle
communiqués back and forth.

As for the wisdom of trying to forestall Soviet incursions into the

Gulf through a "diplomatic" arrangement, it is not clear why the alliance should rest its hopes upon the durability of such an accord if it lacks capacity to enforce its terms at the spot.[16] Nor is it clear how an accord among the US, the Europeans, and the Soviet Union on Gulf affairs would cope with the threat to oil supplies resulting from domestic upheavals, unless one assumes that the Soviets are indeed behind all unrest in the region; or that domestic upheavals will not have a significant impact upon oil supplies, and therefore are not a matter of concern.

Establishing a presence in the Gulf and bringing military force to bear are significant problems. Permanent facilities at key points within the Gulf states would be desirable from a logistics standpoint, but why would governments in the region be willing to accept American bases until the US shows it is prepared to throw its weight behind friends and allays suspicions that US troops would be an army of occupation to ensure oil flows. United States presence in the Gulf will have to be established obliquely, which is to say, at the beginning US capabilities will lag behind the foreseeable threats, and the initial investments, political and financial, will be quite high in comparison to tangible returns.

Again, Reagan policies have laid down a good foundation. The decision to sell AWACS aircraft to Saudi Arabia engaged the Reagan administration in a bruising battle with Congress that was counterproductive in important ways. Debate within the US was demeaning to the Saudis when it stooped to stereotypic views of Arabs and called into question the ability of the House of Saud to rule wisely. And the Saudis should have asked themselves whether the interpretation that might be put upon the event—i.e., that for the US, old allies mattered less than new opportunities—would not tarnish their triumph. However, Reagan wisely tackled the Saudi request early in his term, at a point when Congress would still be reluctant to challenge his mandate. The intensity of congressional opposition was at first badly misjudged by the administration. Yet by winning the vote in a brawl, Reagan succeeded in a demonstrative point about presidential primacy in foreign policy. The request for AWACS was understood by the Saudis and others in the region as proof that the US would accept partners with autonomous interests among Arab states, not just clients. (In this regard, Sheikh Yamani's remark in the midst of congressional debate, that Israel remained Saudi Arabia's primary enemy, was perverse but crucial.)

Building upon Carter's initiatives, the Reagan administration has negotiated agreements with states on the periphery of the Gulf, receiving rights of access in exchange for upgrading local airbases and other military facilities. This may well be less satisfactory and more expensive than obtaining bases directly in the region, but it wisely avoids the higher political price that both the US and host governments in the Gulf would have had to pay for full US basing rights. For the moment, the Reagan administration's emphasis upon naval forces and air- and sealift to bring power to bear is the sensible course. If, as seems likely, land bases cannot be obtained until the US establishes a credible presence in the region, then maritime forces are indispensible. In any case, there are some causes of political volatility in host states over which the US will have little influence, so it will always be prudent to retain a good portion of US capabilities off-shore. Finally, the administration's arrangement for joint military exercises in the region (such as the Bright Star exercise with Egypt) are well-devised. In addition to whatever military preparedness they foster and symbolic support they grant to host governments, they again remind the American public that being a superpower entails a global presence and provide concrete signs of support for friends.

The backbone of US schemes for the defense of the Gulf is the Rapid Deployment Force (RDF). Reagan has wisely adopted plans, set down by Carter in 1979, to construct the RDF not from new units but from existing military forces, including some available in principle as reinforcements for Europe. This scheme in fact excuses the Europeans from most burdens in defending "out-of-area" interests. The Reagan administration seeks only the use of NATO facilities for Gulf contingencies and arrangements for the Europeans to mobilize and reinforce their own national forces to fill gaps left when the US must respond in the Gulf.

Reportedly the Europeans have resisted planning for the diversion of US forces to the Gulf.[17] If so, they have good reason to resist. The competence and duration of any American intervention cannot be guaranteed by the Europeans, and so any collaboration by NATO risks harm to all within the alliance, without assuring commensurate influence over US decisions. There is also the wish, expressed by Europeans in some quarters, to tell the Soviets that while "no distinction should be made between the Middle East and Europe when it comes to assessing Soviet offensive behavior and its impact on Western policy," nonetheless the alliance would like to keep the Middle East *militarily* separate from Europe.

> ... [T]he West has an obvious interest in maintaining an option of limiting any possible military conflict between East and West to the Middle East, and of preventing its automatic spillover to Europe.... It lies in the logic of a policy of geographical limitation of military conflict in the Near East that Europeans and Americans maintain a military capacity either within the Middle East or available in regions outside the European theater in order to act without automatically using forces stationed in Europe. Such forces should be designed to deter a conflict *and contain it if necessary*, as well as to help achieve political objectives in the region.[18]

Presumably, a massive shift of US forces from Europe to the Gulf would either be in response to a Soviet incursion or could provoke one, which is to say, US contributions in Europe would be reduced precisely when the dangers of Soviet adventurism were highest. All of this would supposedly argue for an RDF composed of new forces, independent of NATO obligations.

Discussion of these issues cannot fail to provoke irony and *déja vu*. Of course it is desirable to keep any conflict with the Soviet Union "limited," but do the Europeans suppose it will be any easier for Arab states in the Gulf to accept such "limited war" doctrines than it has been for the Europeans to endorse American "limited war" policies in Europe? Would not keeping the conflict "limited" require a show of willingness to accept escalation if forced to it? Perhaps even some limitation on the size of forces in the Gulf, just enough to serve as a "tripwire," so the Soviets would be deterred by the fact that the West had no alternatives but to escalate? And given the Soviet advantages in geographic proximity and larger conventional forces, is it realistic to think the alliance could afford the military forces required to "contain" a Soviet attack in the Gulf? Is it wise to "decouple" Gulf security from NATO in this way? In deciding upon a strategy for the defense of the Gulf, NATO seems destined to replicate all the poisonous debates over its own defense. It is just as well, therefore, that the Reagan administration has stuck to plans for the RDF to be composed predominantly of strategic reserve forces in the US and that requests for contributions from the allies will be minimal.

Even in its disasters, the Reagan administration can show some redeeming virtues. The manner in which the administration went about the Polish sanctions, especially the gas pipeline affair, will occupy a special niche in European memories, no matter what triumphs or tragedies follow. Yet it was Reagan and not the allies who understood this as a test of the alliance's moral character. In a period when the Europeans are able to act as "spoilers," and are pressured to do so by domestic political considerations, the alliance needs a solid moral anchor to keep it from drifting entirely at the mercy of narrow self-interestedness. It was easier for the US to neglect the moral component in the past, in part because open or implied threats of US troop withdrawals brought allies into line. That tactic was corrosive and demeaning even then; in the current period, it is hardly sensible for the US to try to reassert leadership by threatening to withdraw it.

Evoking a common sense of moral purpose within this diverse alliance is not easy. Hallowed recollections of the comforts and salvation that allies brought in the time of Europe's last trial are lifeless history for that half of the alliance's population too young to remember WWII. Despite its growing military strength, the Soviet Union is less blatantly menacing toward Europe, less brutal in its behavior than one or two decades ago. The political principles of Soviet rule are anathema, but vigorous anti-communism from an American president is bound to feed European suspicions that the US seeks a return to the Cold War period of Europe's subordination. Reagan's style is nostalgic, his experiences are of a generation past, his voice is pure American heartland—on every count he seems an unlikely prophet for the alliance.

Yet in his speeches on his European tour in mid-1982, Reagan showed his weaknesses but also his great potential as a moral voice. Before the British Parliament, he stumbled badly. By echoing Churchill's Iron Curtain speech, Reagan pricked fears that he sees the world as unchanged from the 1940s or 50s. By altering Churchill's ringing phrase to read "From Stettin on the Baltic to Varna on the Black Sea," Reagan clumsily undermined his own point about unrelenting Soviet dangers; and dwelling on the failings of the Soviet economy is a fine way to evoke smugness, but could hardly produce a restorative sense of moral purpose. Reagan's closing call for a "crusade for freedom" was a graceless echo of cold warriorism.

Before the German Bundestag, however, the President found the proper voice. He opened with a tribute to the German immigrant heritage in America, closed with a haunting image of German culture standing against the destruction of war, and reminded the Germans of today that they are the "founding fathers" of Germany's future. This was nostalgia at its finest, recalling the past in order to invigorate the alliance as the bearer of noble things into the future. Rather than merely longing for a resurrection of the past, it offered the vision of a future enriched by our steady improvement upon the past. Reagan celebrated the alliance this time by recalling its achievements in the face of trials, not by deriding the Soviet Union. His call to action was faultless: "the noblest objective of our diplomacy is the patient and difficult task of reconciling our adversary to peace." There are some political tasks for which Reagan's natural sentimentality are finely suited.

The Polish sanctions, and even the pipeline affair, began in the same tone. In announcing the sanctions in December 1981, Reagan reminded the alliance of the political heritage they shared, contrasted this with Poland's plight, and insisted that the freedom and abundance enjoyed in the West "bring with them a solemn obligation . . . to the heritage of liberty and dignity handed down to us by our forefathers and an obligation to the children of the world, whose future will be shaped by the way we live our lives today." Again, the reminder that the alliance stands as both the beneficiary and the trustee of a rich heritage was an effective use of nostalgia to provide a moral community with a sense of obligation and a vision of the future. Although Reagan clearly sought to inflict pain on the Soviet and Polish governments for their policies, his theme was moral obligation—"free men cannot and will not stand idly by." Regrettably, the alliance promptly reduced discourse to whether suspending fishing rights and airline service would compel an end to martial law. It would be a fine and just world if expressions of moral outrage invariably halted outrageous behavior, yet outrage can have an important effect in binding and rejuvenating a moral community, even when it cannot reform the world. The alliance's purpose is to contain Soviet power, but the deeper reason for resisting that power is the manner in which it is used by the Kremlin against its subjects. If the alliance dulls its sense of outrage at the way Soviet power is used, it risks losing its moral core and sense of caution and purpose as it expands trade and political contacts with the Soviet bloc.

A European argument has been made that, by invoking sanctions which can have no effect on the Soviets, the alliance forgets that "the rest of the world is likely to regard a policy which conveys only intentions or emotions as signals of confusion and impotence rather than of decisiveness and strength."[19] Perhaps this is so. Yet without some gesture, the alliance would have appeared decisively indifferent, and that is not in its long-term interests, even moral concerns aside. The European argument for undisrupted ties with the Eastern bloc is that over the long term, these contacts will produce gradual reform and moderation of political repression that will ease Europe's division and danger. It seems more likely that carrying on business more or less as usual in the Polish case will engender resentment against Western Europe by the Polish people and even by the Polish and other East European governments, who may see this as a case of West Europeans abetting the Soviets.

Unfortunately, the Reagan administration quickly squandered whatever potential there was for galvanizing the alliance in the Polish sanctions case. What should have been an exercise in moral persuasion and education became blunt coercion when legal restraints on pipeline equipment exports were imposed. And when American grain sales to the Soviets were exempted from restraint on the dubious argument that such sales actually harmed the Soviets economically, the Reagan administration reduced the case to one of domestic political self-interest. At that point the policies lost their moral effect and instead gave the Soviets incentive to prolong martial law in Poland, to keep bitterness brewing within the West and to force the US into an embarrassing retreat.

Something else was lost in the pipeline affair: a reputation for constancy that is crucial if the accomplishments of the Reagan administration are to be taken seriously by Europe. It is possible that the Europeans might have been induced to follow American leadership on the gas pipeline had the US made its resolve and intentions clear before the allies were locked in by contracts and domestic policies. But instead, when the final contracts were being signed in late 1981, the State Department's assistant secretary for economic and business affairs was asserting that

> ... [W]e do not regard this as an issue which should be resolved by the United States attempting to dictate what Europe should do.... We recognize also that the final decision on the pipeline is Europe's and that the consequences of their decision, for good or ill, will be felt primarily by Europeans, not Americans.[20]

For European governments, it can be difficult enough to reconcile domestic opinion to compliance with American policies without the added burden of then seeing the US reverse course and reduce all previous arrangements to nonsense. In assessing the Reagan administration's accomplishments in dealing with Europe, therefore, we must ask not only "Is it enough?" but also "Will it last?" Midway through his first term, it does not appear that Reagan's achievements are either sufficient or firmly grounded.

The Reagan administration has made the restoration of American military strength the centerpiece of its foreign policy. Indeed, it has behaved at times as if it intended to hold all other policy in abeyance until its military programs were completed. Certainly the achievements so far in boosting military spending are impressive, but do they really show sufficient and lasting resolve? Whether spending $1.6 trillion over five years is "sufficient" or not is a question too closely tied to specific doctrinal viewpoints to be answered objectively. But allies, would-be-allies, and even the Soviets looking to whether long-term trends favor the rise or demise of US military potential could turn to the administration's own figures on comparative American and Soviet military spending. What they would find is that the administration, even with its own projected efforts, expects the gap between total annual US and Soviet spending to narrow but not close by the end of the decade; expects the gap in investment (i.e., procurement, military construction and RDT&E) to remain unchanged; expects the gap in RDT&E to widen; and expects the gap in strategic forces spending to narrow slightly but remain enormous.[21] Moreover, while the American military effort has lagged over the past decade, the Soviets established a widening advantage in the ratio of US-Soviet total accumulated military investment. By the administration's own estimates, if the Soviets hold their rate of investment steady, the US would have to have an annual investment growth rate of 14% to restore a one-to-one ratio in accumulated investments, and even then it would not reach parity until the mid-1990s. In fact, the current and projected US investment growth rate is only about 10%. Research and development innovations that would render whole portions of the accumulated Soviet forces obsolete would help restore the balance more quickly, but, as noted, the gap between American and Soviet RDT&E effort will widen.

What are allies to make of this? Comparisons based upon dollar estimates of Soviet military expenditures are the mushiest of data. In its zeal to emphasize military dangers and the urgency of reform, the administration has painted a bold picture instead of a long American recessional. At the same time, allies who have watched Reagan's domestic policies closely would have to doubt that he has laid the political groundwork for sustained military spending. Historically, the American electorate has been willing to insulate decisions on guns from decisions on butter, so long as the pool of tax revenues kept expanding and deficit spending was tolerated. The Reagan administration has changed these two conditions and thus cast the competition between military and social welfare spending in sharper relief than perhaps any postwar administration. Of course, for Reagan the two are not in competition. His tax cuts and assaults on social programs are part of a political doctrine regarding improper governmental intrusion in the lives of individuals. A large share (about 38%) of the voters who elected Reagan, however, did so out of exasperation with Jimmy Carter, not because they endorsed Reagan's broad ideological stands on social or economic issues.[22] When the administration's vigorous efforts to keep tax cuts, trim deficits, *and* keep Department of Defense spending high led it willy-nilly to cut into social welfare programs largely without discrimination, Reagan and the electorate parted company, for the public had a different idea about how to balance budgets while financing higher military spending: postpone tax cuts.[23]

If it comes to pitting guns vs. butter directly, child nutrition programs against army tanks, the Defense Department will lose. Those favoring enlarged social programs can invariably produce heart-rending cases of genuine human need. By contrast, Department of Defense programs will always seem postponeable and trimmable, and it will be hard to argue that national security is palpably reduced by, e.g., one submarine per year rather than two. Moreover, the major source of competition in future years for treasury dollars will be entitlement programs with powerful constituencies, not the "social engineering" programs that Reagan believes the electorate abhors.

To protect the high levels of military spending that he favors over the long run, Reagan would have to convince the electorate that federal social welfare assistance was undesirable in and of itself, no matter what the pleas of human suffering. Reagan has argued for the state governments, corporations, and private charities to take up assistance programs, with appropriate conservative arguments about local control and efficiency. But state governments, businesses, and charities have been devastated by the same economic slump that pushes up demand for social services. Rather than providing a convincing case that the burdens shucked off by the federal government can be readily taken up by local effort, Reagan has engineered a refresher lesson on why these burdens were passed to Washington in the first place.

Reagan has repeatedly asserted that economic revival is a prerequisite for reestablishing US leadership and military strength. This is true with a vengeance. Unless economic activity and the pool of tax revenues expands, the administration cannot escape the clash between guns and butter. Without recovery, it is improbable that either Reagan or his military spending programs will survive the 1984 elections. And the demise of either or both will intensify doubts about the American capacity for sustained leadership.

The administration is also on unfirm ground in its handling of two broader aspects of US-Soviet relations vital to the Europeans: East-West trade and arms control. During the presidential campaign, Reagan remarked of East-West trade: "Why shouldn't the Western world quarantine the Soviet Union until they decide to behave as a civilized nation should?" "Why not . . . a complete cutoff of trade? It sure beats war."[24] Since his election, Reagan and his spokesmen have characterized their trade policy in various ways.

> . . . We must not subsidize the Soviet economy. The Soviet Union must make the difficult choices brought on by its military budgets and economic shortcomings. (President Reagan, Eureka College, May 9, 1982)

> We must force our principal adversary, the Soviet Union, to bear the brunt of its economic shortcomings. (William Clark,

speech at Georgetown University, May 21, 1982)

... [O]ur strategy must see to it that productivity and technological creativity of free societies are not exploited to make good
the chronic deficiencies of the communist system. ... If the Soviet
Union earns foreign currency by exporting raw materials to our
allies, it can purchase more equipment to facilitate its arms
production. ... The Soviet leaders must know full well by now
that their central planning system is fatally flawed. But their system cannot be reformed without liberalizing Soviet society as a
whole. Hence, without access to advanced technology from the
West, the Soviet leadership would be forced to choose between its
military-industrial priorities and the preservation of a tightly-
controlled political system ... in a reversal that is testimony to the
degree of past blindness to reality, it is the Soviets who do the
manipulating [of trade levers]—and with considerable success—in
spite of their inherently weak bargaining position. ... I must also
remind you that whatever strengthens the Soviet Union now, weak-
ens the cause of freedom in the world. (Casper Weinberger, *Annual
Report to the Congress, FY 1983*, pp. 1-22 and 23)

"Economic warfare" has also found its way into the Defense
Department's long-range Defense Guidance document for 1984-
1988, cited as one means by which the US will restore military
balance—a tacit admission, some might infer, that the administration's weapons programs are themselves inadequate to the task.

It is already evident that the debate with the Europeans over East-
West trade could wreck the alliance by aggravating points of fundamental disagreement about the nature of the Soviet Union and hence
about the Soviet threat. The administration says it rejects the European view that "strong economic ties can moderate political attitudes
and behavior among the Communist states."

Unfortunately, in the case of the USSR, such moderation has not
occurred and the era of detente has been a period of unprecedented growth of the Soviet military, coupled with increased ad-

venturism worldwide.[25]

Other Western policies have not been successful. East-West trade was expanded in the hope of providing incentives for Soviet restraint, but the Soviets exploited the benefits of trade without moderating their behavior. . . . Both the current and the new Soviet leadership should realize that aggressive policies will meet a firm Western response. On the other hand, a Soviet leadership devoted to improving its people's lives, rather than expanding its armed conquests, will find a sympathetic partner in the West. The West will respond with expanded trade and other forms of cooperation.[26]

Despite its derogation of the European view, the Reagan administration supposedly still has room in its own policy for substantial trade with the Soviets. Its approach assertedly is "to broaden certain economic ties that will permit us to exercise greater leverage and influence on Soviet behavior," which presumes that indeed trade will be significant enough economically to the Soviets so that Kremlin behavior will be moderated by these trade levers. Grain sales are cited as an example: they involve "non-strategic" goods, remind the Soviets of the benefits of East-West cooperation, and by requiring "cash on the barrelhead," the sales drain hard currency that might otherwise go to enhance Soviet military forces.[27]

Then what are the consequential differences between the Reagan administration and the Europeans? One is the underlying economic pressure for trade. The Europeans are more dependent upon foreign trade generally, their economies tend to complement the Eastern bloc but are competitive with the US (Germany's exports to the US in 1981 were only 1% larger than exports to the Soviet bloc, and imports from the US only 8% larger), and alternative markets in the third world are drying up. Not surprisingly, the Germans, who rely upon export trade for 25% of their GNP and who conduct half of all the West's trade with the Eastern bloc, have repeatedly stated that trade restrictions and embargoes must not become a normal means of conducting foreign policy. A second difference lies in assumptions about the timing and effect of East-West economic exchanges. The

Europeans view trade as a device for provoking reform in Soviet policies; the Reagan administration would grant trade as a reward only after reforms are manifest. Europeans take a long view, believing that trade ties work their change slowly and that Soviet reform will emerge as domestic groups benefitted by Western trade push to the top; Reagan sees the Soviets as being in such dire economic straits that immediate pressures ought to compel reforms.[28] And the Reagan administration has a more expansive view of what ought to be restricted. It would halt sales of energy exploration equipment and would expand the COCOM restrictions to cover not only specific items judged useful to the Soviet military effort, but also some dozen "critical technologies" embodying the high-tech advantages of the West, even if intended for non-military use. When it speaks of economic warfare, the administration goes further yet, to include any items that conceivably permit the Soviets to earn or divert funds into military forces. In its extravagant language of "economic warfare," the Reagan administration departs most fundamentally from Europe in goals and perceptions when it sets out to ease the Soviet threat by razing the economic and political structure of the Soviet state. The line of argument recalls "The Sources of Soviet Conduct" and 1947. Europeans, whose attachment to detente impels them to view the Soviet Union as more a traditional than an implacably revolutionary state, cannot possibly accept the Reagan approach. Success of such an assault upon the economic and political core of the Soviet Union is improbable; Europe in its exposed position would face the gravest risks, and the collapse of the Soviet Union would only make Europe's position vis-à-vis the US more problematic.

The postures on both sides of the Atlantic are faulty in parts. Some claim perhaps can be made that during the early days of detente, the prospect of enlarged East-West trade exercised some influence at the margins upon Soviet policy. Less of a claim can be made that the selection or advancement of Soviet elites is significantly determined by this factor, so that if trade only continues long enough, Soviet behavior is bound to moderate. In addition, if the Europeans (and the US) hope to continue spending small portions of the GNPs on defense, and particularly defense investment, in the face of large Soviet efforts, then the West must protect its technological edge. Bans on the sale of specific military-related equipment are useful but can be evaded by a determined Soviet Union. Since the more effective constraint upon the Soviet military appears to be the generally backward state of the Soviet technological base, the West cannot be indifferent to the secondary consequences of trade, while the long-term moderating effects upon Soviet foreign policy behavior remain uncertain. Attempting to retard the general advance of the Soviet technological base does make sense—if it is feasible.

On the other hand, the Soviet Union is not on the brink of economic collapse, though it is not hard to see why Reagan prefers to argue that it is. According to its own assertions, the administration intends to sell the Soviets nothing even remotely helpful to the Russians' military efforts or remedial of their economic shortcomings, nor anything that would give the Soviets reverse leverage on Western producers or policies. Yet supposedly the products will still be so vital to the Kremlin that they will yield leverage for the US to, e.g., force moderate behavior and draw the Soviets into deep reductions in the START talks. It is hard to imagine how all these conditions could be fulfilled *unless* the Soviet Union were experiencing fundamental collapse and therefore would be grateful for the most basic and innocuous of goods in trade.[29]

Of course, the Reagan administration's contorted justification for resuming grain sales fails by its own announced standards. The Soviets will invest $320 billion in agriculture under their current five-year plan, adding to the $450 billion invested since 1965. Even so, the performance of the agricultural sector is abysmal, and the Soviets have been importing grain in amounts equal to one-fourth of total domestic production.[30] Surely the Soviets should be credited with figuring out that the $8-12 billion cost of imported grain, even if paid in hard currency, puts less of a strain on the Soviet economy than the levels of agricultural investment needed to ensure higher grain production.[31] Any grain sales, indeed, any foreign trade at all, in this sense amounts to a "subsidy" that permits the Soviets to divert funds away from civil uses and into military investment. Setting such restrictive standards for East-West trade is an unfruitful line of policy with no chance of being accepted by the Europeans. Nor could the administration serve its other purported goal of developing trade levers over Soviet policy. Relieving itself of "its own economic shortcomings" is precisely what every nation tries to do in international trade. The Soviets would have no incentive to moderate behavior if the Reagan administration announces in advance that, in effect, it is conducting economic warfare and will grant no trade in items the Soviets truly need.[32]

There is no harm in trying to get the Europeans to widen the COCOM categories and generally to rein in trade and credits with the Soviets as an element of general East-West policy. (Though why the allies should try to put a crimp in Soviet domestic energy production through trade restraints, when the alliance has so little capacity to protect supplies in the Gulf, will take a lot of explaining.) But such restrictions are notoriously leaky; inevitably they rest more heavily upon some economic sectors and thus more upon some states than others, and domestic political pressures upon the allies to thwart restrictions will be great. If the Reagan administration continues to persuade itself that the Soviets can be pushed over the economic precipice with just a bit more shove, or insists upon making up for shortcomings in American military spending by curtailing European trade in order to blunt Soviet military programs indirectly, then it is surely headed for unending strife with the allies.

The Reagan administration has found itself in a quandary over arms control, the other US-Soviet issue vital to alliance relations. On the one hand, Reagan himself has a broad if diffuse animus toward the concept of arms limitation. Even when announcing his own strategic arms control initiative in May 1982, Reagan could not refrain from a sweeping condemnation of past efforts:

> . . . [S]o far, the Soviet Union has used arms control negotiations primarily as an instrument to restrict US defense programs and, in conjunction with their own arms buildup, as a means to en-

hance Soviet power and prestige.[33]

This is faulty arms control history. Left-wing critics are more accurate in their assertions that superpower arms control has served more often to ratify decisions already made about weapons programs. But it doesn't really matter. Arms control is not a conservative's issue. Rather than viewing it as an adjunct to wise military planning, Reagan sees arms control as a self-imposed, self-denying constraint upon the American genius for competition.

On the other hand, as Reagan discovered during his first year, it is no longer possible to sustain American and European public support for military programs without some sign that the arms control alternative is being explored. Reagan now has pressure from two directions to show not just motion but results in arms limitation efforts. One source of pressure is the allies. When Pershings and cruise missiles are ready for deployment in 1983, the US will have to show that it has lived up to the spirit of NATO's two-track decision in 1979—that it has negotiated arms control in good faith before going through with deployments. The other pressure will come from the American public when, as now seems unavoidable, the administration will be able to sustain its high military budgets only by asking greater sacrifices in the form of higher deficits, even deeper cuts in social welfare programs, assaults upon entitlement payments, or prolonged economic malaise. Yet if it holds to its current tactics, the administration stands no chance of succeeding in either the INF (Intermediate-range Nuclear Force) or START (Strategic Arms Reduction Talks) negotiations, or improving public opinion of its efforts.

There is little hope for agreement in the INF talks because there is no "give" in the positions of the sides. No precedent exists in modern arms control experience to suggest that the Soviets will dismantle all or most of their newly-deployed SS-20s in order to forestall NATO's INF deployments. Moscow would insist upon retaining SS-20s targeted against China; but since the SS-20s are inherently transportable, NATO must see a danger of redeployment west of the Urals in a confrontation. To improve their bargaining posture, the

Soviets must argue that French and British missile forces, as well as all of NATO's nuclear-capable aircraft, are included in the NATO total; otherwise the balance would appear to be grossly disproportionate in Moscow's favor. But the US will argue that none of these other systems are subject to negotiation; otherwise there is little prospect of setting ceilings that will cut into the SS-20s. The Soviets have little to gain from these talks anyway. The Reagan administration has ensured, with its programs to deploy hundreds of long-range cruise missiles on American submarines and surface ships, that the Soviets will soon face vast numbers of cruise missiles in the NATO region, no matter what becomes of land-based INF. The Pershings, with their short flight times and relative invulnerability to defenses, pose a more potent threat to the Soviet leadership and are undoubtedly the real focus of Soviet anxieties. But restraints that would cut deeply into the Pershing deployments without exacting a high price in SS-20s would be hard to extract from NATO. From the Soviet perspective, then, stewardship of the Soviet INF negotiating team might just as well be assigned to the ministry of propaganda. Any limitations on NATO's INF will be won in the streets and parliaments of West Europe, not at the green baize table in Geneva.

The Reagan administration was dealt a weak hand in all this by prior NATO decisions, but it has not done much to improve its position. When NATO faces the reckoning in 1983, the US will need a compelling military justification for the deployments and proof that Soviet unreasonableness has blocked the arms control track. Unfortunately NATO's decision to deploy precisely 572 missiles in 1983 was blatantly political rather than military. The imbalance of forces being rectified was "perceptual," the deadline for deployments was set by RDT&E schedules rather than calculations of maximum danger, and 572 was a number conveniently divisible into large and small shares for large and small allies. The weakness of these justifications was reflected in Reagan's attempt to find compelling arguments when announcing his "zero option" proposal in November 1981:

The only answer to these . . . SS-20 intermediate-range missile systems is a comparable threat to Soviet targets. In other words, a deterrent preventing the use of these Soviet weapons by the counterthreat of a like response against their own territory. At present, however, there is no equivalent deterrent to these Soviet intermediate missiles.[34]

This argument could hardly suit Soviet purposes better. It rests upon a strained distinction between intermediate-range missiles and all other nuclear weapons on NATO's side. By asserting that "no equivalent deterrent exists," Reagan fuels suspicions that US strategic nuclear forces are indeed "decoupled" from Europe's security. The Soviet's counter-argument—that NATO already has an array of intermediate-range weapons, including French and British missiles— is not hobbled by such strained distinctions, is bound to seem more reasonable to public opinion than NATO's refusal even to discuss French and British weapons, and in its way offers psychological comfort by reminding Europeans that even without Pershings and cruise missiles they are hardly defenseless.

The Soviets can also shift the burden of "reasonableness," and postpone NATO's deployments indefinitely, by insisting that the INF and START negotiations be melded together so that all nuclear systems relevant to NATO and Soviet security are discussed. Here again, Reagan has a weak position, though largely of his own making. The specific proposal Reagan put forth for START (850 ICBMs and SLBMs; 5,000 total warheads, no more than half on land-based ICBMs; later reductions in total throw-weight and warheads; plus other limits) could not be transformed into a treaty by the end of 1983—or even by the end of Reagan's administration. Even if the Soviets could be induced to accept such drastic reductions and restructuring of their strategic forces, such low force levels would entail significant rewards for cheating and thus would require verification methods of the most intrusive sort. The Reagan administration fully understands this, and surely must also be credited with understanding that such intrusive inspection practices are unnegotiable with the Soviets (or even with the Pentagon).

If Reagan seeks by this posture to make a point about the infeasibility of meaningful arms control, there is nothing wrong with that in principle. Ascertaining whether the Soviets are willing to accommodate genuine Western security concerns is precisely what the US should be using the Geneva negotiations for. However, the shortcomings of Reagan's START proposals are that they do so little to address genuine security problems. The proposed limits would prolong the strategic instability posed by ICBM vulnerability, would not significantly reduce the destruction from all-out nuclear war, and would not make the defensive task (through ABM and/or civil defense) that much easier. Indeed, if strategic bombers and cruise missiles remain largely unrestrained, START might not even yield overall reductions in total strategic forces. Because his proposals seem to serve so few other purposes, Reagan has aroused suspicions that his START position was designed primarily to paralyze arms control rather than to advance it. A Soviet proposal to meld the INF and START talks thus becomes doubly attractive to American and European arms control proponents: it postpones INF deployments and compels the US toward more reasonable START proposals.

The US surely could adopt a more ingenious posture on these matters. First, the US has in effect tabled two INF proposals—572 NATO Pershings and GLCMs for 300 + SS-20s, or zero NATO missiles for zero SS-20s. The Reagan administration should devise other trade-off formulas, indeed a whole list of them. Nothing would serve better, if the US must buy time in 1983 without appearing to back down on INF deployments, than a flurry of new INF initiatives, each requiring further negotiation. Bureaucracies do not care to consider (or announce) new initiatives until prior ones are clearly dead, but Presidents are free to do so.

Second, the US might announce that all intermediate-range (i.e. over 1,000 km.) nuclear-capable systems in Europe should be taken into account in negotiations. By the Soviet tallies, this would raise the NATO total currently to 806, including 550 US aircraft that the Soviets claim are dual-capable. But the Soviets concede already to having 975 such systems, and the burden of proof would be upon them to show why an additional 980 + SU-24s and MiG-27s, judged by NATO to be dual-capable, should not be counted as well, bringing the Soviet total to around 2,000. This tactic will not produce cuts in the SS-20s, but it would improve the US justification for then following through with Pershing and cruise deployments. The US cannot sign a bilateral treaty binding the French and British, of course, but nothing prevents the US from offering an accord that takes third-party totals into account in the determination of ceilings for both sides.

Third, Reagan could accept advice which he earlier rejected and improve his START position by dropping the 850 ceiling on ICBMs and SLBMs, while pushing for reductions in total throw-weight and warheads and a warhead size limit (e.g., 200-400 kg). This would nudge the evolution of strategic forces toward smaller, single-warhead missiles, still a radical restructuring but far more stabilizing and beneficial to the US than the current proposal, and thus more convincing as a good faith effort at arms limitation.

Finally, the administration should hold firm on its plans for cruise missile deployments on US submarines and surface ships. Perceptually, off-shore forces are not the equivalent of land-based INF, and they reduce Soviet incentives to negotiate seriously. Nevertheless, SLCMs provide a plausible line of retreat for the alliance, far preferable to wrecking governments and splintering allies by forcing land-based deployments, according to an artificial deadline, in the face of massive European anti-nuclear resistance.

It is not clear that Reagan has yet found solid ground in his Middle East policy either. Here the administration needs three achievements. The first is a demonstration that the long-held US policy of refusing to deal with the PLO, of trying for a step-by-step resolution of the Arab-Israeli conflict within the context of Camp David, and of excluding the Soviets from a role in a negotiated settlement has not retarded the prospects for peace. Long years of unwavering US support for Israel's posture on Palestinian self-determination have been justified on grounds of sympathy for Israel's travails and concern for its bargaining position. More recently, however, American diplomacy had appeared more pliant than powerful in dealing with Israel, because the US could not bring itself either to boldly support or criticize and constrain Israeli actions. The US should not forget that the reason its Middle East policy has succeeded thus far is because the US is perceived by the Arabs as the only party capable of bringing Israel to terms. President Reagan's letter to Saudi King Fahd during the Lebanon crisis in July 1982—asserting that if the Saudis could not find a refuge for the PLO promptly, the US could not be responsible for Israel's actions—may have seemed like a clever negotiating ploy, but its long-term effects upon Arab opinions of US power could only be harmful. The Reagan administration needs success in its Israel policy at least as much to make a point to the Gulf states as to mollify its European allies.

The second achievement is to make it clear that the US intends to have an abiding interest in the stability of the Gulf region, not simply as a fiduciary for Israel or the Europeans, but in its own right. Were the US to remain tied to the Gulf for oil imports, its durability as a guarantor of Gulf security would be more credible to the Europeans and the Soviets. (Currently 21% of US oil imports, but only 9% of its total oil consumption comes from the Gulf, almost all of it from Saudi Arabia.) So long as arrangements are made to survive disruptions of imported supplies, continued or even enhanced reliance upon Gulf producers need not be a hazard. Granting some preference or quota to Gulf suppliers would also free up other sources for European consumers and diversify their dependency.

A policy of this sort starts from the premise that oil is a security matter and not just a consumer product. The Reagan rhetoric on energy often runs in exactly the opposite direction. In campaign addresses, Reagan argued that the US need not have to live with scarcity, foreign dependence, or governmental intrusion into oil industry decisions if American free enterprise is unleashed to search the republic for new oil supplies. The collapse of oil exploration and alternative energy ventures as the world economic slump deepened during 1982 pointed to a basic weakness of Reagan's free-market notions: the market responds to price, but current oil prices are poor predictors of future political turmoil and disruptions in supplies. What the US needs is a creative response to continued import reliance that will serve broader security interests by turning necessity into opportunity.

The Reagan administration made a proper step in that direction by speeding up acquisitions for the Strategic Petroleum Reserve (SPR). Yet even here the ideological views of the president have led him to oppose any planning now on how the SPR might be allocated in emergencies, and in March 1982, Reagan vetoed the Standby Petroleum Allocation Act, which did little more than authorize the president to prepare emergency price and allocation schemes for congressional consideration, on the grounds that "our marketplace and the good sense of the American people provide our best lines of defense against any future interruptions of energy supplies"[35] If purchases for the SPR remain at target levels, by 1989 the US will have 750 million barrels of oil in reserve, augmented by an equivalent volume of oil and products in private stocks. The total is an impressive amount, equal to perhaps six month's consumption of imported oil. It ought to be encouraging to European allies, with whom the US has emergency oil sharing obligations under the International Energy Agency. But much of the effort is dissipated by what the Europeans will view as a quirky ideological refusal to think seriously and specifically about how the US will cope with the next oil disruptions.

The third achievement that the Reagan administration needs in its Middle East policy is to convince the Europeans that the US has prudent responses to the problems of regime stability in the Third World. Even if the US is bearing the major burden of "out-of-area" military preparations, the Europeans will remain extraordinarily sensitive and vulnerable to the consequences of any US policy in the Gulf, no matter who finances it. The oil disruptions of 1973 and 1979 have established that the Europeans will be held hostage to, and will suffer the consequences of, US policy, even when they disagree with it and attempt to separate themselves from it. Since the economic ties, weapons sales, and historical entree of the Europeans in the Gulf region is in many cases greater than that of the US, their capacity as spoilers is substantial.

Here again, Reagan got off to a bad start. In October 1982, the President added the Reagan Protocol to the Carter Doctrine by asserting that the US would not permit Saudi Arabia to become another Iran. Making such a commitment in a seemingly offhand manner at a press conference was bound in itself to raise questions about Reagan's judgment. Moreover, the comparison with Iran revealed again the scope of Reagan's belief that all the world is malleable beneath the hammer of American power. For the Europeans, who have learned something in the postwar years about the limits of western influence in the Third World, the simplicity of Reagan's views could not be encouraging: ". . . the Shah fell when Carter pulled the rug out from under our ally of thirty-some-odd years standing. All he had to do was stand up and stand beside the Shah's government and there wouldn't have been a successful revolution."[36] No doubt the US could have handled its affairs in Iran in a wiser fashion. It ought to have recognized earlier, for instance, what became evident at the Shah's fall—that even the middle class that had profitted most from the Shah's rule would not rise to his defense, because not a family had been untouched by the spreading crudities and cruelties of SAVAK. As important as Reagan's simplicities, however, is the fact that an American public encouraged to believe all will yield before American power is bound to react to failure by yet another retreat from global involvement. The problem isn't just that simple views lead to wrong policies; simple views presage failure and undermine the reliability of American leadership. In making its case to the Europeans in this matter, the Reagan administration actually has some advantages. Clearly the initial test of American prudence in dealing with turmoil and transition in modernizing nations will be in Central America, where the US enjoys historical experience, proximity, and friendly states in the region to serve as mediators and interpreters. France's decision to challenge the Reagan administration in Central America will make it an intriguing test of policies.

Reagan still lacks a European policy—that is, a policy which focuses on Europe as Europe and shapes US actions according to a (reasonably) coherent vision of what Europe is, where it is going, and where the US wishes to stand in relation to it decades hence. Reagan's policies do have parts that might be assembled into a functional substitute for a coherent European policy. The most important elements are a commitment to restoring military balances; a recognition that the Gulf is the most probable region where the alliance will be tested in the coming decade; an appreciation that the West must closely examine the character of its associations with the Soviets, even as it expands them; a subtle hand in encouraging the American public and Congress to think once again of the US as a nation with global responsibilities; and a certain boldness and stubbornness in personal style that are indispensible to true leadership. The very fact that Reagan lacks a true European policy, and has fixed his gaze instead upon the Soviet Union, could even be a virtue—it at least might avoid the hubris of Americans supposing that they know perfectly well what is good for Europe.

Unfortunately, the Reagan administration falls too often from virtue to vice through excessive zeal. By riveting its attention upon the Soviet Union, and upon military strength as the centerpiece of policy, the administration has been drawn into viewing Europe as a mere instrument of US efforts to garner power vis-à-vis the Soviets. It is a short step from this view to an attitude that if the Europeans will not go along with the US in carrying out America's Soviet policy, then the US will find better instruments.

But Europe and the alliance are not just tools of America's policy; they are the very measure of its success. American containment of the Soviet Union is evaluated in the concrete. The measure is whether the Soviets succeed in accreting power by absorbing or dominating nations on their periphery. Europe is unquestionably the quadrant of that periphery which matters most. It is inconceivable that the US could resist the Soviets if it lost Europe, just as it is inconceivable that the US could deny Europe to the Soviets without the alliance. If Reagan genuinely believes, as he remarked in January 1980, that "we now enter one of the most dangerous decades of Western civilization," then he ought to prize the cooperation of the Europeans even more. The allies have available far too many ways to spoil US policies toward the Soviets, if their views and sensitivities are ignored. And harmonious ties with the Europeans are themselves a significant offset to Soviet military power in a period when balance is in doubt. Close relations among the allies enhance deterrence by heightening the credibility of mutual promises that all will make sacrifices in the common defense. A potential breach within the alliance on fundamental questions of how to contain and tame Soviet power, of which fissures over Afghanistan and Polish sanctions are symptoms, ought to call forth more attention to a European policy, not less.

Complete harmony among the allies is unachievable, given the centrifugal forces inherent in the alliance's distribution of power and Europe's dependent and exposed position. The extent to which the Europeans will strike out on their own paths will be set very much by how efficacious and constant American leadership is, and by the transformations that American policy will work on European opinions regarding the limits of proper conduct in dealing with the Soviets and breaking ranks with the US. Perhaps obsessed with intimations of its own mortality, the Reagan administration has unfortunately preferred impatience, simplistic assumptions that sweeping changes in the world can be wrought by a few deft strokes, radical demarches of policy for which little groundwork has been laid, and a narrow focus on the Soviet Union. Such governance by *coups de main* expends consensus rather than creating it. Ronald Reagan's innate sense of the importance of moral cement for the alliance, supported by the bulwark of American military strength, ought to have served him better in alliance affairs than it has so far. He has regrettably forgotten the words of Walter Lippmann: "The final test of a leader is that he leaves behind him in other men the conviction and the will to carry on."[37]

NOTES

1. Ronald Reagan, acceptance speech before the Republican National Convention, July 17, 1980. *Vital Speeches*, Vol. XLVI, No. 1 (August 15, 1980).

2. Henry A. Kissinger, *Years of Upheaval* (Boston: Little, Brown, 1982), p. 235.

3. Kissinger, *Years of Upheaval*, p. 245.

4. Helmut Schmidt, "A Policy of Reliable Partnership," *Foreign Affairs*, Vol. 59, No. 4 (Spring 1981), p. 755.

5. André Fontaine, "Transatlantic Doubts and Dreams," *Foreign Affairs* (America and the World 1980), Vol. 59, No. 3, p. 593. Fontaine is editor-in-chief of *Le Monde*.

6. Rowland Evans and Robert Novak, *The Reagan Revolution* (New York: E.P. Dutton, 1981), p. xiii.

7. John Sears, quoted in Hedrick Smith *et al.*, *Reagan the Man, the President* (New York: Macmillan, 1980), p. 109. John Sears was Reagan's initial campaign manager in the presidential race.

8. Reagan, quoted in Hedrick Smith *et al.*, p. 100. One of its early embarrassments came when the administration translated these views into the assertion that the Soviets were behind most terrorism in the world—an assertion that the administration was subsequently unable to document.

9. Reagan, quoted in Hedrick Smith *et al.*, p. 100.

10. Reagan, interview with Evans and Novak, March 23, 1981. Quoted in Evans and Novak, p. 237-238.

11. Reagan, commencement address, Notre Dame University, May 17, 1981. See also " . . . communism is an aberration—it's not a normal way of living for human beings, and I think we are seeing the first beginning cracks, the beginning of the end." Reagan, press conference, June 16, 1981.

12. Reagan's itemizations of Soviet difficulties are echoes of Kissinger's own, with one notable exception: Kissinger does not prophesy

imminent Soviet collapse. See Kissinger, *Years of Upheaval*, pp. 242-244.

13. "The Soviet empire is faltering because it is rigid—centralized control has destroyed incentives for innovation, efficiency, and individual achievement." Reagan, address at Eureka College, May 9, 1982.

14. Venice Declaration of European Council, June 13, 1980.

15. Those addicted to reading bureaucratic entrails for augeries of policy will note that in the FY 1983 Annual Report of the Secretary of Defense, precedence of place is given to conventional forces over nuclear forces in the layout of text on military requirements and programs. This unprecedented shuffling of the hierarchy was deliberate: "It is by intention that I have not treated nuclear strategy until now . . . in this report . . . This administration does not regard nuclear strength as a substitute for conventional strength." *Annual Report FY 1983*, p. I-17.

16. Michel Jobert, currently France's foreign trade minister, has urged the Gulf states to join with France in asserting political independence from both superpowers and excluding both from any presence in the Gulf. Of the possible Soviet threat to the Gulf, Jobert merely asserts: "At this moment, the Soviet Union, besides its growing difficulties in Afghanistan, is fully conscious . . .that the oil supply to the West from the Middle East is of such importance that its interruption, either at the source or through control of the shipping routes, would launch a military intervention." M. Jobert does not explain who would undertake this "intervention" nor how it would be accomplished if the only power capable of countering the Soviets—the US—has been systematically excluded from political associations in the Gulf by its European allies. See Michel Jobert, "Oil Prospects in the Gulf: The EEC and the Gulf," in Abdel Majid Farid, ed., *Oil and Security in the Arabia Gulf*, (New York: St. Martin's Press, 1981), pp. 119-20.

17. New York *Times*, May 16, 1982.

18. Karl Kaiser *et al., Western Security: What Has Changed? What*

Should Be Done? (New York: Council on Foreign Relations, February 1981), p. 33; emphasis added. One must wonder what message the Soviets hear when told that Europe will regard offensive military acts in the Gulf as conceptually equivalent to offensive acts in Europe itself; but that doesn't mean Europe is serious enough about the Gulf to behave as if it were defending itself.

19. Edward Heath, "The Changing Basis of Power in International Affairs," 38th John Findley Green Lecture, Westminster College, Fulton, Missouri; March 2, 1982. *Vital Speeches*, Vol. XLVIII, No. 13 (April 15, 1982), p. 390.

20. Assistant Secretary of State Robert D. Hormats, "Soviet-West European Natural Gas Pipeline," *Department of State Bulletin*, December 1981, p. 52. Hormats' testimony was before the Subcommittee on Energy, Nuclear Proliferation, and Governmental Processes of the Senate Committee on Governmental Affairs, October 14, 1981.

21. *Annual Report FY 1983*, Charts III.J.1&2, p. III-124 and pp. III-125. Soviet spending figures are for estimated dollar costs of Soviet expenditures, in billions of 1983 dollars.

22. New York *Times* poll; New York *Times*, November 9, 1980.

23. New York *Times/CBS* poll, *May 19-23, 1982;* when asked to choose among three alternatives for reducing the size of the federal deficit, 55% of the respondents said they would be willing to eliminate the tax cut planned for July 1983; 48% were willing to reduce proposed military spending; and only 31% were willing to reduce spending on programs for the poor.

24. Reagan, quoted in Evans and Novak, *p. 201*.

25. Undersecretary of State for Economic Affairs Myer Rashish, "East-West Trade Relations," *Department of State Bulletin*, November 1981, p. 23. Rashish's statement was before the Subcommittee on International Economic Policy of the Senate Foreign Relations Committee, September 16, 1981.

26. Reagan, address at Eureka College, May 9, 1982.

27. Reagan, press conferences, June 30 and July 28, 1982. New

York *Times*, July 1 and July 29, 1982.

28. Contrast the following, for example. First, Reagan: "... the Soviet Union is very hard pressed financially and economically today. They have put their people literally on a starvation diet with regard to consumer items, while they poured all their resources into the most massive military buildup the world has ever seen." Press conference, June 30, 1982. And second, a European view: "... on the whole and within certain limits, trade does indeed encourage the growth, inside Soviet society, of forces and views naturally oriented toward the pursuit of more peaceful relations with the rest of the world. It is not so difficult to identify, in the Soviet hierarchy of power, those economic and technocratic groups which are in favor of strengthening ties with the West for economic reasons, in order to develop Soviet technology and, in general, to compensate for Soviet economic failures and backwardness. If these people and groups have a certain influence on Soviet policy—and they presumably do have one—theirs is bound to be an influence for detente and peace, rather than for actions leading to a 'cold war' atmosphere." Giovanni Agnelli, "East-West Trade: A European View," *Foreign Affairs*, Vol. 58, No. 5 (Summer 1980), p. 1026. Agnelli is Chairman of the Board of FIAT and former Chairman of CONFINDUSTRIA.

29. Nor would the CIA support Reagan's view. A CIA study of the Soviet economy, delivered to the Joint Economic Committee of Congress in December, 1982, noted that while imports from the West could play an important role in improving Soviet economic performance, the ability of the Soviet economy to survive even in the absence of all imports was much greater than that of most, possibly all, other industrialized economies. "In fact, we do not consider an economic 'collapse'—a sudden and sustained decline in . . . Soviet GNP—even a remote possibility," asserted Henry Rowen, chairman of the CIA's National Intelligence Council, when presenting the report. New York *Times*, January 9, 1983.

30. New York *Times*, June 1, 1982.
31. Certainly the Europeans have figured this out. See *Sueddeutsche Zeitung*, (Munich) August 1, 1982: "The grain deliveries strengthen the Soviet Union because it is cheaper to pay for the grain, in spite of the loss of hard currency, than it is to reform their agricultural economy. In any case, a country of the size and potential wealth of the Soviet Union cannot be forced to its knees in this fashion." An analysis prepared by Wharton Econometrics, for instance, estimated that the 46 million metric tons of grain imported by the Soviets in 1981 had a crude oil equivalent value of about 29 million metric tons of oil. The resources, in labor and capital, required by the Soviets to produce an additional 46 million metric tons of grain, however, are estimated as equal to those required to produce roughly 160 million metric tons of oil. Thus, by producing oil for export sale and using the revenues to import grain rather than producing it, the Soviets save resources equivalent to about 131 million metric tons of oil, or about $32 billion in savings. See the letter of Jan Vanous, New York *Times*, November 19, 1982.
32. The Administration's policies seemed to remain unchanged even when George Shultz—with his reputation for judicious accommodation—replaced Alexander Haig as Secretary of State. At his first meeting with the NATO foreign ministers in Canada in October 1982, Shultz reportedly outlined the following principles which he hoped the Allies would adopt on East-West trade: i) there should be no trade that adds to the military or economic capacity of the Soviet Union; ii) there should be no trade or credits that would "subsidize" the Soviet economy; and iii) there should be no trade that would enhance the Soviet "security posture." Fundamentally, these principles are no different from previously enunciated US policy. New York *Times*, October 22, 1982.
33. Reagan, address at Eureka College, May 9, 1982.
34. Reagan, speech before the National Press Club, Washington, DC, November 18, 1981.

35. Reagan, veto message, New York *Times*, March 25, 1981.

36. Reagan, quoted in Hedrick Smith *et al.*, p. 101. Reagan's comparison between Saudi Arabia and Iran also maladroitly provided grist for accusations that the US Rapid Deployment Force is intended in part as an army of occupation to ensure US oil supplies. The administration's own classified Five-Year Defense Guidance plan, liberally leaked to the press, offers cold comfort on this point to sensitive Gulf states. On the one hand, the plan reportedly asserts that "it is essential that the *Soviet Union* be confronted with the prospects of a major conflict should it seek to reach oil resources of the Gulf." Yet in another ambiguous phrase, the plan affirms that "*whatever the circumstances*, we should be prepared to introduce American forces directly into the region should it appear that the security of access to Persian Gulf oil is threatened." New York *Times*, October 25, 1982; emphasis added.

37. Lippmann, "Roosevelt Is Gone," April 14, 1945.

A Proposal To End The Danger Of War In Europe

By

MORTON A. KAPLAN

The recent anti-nuclear demonstrations in Western Europe and the United States have aroused much controversy. Their proponents argue that they are the beginning of a popular tidal wave that will eliminate, or at least reduce, the danger of nuclear war in Europe. Opponents argue that, even if the drive is not being orchestrated from Moscow, it will have asymmetric effects that will weaken the defensibility of the West and increase the chances of war, including nuclear war.

Although the size of the demonstrations is clearly disproportionate to the actual risk of war in Europe, the concern that is being expressed is warranted by the nature of the catastrophe that would occur if war, and in particular nuclear war, broke out in Europe. Yet history provides little support for those who believe that reducing numbers of weapons or refusing to engage in an arms race lessens the probability of war. Most analysts now agree that political lack of support for rearmament in the democracies in the 1930s played a significant role in reinforcing Hitler's plans for conquest. Even if we dismiss, as I would, the argument some make that the Soviet Union is planning additional conquests in Europe, the repeated crises within eastern Europe and the dismal state of the Soviet economy might lead the Soviet high command—if the West is weak or seems irresolute—to seek a solution to its problem through threat, bluff, or extortion. And, even if this is not very likely, the demonstrations would make no sense if the risk of war is negligible. Surely no one in his right mind expects NATO to attack the East.

There can be no doubt that the present heavy concentrations of military force in Europe, which are driven by the huge size of the military forces that the Soviet Union unilaterally built up, are morally obscene. Justifications for this build-up often refer to Russian history. The Russian concern with military space for defense is understandable in these terms. Both Napoleon and Hitler invested the Moscow area, and only defensive territorial space saved Russia.

Today, however, it is Western Europe that lacks space for defense. From the border between the Germanies to Paris is less than 300 miles or roughly the width of the state of Pennsylvania. Contending armies, even without the use of nuclear weapons, would employ unprecedented explosive power in areas of concentrated population. It is little to wonder, therefore, that some in Western Europe worry about the new Pershing II nuclear launchers that have been proposed for Europe. They are provocative because they can hit Moscow, dangerous because they can be hit by preemptive attack, and are seen as signifying—even though this is factually incorrect—an American willingness to engage in nuclear war that would be limited to European terrain. Western European demonstrators have particular reason to be concerned given the unprecedented and unnecessary concentration of Soviet nuclear power directed against them, not merely in tactical nuclear weaponry, but in the MIRVed SS-20s as well.

No Reasonable Objective Can Validate the Risk of War

It can be taken as a given that no European nation will today begin a war for the reasons that led to the wars of the last century and this. Not trade, colonies, space, or other similar motives will lead the authorities of either East or West deliberately to initiate a war in Europe. War in Europe, if it comes, will come from miscalculation or from some uncontrollable incident. Although an equilibrium in strength between NATO and the WTO (Warsaw Treaty Organization) is a bulwark against a war by miscalculation, it not only is no guarantee against war arising from an uncontrollable incident but provides a large part of the explosive power that would be set off by the flame arising out of an incident.

There is a plan presented here that will guard against both war by miscalculation and war arising from an uncontrollable incident. It will be consistent with the national security of all the nations of Eastern and Western Europe. In addition, by reducing drastically the huge expenditures for military forces, it will release the economic and creative energies of the populations of both areas.

This plan may not be received with enthusiasm by the leaders of either bloc. Leaders of large entities tend to be extremely conservative and often lack imagination. They tend to be responsive to vested interests that have a stake in the current situation. And it is possible that the non-legitimate nature of Soviet rule may inhibit acceptance for fear of loss of personal political position and power. I am not, therefore, arguing that the plan will be accepted, at least initially, but only that it is acceptable in terms of the national, international and human interests of the parties to whom it is addressed.

The threat of war stems from the huge build-up of forces in Europe, not from nuclear weapons as such. In the absence of a massive confrontation in Europe, even entirely conventional, nuclear war in Europe would not be a threat.

It is inconceivable that the leaders of East or West would resort to the use of nuclear weapons over a European issue unless a conventional European war were in progress or about to be initiated. If only modest forces were present in Europe—so small that they would be incapable of producing the conquest of other nations—then it is difficult to believe that nuclear weapons would be resorted to. It is only in a disordered fantasy that one imagines leaders in Moscow or Washington pressing the red button in the absence of a threat to the survival of the nation.

However, if survival is threatened, the resort to nuclears is not unlikely. Because the losing side is not unlikely to resort to nuclears, the attacking force is motivated to preempt whether or not it has agreed not to use nuclear weapons first. Even if all nuclear weapons are removed from Europe and strategic forces savagely reduced, the losing party is still likely to resort to strategic nuclear weapons, whether sea- or land-based.

Therefore, if one wishes significantly to reduce or to eliminate the threat of nuclear war in Europe, the first step is to reduce or eliminate the threat of war in Europe; and this threat lies in the conventional confrontation.

The possibilities just sketched are sufficient reason for proposing a conventional disarmament plan such as the one in this proposal. However, the next generation of nuclear weapons constitutes an additional reason for considering nuclear disarmament proposals—valuable though they may be as auxiliary considerations after conventional disarmament—as largely irrelevant to the avoidance of nuclear war.

I am indebted to General Gallois for a better understanding of the sub-kiloton nuclear missiles that are on the horizon. These weapons are so small they can be easily shielded and hidden. A freeze to prevent their manufacture cannot be verified effectively for control purposes. They can be fired from dual-purpose launchers so that no distinction can be made between conventional and nuclear launchers. And they can be shot accurately from Western Europe to Eastern Europe and the Soviet Union and vice versa with little likelihood of extensive collateral damage.

Thus, they may produce a preemptive hair trigger in a crisis if they are deployed or presumed to be deployed. The preempting side may believe that it can avoid disaster, change the European balance, and run only a slight risk of strategic nuclear retaliation if there has been only minimal civilian damage. This estimate may be correct and that would be bad enough for the losing side. But it may well be wrong and then the nuclear holocaust would be upon us. However, in the absence of targets requiring nuclear attack to be disabled and also of the extensive forces needed to consolidate gains—and both would be absent with the present proposal—the hair trigger is gone, for both the threat and the targets that invoke it are gone. (This is an additional reason for the removal of tactically-oriented nuclear weapons to the seas in the back-up proposal; but the best solution is that of massive conventional disarmament.)

CONVENTIONAL ASPECTS

Except for 10,000 American and 10,000 Soviet troops in the respective Germanies as guarantees against forcible attempts to reunite Germany, all US ground forces would be removed from Europe and all Soviet ground forces from areas west of the Urals. The Soviet armies must be behind the Urals because otherwise they would constitute a threat to other European nations. Such major reductions by the United States and Soviet Union obviously would be dependent upon the minimization of the other conventional armies in Europe either as a threat to each other or to the Soviet Union, although it is difficult to imagine that the Poles, Rumanians, or Bulgarians would attack the Russians, even if the Russian armies are behind the Urals. Moreover, one might perhaps admit 50,000 to 100,000 Russian soldiers on the frontier as part of this proposal. In any event, therefore, the other European armies would require substantial limitation. Although this would have to be negotiated with them, one possibility is that all national European armies other than the Soviet be limited to 50,000 men on active duty and 200,000 men in reserves. Furthermore, except for the Soviet Union, all forces under ministries of the interior and all national police forces, except for small customs and air and seaport forces, should be eliminated because they might serve as disguised armies. Police forces should be local only.

All tanks should be removed from Europe within the specified area. In addition, the Soviet and United States tank forces should be limited to 1,000 tanks apiece. All other tanks should be destroyed. No armored equipment should be permitted in excess of 5 tons. All guns larger than two inches should be removed from the specified areas.

All combat aircraft should be removed from the specified area. The Soviet Union and the United States should be restricted to one thousand fighter aircraft apiece and one hundred medium-range and one hundred long-range military aircraft apiece.

The ground forces of the United States should be restricted to 1,000,000 men in the continental United States and of the Soviet Union to 1,000,000 men, who would be east of the Urals. The reserves should be restricted to half a million men. Following such European agreements, sustained efforts should be made to reach similar agreements in Asia and particularly on the Soviet-China border. If this can be done, the American, Soviet, and Chinese forces should be reduced to 250,000 men and the reserves reduced accordingly.

Adequate on-site inspection and also remote sensor inspection arrangements must be agreed to.

All European nations and the United States should sign agreements to the non-first-use of force and to non-interference in internal political changes within other nations, even those involving system changes.

There should be an agreement to arbitrate all disputes that might lead to war.

This should be a first stage in an effort to remove the threat of major war from the world. In particular, proposals should be explored for the Middle East and Asia, areas that, although not as likely as Europe to lead to nuclear war, cannot entirely be excluded as danger zones.

The parties to the agreement should pledge themselves not to sell the weapons that are eliminated but to destroy them and also to permit inspection of resupply facilities. In addition, they should pledge themselves to bring within strong control the sales of armaments abroad. It is assumed that the arrangements they have agreed to would make this advisable, particularly because the great comparative advantage that the United States and Soviet Union have over other nations would be greatly reduced.

Some European analysts believe that the force levels proposed here for Europe, exclusive of Russia, are so small that Russia quickly could invade Western Europe anyway. However, although the size and composition of the reduced European forces certainly require extensive discussion, the subsequent potential threat from the Soviet Union should not be exaggerated. If Russia does not mobilize, it will denude its Asian front. If it mobilizes, there likely is time for European and American mobilization. The Soviet Union, moreover, would have to move through an independent Poland and this would provide both a time and space buffer. In addition, the major Soviet threat is not of an actual attack but of political blackmail and of the threat of attack. This would be far more difficult at a distance. And it is hard to think of the precipitating factors.

Furthermore, the proposal could include provisions for civilian reserves trained in and equipped with small arms and anti-tank weapons, which could be so widely dispersed that the preemptive strike mentioned earlier would not be feasible. Other weapons more effective in defense than offense and for use by civilian militias might also be permitted. It is true that these details are important and require extensive discussion, as do the actual sizes of the reduced European forces, but the general thrust of the proposal seems superior to present arrangements.

NUCLEAR ASPECTS

All land-based nuclear weapons should be removed from Western and Eastern Europe, including Great Britain and the Soviet Union west of the Urals.

The sea-based weapons of France and England should not be eliminated by this proposal; but neither should Russian sea-based weapons. In any event, the land-based weapons are the ones that may provoke a preemptive strike in Europe.

A world in which this proposal is accepted is a world in which it will be enormously easier to negotiate massive nuclear reductions and to inhibit proliferation. In a world in which there are few conventional arms, it is inconceivable that nations would lob nuclear weapons at each other. If this does not make the issues of nuclear balance meaningless, it certainly makes them much less critical than in the current world. Because the minor nuclear powers can never compete with the major ones anyway, the reduction or elimination of their systems as a condition for the reduction or elimination of the systems of the major powers may succeed in reducing or eliminating the serious threat of nuclear proliferation. The small powers may well accede to this pressure because they will not wish to live in a world in which the major powers can punish them severely if they use nuclear weapons. This will be particularly true if they receive guarantees of assistance if invaded and promises of sanctions against invaders.

SOVIET RESPONSE

Although the Soviet Union initially may turn this plan down for fear of its consequences in Eastern Europe, or even inside the Soviet Union, its eventual implementation would enhance the national security of the Soviet Union and remove an albatross from the neck of its economy. Even though the Russian public does not directly determine national policy, the plan, if beamed in by broadcast, or even eventually by a kind of osmosis, likely will become enormously popular with a people that has long suffered from immense economic hardships, a decreasing life span, and great harshness in living conditions. The West, therefore, should manifest great persistence in pursuing this plan and, if necessary, might even attempt to implement it by stages—if they are not destabilizing—as an alternative to the cosmetic SALT and MBFR (Mutual Balanced Force Reduction) negotiations. (The current START proposals may widen the window of vulnerablity and may produce less flexibility than proposals similar to the back-up proposal that is specified below.) These in fact are mostly propaganda ploys: offensive on the part of the Soviet Union, which is attempting to disrupt Western unity; and defensive on the part of a NATO that is trying to prevent a deterioration in its position. Although the confidence-building measures proposed by the Rumanians, and elaborated on recently by President Reagan, such as notices concerning maneuvers, are certainly valuable, they are only marginal with respect to the threat of war. Europe certainly deserves something much better.

There is a good reason why Russia would stumble over its own feet in rejecting this proposal, as it likely will do initially. Russia is still committed to the Litvinov proposals of the 1930s for complete and absolute disarmament. Although this proposal does not go that far, it takes a giant step in that direction. Furthermore, there is no reason why the West should not offer to work toward that goal with a proposal similar to this one as a major step in that direction.

EUROPEAN TRANSITIONS AND EASTERN EUROPE

In my opinion the threat of war in a Europe from which both the United States and the Soviet Union have removed their forces and in which the Soviet relationship with Eastern Europe has been attenuated would be minimal. However, because of the highly urbanized character of Europe, the dangers involved in modern weapons technology, and the aspirations of the peoples of the area, it would nonetheless be immoral not to attempt to reduce even that minimal risk. Therefore, even a joint US/USSR withdrawal should be accompanied by a series of intra-European arms control and confidence-building agreements.

Furthermore, although differences in the natures of the Eastern and Western economies would make difficult any intimate linking` between the Common Market and the Eastern European economies, a military withdrawal should be accompanied by a series of intra-European economic measures. Our object throughout should be to leave behind a safer, and more independent, Europe.

At least two European regimes likely would collapse during this process with dire consequences for the leaders of these regimes: East Germany and Czechoslovakia. Therefore, it would be important for some tacit, if not formal, agreements between the United States, the Soviet Union, Poland, and the democracies of Western Europe to be reached to insure continued consultation and process insulation in order to minimize the potential destabilizing consequences of collapses of those regimes. That might place limits on the free popular choices of the people of the two countries that it would be difficult to justify theoretically. But it would be far less moral to leave Soviet hardliners with an argument for war in order not to fail completely in their obligations to their clients.

BACK-UP PROPOSAL

Suppose that this proposal is rejected and that no significant arms control proposals appear likely of joint adoption by the United States and the Soviet Union. What are the things that the United States and its allies could do unilaterally that would increase deterrence, decrease the provocatory character of present arrangements, place European nations in control of their own destiny, and not reduce the comparative war capability of NATO?

NUCLEAR POSITIONING

Some of the suggestions made here have been made previously by me; I refer briefly to their history only to indicate my persistent interest in such measures. As early as 1971, I suggested to the Pentagon that the Pershing and Sergeant weapons be eliminated from the NATO arsenal and that the nuclear-armed QRA (Quick Reaction Aircraft) be withdrawn to Great Britain or the United States. That proposal is repeated now with a further specification for the unilateral removal of all nuclear launchers with ranges exceeding 250 kilometers. Weapons of this kind that are easily located and that can hit the Soviet Union are obvious targets for a Soviet first strike. In the original proposal I argued that the presence of these weapons might have destabilizing effects during periods of tension. On the other hand, removing the QRAs to Britain and the United States not only removes them from the sites of likely targeting but permits their potential recall as an element in deterrence.

Any required nuclear targeting in the event of a war in Europe, with the exception of massed tanks, can be accomplished through the employment of Poseidon and/or Trident missiles. It may be that the US may wish to reconsider the actual number of nuclear missile submarines to be employed within this strategy and that some of its allies may wish to assist in the financing of them.

The great threat that the arrangements specified here do not account for is that of massed tank attacks. Shorter range Lances can be used for this purpose. If it were not for the propaganda tag that has been tacked on to the neutron bomb (or the enhanced radiation weapon), it would be the weapon of choice. It is not true that it was developed to kill people while leaving buildings intact. The object was rather to develop a weapon the lethal effects of which could be more narrowly contained than is the case with standard nuclear weapons. If the alliance should decide to resort to this weapon system, it should recommend as part of its declaratory policy that the Soviet Union remove its standard nuclear shells and replace them with neutron shells. Although there is no possibility that NATO forces will attack eastward, reasons of appropriate symmetry recommend this. In time, smart conventional weapons may be able to do this job.

It is true that the previous proposals run counter to the sentiment of many Americans for a nuclear non-first-use proclamation by NATO. Such suggestions have been made in an effort to reduce the risk of nuclear war. However, such a proclamation would be counterproductive. It is extremely unlikely that the Soviet Union would begin an invasion of Western Europe if it could not mass its tanks. The only current significant threats to massed tanks are nuclear mines and shells. Although a nuclear non-first-use proclamation would not in fact necessarily stop us from resorting to nuclear weapons if a successful Soviet campaign is launched against the West, the belief that we might not resort to such weapons is likely to reduce substantially deterrence of a Soviet attack and to increase, rather than to reduce, the risk of war—and hence of nuclear war—in Europe. The proclamation in 1982 by Russia of a non-first-use doctrine, however, was cost free; for the West will not attack the East and the WTO has superior conventional forces. Some proponents of the nuclear non-first-use proposal argue that it will not reduce deterrence because the Russians are unlikely to believe it. This is too tricky.

A careful reading of the debates between Admiral Yamashita and his staff and the Japanese naval general staff on the Pearl Harbor campaign indicates the extremely dubious character of the venture. If it had not been for Admiral Yamashita's great prestige, the attack would not have been approved. Even so, the attack would not have been launched if the fleet had not been stationed in bases, if it had not regularized its activities, and if other defensive measures had been taken. This is merely one example in military history that illustrates (a) that risky operations *do* get undertaken and (b) that both their success and their initiation could have been avoided by appropriate measures. Wishful thinking does not make good policy. And unnecessary marginal reductions of deterrence can invoke very heavy costs. However, if smart weapons actually develop sufficiently they can and should substitute for nuclear weapons in Europe.

It would be better to make an announcement that can be believed because it is inherently credible. NATO should announce that it will not initiate the first use of force or the threat of force in the entire NATO/WTO area; that if the Russians use modest local force in the

NATO area, NATO will respond in kind without escalation; that if the Russians attempt to change NATO boundaries in Europe by the use of force, NATO will do whatever is required to defeat this. In the attempt to defeat this, nuclear weapons will be employed only if necessary. NATO should also announce that it knows that Russian operational manuals specify, and that their war-gaming employs, nuclear weapons in the event of a central, that is, European, war and announce that a significant employment of nuclear weapons in Western Europe will invoke the use of nuclear weapons against the territory of the Soviet Union.

DISSUASION

Because of WTO conventional superiority, it is important to reduce WTO cooperation with the Soviet Union in an attack on the West. Because of the number of targets in Eastern Europe, there are prospects for dissuading Eastern European nations from cooperating with a Soviet attack.

In a prolonged central war, missiles from submarines would be aimed at the Soviet Union and at choke points in Eastern Europe, including marshalling yards, large military dumps, and naval and air bases. Similar facilities within the Soviet Union would also be subject to such attack.

In a variant of the dissuasion strategy I first proposed to the Pentagon in 1971 and then publicly in 1973, the list of targets in Eastern Europe subject to these attacks would remain quite limited to prevent extensive collateral damage provided that these countries refrain from actively assisting the Russian attack and that their forces do not hold border areas essential to NATO counterattack. Under these circumstances, we would also guarantee them from other consequences of belligerency. The East Germans would be particularly vulnerable inasmuch as their territory would be the only effective staging ground for a WTO attack on the West (with the exception of a direct Russian attack on the northern flank). It is extremely unlikely that the Russians would mount such an attack on the central NATO front without the cooperation of the East Germans; and this is a lesson that should be taken closely to heart by the East Germans, lest they be subjected to severe damage. Inasmuch as the East Germans, unlike the other Warsaw Treaty Organization states, seem unlikely to cooperate with a dissuasion strategy, it perhaps may be the case that NATO would agree to limit counterattacks in East Germany if there were massive civilian resistance and sabotage. This is an instance in which the dropping of anti-tank and anti-aircraft weapons might play an important role.

After this tactic was publicly proposed in 1973, NATO officers in Washington got feedback from Eastern European nations' officials many of whom began to ask what they would have to do to stay out of the line of reprisals. This type of reaction is one that the Russians would have to take very seriously. They could not remove these governments during times of calm, for that would be excessively costly because of active and passive resistance and the need to maintain a minimum of consensus. During a crisis, it would be too late to do this effectively because it would be a sign of disunity and, thus, would weaken the WTO threat to their West and their assurance in threatening or conducting war.

THE COUPLING PROBLEM

The dispute between the Soviet Union and the United States over the installation of Pershing IIs in response to the Soviet SS-20s is primarily political rather than military or strategic. The Soviet Union is fully capable of saturating Western Europe with nuclear weapons other than the SS-20s. And the targeting that will be assigned to the Pershing IIs could be taken over by the American submarine fleet.

The Soviet objective in implanting massive numbers of SS-20s is to convince the Europeans that they are decoupled from American strategic deterrence. The objective of the United States in putting Pershing IIs into Europe is to convince them of the contrary. The

Soviet Union behaved in a threatening way before the recent German elections in the hope that Germans would be frightened into voting for the Social Democrats, who in turn would back off from the decision on the Pershing IIs.

When the former tactic failed, at least in part, because of the Christian Democratic victory, the Soviet Union turned its threats against the United States by proposing that the use of the Pershing IIs would lead to a nuclear counterattack against the United States. This represented an effort to influence the debate in the Congress over a nuclear freeze. If the freeze won, the Russians hoped that its advocates would resist new deployments while negotiations were in progress.

The political asymmetries between the NATO and WTO blocs has concerned me since the late 1950s, when I made the first proposal for a joint-NATO nuclear force, a force that would have operated under NATO command without veto under certain standardized conditions.[1] By the time this proposal emerged from the bureaucratic process as a multi-lateral fleet that operated on the surface and with six vetos, I disowned it.

In 1971 in a project that was done for the army, I advocated pulling the Sargeants and Pershings out of Europe, rebasing the quick reaction aircraft in England and the United States, and doing NATO strategic nuclear targeting from the seas. My argument for this was that nuclear weapons in Europe, particularly if they could hit the Soviet Union or were highly vulnerable, would be such a visible target that they would be divisive of the alliance during a crisis. And the Russians would particularize their threats to heighten this divisiveness. To maintain the strategic coupling, I proposed a quick transfer capability for nuclear submarines. There would have been previous training of officers of a particular nation if it was attacked or under immediate threat of attack.[2] This was nearly accepted by Operations and Plans, but ultimately it proved too difficult to get the army to give up its intermediate range nuclear weapons in a world in which the air force and navy had intercontinental missiles.

Recently I revived that proposal.[3] In a discussion of the plan in

Europe, the major criticism was that in a crisis the United States might not turn the submarines over.

There is a solution to the problem and I propose it here. Any NATO ally that so wishes may place on an agreed number of American nuclear submarines a parallel command officer and fire-control officer plus a certain number of other personnel. There will be a treaty between the United States and each ally that specifies that, under an attack of agreed dimensions, according to the NATO situation report, that ally may take command of the particular submarines and use them according to national orders. Each member of the crew of each appropriate submarine must attend a briefing on the arrangement and sign a statement specifying that the treaties of the United States are the law of the land and that he will obey the command of the treaty-designated command officer.

This proposal, in addition to being enforceable, has an additional advantage over my earlier proposal. Command of specified submarines would be taken over not merely by the nation under immediate threat but by any other NATO ally that considers the attack against that nation to be threatening to its interests. As a consequence of this, the Soviet Union would not be able to direct its retaliatory threats against a particular NATO country because it could not know which NATO country might fire. Moreover, because any substantial conventional attack on NATO would threaten the Soviet Union with intercontinental warfare, the extremely high deterrence that the United States had in the middle 1950s when it had nuclear superiority would be restored. The alliance would be coupled and the Soviet threats would lose their destabilizing capability. We would have neutralized the SS-20s much more effectively than can the Pershing IIs.

CIVILIAN ASPECTS

Although the value of anti-tank and anti-aircraft handheld weapons against mass attacks has been much exaggerated, those weapons can be of considerable use under appropriate circumstances. There should be stockpiles of such weapons in Western Europe. There will be two ways in which such stockpiles can be used. In the first place, there should be large, trained civilian militias that can use them if a NATO nation is invaded. In the second place, they can be dropped into Eastern European countries if Soviet forces attack one of those nations or the West.

There may be better versions both of the principal plan and of the fall-back plan. The present proposals are intended primarily to clarify the character of the options that face us. If statesmen in the United States and the Soviet Union adopt a comparable plan, that would remove the threat of holocaust from Europe and, thus, likely from the entire world. Wars, and even nuclear uses, elsewhere are not as likely to escalate as catastrophically as might be the case in Europe (although such escalation, even in Europe, also is much less likely than many believe). Even the unilateral fall-back position in this proposal, which fails to remove the gruesome threat that hangs over Europe and the world, mitigates that threat to a significant extent by increasing deterrence, by decreasing provocation, by putting European nations in charge of their own destiny, and by maintaining the comparative defensibility of the West at least as well as, and probably better than, existing arrangements.

Notes

1. "Problems of Coalition and Deterrence" in Klaus Knorr, *NATO and American Security* (Princeton University Press, 1959).
2. For a public version of the plan, see *The Rationale for NATO*, AEI-Hoover Policy Studies, 1973.
3. "Comment Mettre Un Terme Au Risque De Guerre En Europe," *Politique Internationale*, April 1983.

COMMENTARY

By
ALEXANDER SHTROMAS

The disarmament problem is too big and too vital to leave to games between governmental establishments or propaganda exercises of demagogues, who dress themselves in the costumes of peace campaigners and who thus exploit the natural anti-war sentiments of the public. What the public on both sides of the Iron Curtain needs most today is an unbiased and fair program for disarmament and the prevention of war, a program with which this public could identify itself and around which it could rally. Dr. Kaplan's program is one of the first such programs and therefore should be discussed seriously.

I have very few quarrels with Dr. Kaplan's proposals. Therefore, I shall concentrate on some elaborations. In the first place, it is a proposal that the West could accept. But of course, as Dr. Kaplan pointed out himself, it most likely—and I have no doubt about it —will be rejected by the Soviet Union. The Soviet Union will attempt to avoid negotiations over such a plan because the process of negotiations would expose the inconsistencies in the Soviet position.

Alexander Shtromas is Professor of Politics and Contemporary History at the University of Salford, England.

The Soviet Union would lose its credibility on the peace issue with both Western idealists and its own unhappy subjects. The credibility of the Soviet Union as a peaceful country—with a government that opts for peace and campaigns for peace—is one of the basic foundations of the Soviet government in keeping its own peoples subdued and agreeable to its rule. As long as the Soviet peoples believe that their government is doing everything possible to keep them out of war, of any sort of nuclear holocaust—(and that's the most profound, and probably the only profound, political sentiment the public at large in the Soviet Union holds)—as long as it is at least a bit credible in this respect, it will retain support.

As soon as its credibility on this issue is undermined, it will lose not only its peace policy supporters in the West but also its support by the Soviet people. They will see no point in complying with such an oppressive regime if it is not genuinely working for peace, which is the only guarantee of physical security for those unhappy peoples. If it is made clear that the Soviet Union is not forthcoming in considering seriously proposals that would erode the danger of war, that would cause such image problems for them that it may be forced to reconsider its entire position.

The idea that Dr. Kaplan has presented—that one must push the Soviet Union to negotiate serious and practical proposals for peace that the Soviet Union isn't likely to accept at least at first—is the best way to pursue peace and security even though initial Soviet recalcitrance may frighten the faint of heart.

But Kaplan's proposal is only one effort in this direction. We have to elaborate additional proposals, some of which may be more conventional.

As for the proposal itself, it seems to me that one weak point that should be reconsidered is the idea of reducing to 50,000 soldiers the armies of all the European countries except the Soviet Union. I don't think that this ad hoc proposal—which limits all national European armies other than the Soviet Union to 50,000 men on active duty and 200,000 men on reserve—will be seen by those countries as fair. One has first to involve them in the process of negotiations to let them express their views and positions on what the security of their countries requires in terms of a viable and credible military force and then to proceed to negotiate.

We should restrict ourselves to four major principles. One principle is yes, we have to achieve a very major reduction of military strength on both sides of the East/West divide—a very serious reduction—a reduction of the general size that Dr. Kaplan is talking about.

A second principle that is important and obvious is on-site inspection of the process of disarmament and of the production of arms.

A third principle that has to be applied as part of the plan is the principle of the equality of military strength on both sides of the East/West divide. And here I am very seriously stressing the element of equality because the Soviet Union during the whole history of disarmament negotiations never proposed equalization of forces. What it always tried to present as disarmament is a proportional reduction of forces. One has to make it clear to all who are fooled by those proposals that proportional reductions mean only one thing: the strong side gets stronger and the weak side gets weaker.

One can achieve by disarmament very many goals. Disarmament is valid and viable only if it is aimed at strengthening peace. You can create an imbalance of forces by disarming as well as by an arms race. Of course, it is cheaper to achieve this goal by disarmament but it will be still the same goal as that of the arms race. That goal is not peace but dominance.

May I suggest that this equalization process should be perceived in terms of both nuclear and conventional weapons. The Soviets always say they are ready to abolish all nuclear weapons and to reduce proportionally the conventional ones, which gives them the upper hand because in conventional terms they are much stronger. So, this principle of equality should be stressed very strongly. Then when this principle is agreed upon, one could start a multinational negotiation to discuss how many troops each country should have. It will be very difficult to persuade France and Germany that they should have the same number of men under arms as Denmark or

Holland, for instance.

In addition, by making the country possessing Poseidon missile systems unrecognizable and by training naval officers to be able to use weaponry in their own name, including the Germans, Kaplan's proposal breaches the existing system of agreements about nonproliferation of nuclear arms and breaches the agreement that Germany should never go nuclear. That could be used by the Soviet Union to its propaganda advantage. They might charge that the United States wants to proliferate nuclear arms—that this is part of an effort to start a war. One shouldn't give them this weapon, and so this proposal should be reconsidered.

I would propose globalism as the fourth principle for disarmament negotiations. If we reduce the forces of European nations, if we reduce the forces of the United States and Soviet Union, we will implicitly increase the force of other would-be nuclear and nuclear powers. As Dr. Kaplan has suggested, Argentina and Brazil are going to be nuclear very soon, and Pakistan and India already are surreptitiously nuclear. And what could we say about the Middle East powers and South Africa? Only a disarmament plan that includes all nuclear and all would-be nuclear nations would really promote peace and would keep the balance intact. May I also suggest that one of the very obvious conflicts that will arise in this sort of imbalance is the Sino-Soviet division. Dr. Kaplan does mention China in his paper. However, he mentions it only in passing. An Asian balance is vital to a European agreement. Finally, sustained efforts by experts should be carried out in studying and developing peace programs. Peace is too important to be left to governments.

US Comprehensive Regional Policy for the Middle East

By

EDWARD E. AZAR

Introduction

The United States is facing a period where new approaches are needed to deal with the Middle East. Designing a policy for the Middle East has always been difficult. Certain options may lead to desirable outcomes, but achieving them requires difficult choices.

It is more advantageous both *conceptually* and *instrumentally* for the United States to pursue a comprehensive regional developmental approach in the Middle East in preference to the present bilateral strategic approach. Past interactions with the region have often been fragmented, apparently disconnected, and even contradictory. This has created ample distrust and even dislike of the US and its representatives in some parts of the region, but there is also a deep reser-

---

Edward E. Azar is Professor of Government and Politics and Director of the Center for International Development at the University of Maryland at College Park.

voir of admiration and respect for the US and the West. The US should capitalize on the positive and build comprehensive regional linkages to tackle simultaneously the problems of peace and development. This approach can protect US interests and welfare by increasing the level of stability in the region and by generating admiration and respect from the Middle East people and their elites.

Peace and development in a comprehensive regional plan will accomplish goals that have been cherished by the US for some time. An economically developed and regionally cooperative Middle East will benefit US exporters and help American business flourish throughout the area. A stable, developed Middle East will enhance the political fortunes, and by extension, the security objectives of the West.

It may be argued that certain less comprehensive policies possess concrete advantages. Perhaps the US could benefit by isolating the oil-rich Arabs from the capital-hungry ones. Or, the US, believing that it is a good short-term strategy, could absorb all it can of the surplus of the area during the coming decade. Concluding bilateral political, military and economic deals is easy and appears to work. However, such approaches are doomed to failure.

If the US continues to pursue the present course, the area will become even more impoverished than it is now. This means that American exports to the area will diminish to negligible levels. If the Arab-Israeli war continues, instability will increase throughout the region. Inter-Arab wars will grow in scope and number. Bilateral or multilateral security arrangements with a few regimes that do not deal with regional stability and peace will not endure. Such approaches did not work in the past (e.g., all the American security initiatives of the fifties failed). Why should this approach work now? By pursuing narrow and seemingly disconnected policies in the Middle East, the US is likely to exhaust its diplomatic and political base.

On the other hand, by pursuing a comprehensive regional policy of peace and development, much as the US did in Western Europe after World War II, the Middle East could make gains in the same way that Europe gained. A more prosperous, less repressive and more stable Middle East would behave more as Western Europe did after 1946, i.e., it would befriend the US and the West rather than the USSR and the Eastern bloc states. If the US (working together with the financial resources in the Middle East) advocates and supports a program of creative development, the US will be protecting its own interests in that vital part of the world. Militarily, if the US takes the long-term perspective and devises ways and means of working with diverse regime types, then the defense capacity of the US and the West will be enhanced. Finally, if the US can help solve the Palestinian-Israeli conflict, then it will have neutralized the Palestinians and the Arab left.[1]

Realistic new initiatives for a new US foreign policy in the Middle East are not easily determined. There are serious obstacles. For example:

(a) Analysts inside and outside US governmental agencies have already committed themselves to other approaches;

(b) Many ideas preferred by one branch of the federal government will be opposed by another;

(c) Short-term risks and costs, whether diplomatic, military or economic, are often more compelling and certain than potential long-term payoffs;

(d) Some approaches may appear to be so theoretical that the realities of the Middle East environment make them appear inapplicable;

(e) Translating general policy guidelines into specific policies and actions is impossible without securing wider intra-and-inter-governmental agreement in regional objectives; and

(f) Future events are so unpredictable and yet interactive that the idea of options for the coming decade appears to be an exercise in futility.

Nevertheless, it is difficult to imagine how US regional objectives can be accomplished without a major comprehensive initiative linking peace to security and development for the whole region.

The Developmental vs. the Strategic Approach to Foreign Policy

On the whole, foreign policy fits in one of two categories: the strategic or the developmental.[2] In discussing these approaches the focus here will *not* be on their ethical and philosophical underpinnings, but on their conceptual and instrumental differences. This bypasses what is often a misleading differentiation, namely, the *moralistic* vs. the *realistic* approaches to foreign policy.[3]

The strategic approach to foreign policy focuses on the concept of power or coercion both as an innate drive and a legitimate means to achieve national interests.[4] The strategic approach cannot be reduced to military means only. It incorporates cultural, psychological, economic, and political resources in order to maximize control in international relations. What makes the strategic approach so unique is its exclusive preoccupation with the ultimate goal of control and influence. Security becomes the catchword in evaluating the behavior of self and others in the international system.

The strategic model of foreign policy forces one to focus on *worst case* analysis and therefore provides a partial and very skewed focus for the conduct of foreign policy. The strategic analyst tends to be concerned with such issues as social conflict, modes of change, economic stagnation, distrust and social victimization only insofar as they impact on his immediate interests. Preoccupation with these concerns, however, does not insure the success of the nation since it rests on a distorted version of reality and is short-sighted. Often a strategic analyst seeks in vain to control currents of change only to create extreme frustration and crises.

The developmental approach is rooted in learning theory and it focuses on the common and interdependent fate of mankind, and on the right of individuals and nations to an equal opportunity for development.[5] The developmental approach does not neglect legitimate American interests in pursuit of a secure world environment. On the contrary, we think that American interests are better accommodated when America is identified as a supporter of the legitimate needs of other peoples rather than as a sponsor of a few nonresponsive elites.

The central idea of the developmental approach is that the legitimate interests of all nations can best be reconciled in an international setting governed by principles of justice and coordinated by policies aimed at the betterment of world society and the systematic reduction of violence and instability. The interests of any nation are legitimized and served best when the interests and needs of other states are taken into account. The mutual accommodation of interests is therefore realized within the context of promoting joint efforts toward development. Development is *not*, of course, merely economic growth, but includes also satisfaction of the economic, political and cultural needs of the population.

There are two obvious factors that pose a serious threat to successful policy. First, the modern world system is marked by conflicting models of change in Western liberal, Eastern-socialist and Third World nations. These conflicting models, and policies based on them, have tended to increase domestic ethnic and regional conflicts. Second, the rise in global interdependence has meant that changes in one region, issue-area, or regime affect the arrangements, relations and payoffs in others. This fact deepens competition, dependence and coercion. But global interdependence also makes possible compatible policies and international cooperation for development.

It is important for the US to pursue a grand design which recognizes the diversity of the modes of change, supports democratic institutions, provides active assistance in the area of basic needs, and involves internationally accommodative policies. On the other hand, preoccupation with spheres of influence and strategic considerations can only generate protracted threats and disastrous consequences.

The strategic analyst may point out that the developmental approach would deprive the US of the actual support of many regimes around the world in return for speculative gains. Others may suggest that the developmental approach disregards domestic American interest groups that favor policies abroad which may contradict the logic of the developmental and comprehensive approach. Additionally, it might be argued that this is a costly affair if the US has to shoulder the responsibility of providing sufficient aid and various other support mechanisms to promote development in the Third World.

These objections may prove justified in the short run. However, no one is arguing that the US has to shoulder all the responsibility.

We are arguing that the US design its own comprehensive developmental approach and then assess what is involved and who is to be involved and in what ways. This is necessary because political and social change will be detrimental to US interests if the US does not appear to have a thorough plan to deal creatively with emerging world events. Policies toward the underdeveloped countries of the world that directly or indirectly support insecurity and continued underdevelopment will invite rejection and opposition to the United States. Only tolerance of different types of regimes and regime changes and support for the reduction of insecurity and instability will gain support for American policy in the long run.

US MIDDLE EAST POLICY: WHAT HAS IT BEEN LIKE?

Traditionally, the United States has not succeeded in creating a regional approach to the Middle East. Most American dealings have been bilateral, incremental and fragmentary.[6] This may be due to what is perceived to be pragmatism, or the "muddling through" approach in US diplomacy. Perhaps the problems seem too difficult to lend themselves to a regional, comprehensive and developmental approach. Whatever the reasons, the US approach has played right into the hands of regional rivalries, fear, and distrust of America. It has added to the anxiety and perception of inequities that have helped reinforce several negative images of the US. The worst of these negative images is that US policies have been misguided and the result of incompetence. The idea that the US can promise anything and everything to any or all parties but can deliver very little on its promises is itself a negative image and, in turn, a source of other negative images. The notion that events in the region can go on without the United States being able to do anything about them is also a negative image and the source of much worse images. Why?

The answer is found in the past performance of the US in the Middle East. Whether in response to the USSR or others, the United

States has pursued (and appears to want to pursue in the future) a one-dimensional strategic (military) alliances approach to managing the problems of the Middle East. The US tried this approach in the fifties and failed to accomplish its goals. The US then refrained from active pursuance of the strategy for a few years. Since the early sixties, but more recently, the US has become more involved in alliance arrangements than ever. And although the US prefers regional military arrangements, it has found itself concluding bilateral deals with a few of the states in the region and at the expense of, or in conflict with, other diplomatic or economic and military arrangements concluded by the US with others.

United States military arrangements and arms sales to the Middle East have not provided the US with the desired regional stability. Because there is no systematic and comprehensive American regional policy toward the Middle East (which combines security and development), the past eight years have witnessed a marked increase in the flow of sophisticated military equipment to the region without achieving the stability and peace the US wishes for the region.[7] Consider, for example, US military sales to Iran and Saudi Arabia alone and try to weigh the benefits and costs of pursuing the strategic approach to the Middle East. If arms sales were aimed at making these countries more secure or more capable of defending Western interests, then certainly this has been an utter failure. About fifty billion dollars in US military sales (see Table I) to these two countries alone in one decade has left both countries as fragile as they were before, and Iran is in complete chaos and adamantly anti-American.

One might argue that the arms flow to Israel and Egypt is a hedge against further regional instability, but this has been a failure too. On the contrary, arms races interact with conflict and violence in a vicious cycle: one leads to another without any end in sight except when the faucet is closed or economic disaster sets in.[8]

TABLE I:
US MILITARY SALES AGREEMENTS IN
US$ TO IRAN AND SAUDI ARABIA 1971–79

Year	Iran	Saudi Arabia
1971	363,884,000	15,863,000
1972	472,611,000	371,004,000
1973	2,171,355,000	709,259,000
1974	4,325,357,000	2,031,250,000
1975	2,447,140,000	3,614,819,000
1976	1,794,487,000	5,791,678,000
1977	5,713,769,000	1,898,045,000
1978	2,586,890,000	4,136,567,000
1979	41,520,000	6,419,891,000

Note: Includes $2,106,000,000 (fiscal 1979) in funding for construction projects requested by Saudi Arabia.

SOURCE: Defense Security Assistance Agency

As long as oil money is being used to purchase arms in the Middle East, resources needed for development and for the eradication of illiteracy and poverty are being used instead to overmilitarize the societies and political systems of the region. The present trend is feeding the condition of protracted social conflict and is in effect weakening the position of the West.[9] Without a serious shift in priorities, the Middle East will either experience war or continue on in instability and tension. Either way, the US stands to lose. The threats to oil supplies and US interests in the region are functions of domestic political instability as much as of external threats or global economic and business anxieties. To understand this assertion better, the following topics will be analyzed:

(1) US relations to the region from 1951 to 1981;
(2) Events and problems of the region; and
(3) The manner by which the US designs its response to the Middle East in the context of American goals and interests.

THE US AND THE MIDDLE EAST

A QUANTITATIVE INTRODUCTION

To draw a picture that is sensitive to changes in the behavior of the United States (and USSR) vis-à-vis the Middle East, data on US (and for comprehensive purposes USSR) relations with Egypt, Israel and Saudi Arabia from 1950 through 1978 is provided below. On the basis of the public record of daily relations between countries from 1948 to mid-1979 that is maintained in Edward E. Azar's Conflict and Peace Data Bank (COPDAB), average annual cooperative and conflictive interactions for five time periods since 1950 have been constructed. In addition, these have been divided into quantities of conflictive and cooperative relations in terms of the general categories to which they belong, namely, economic, political, and military. Thus, the data in Table II provides us with indices of the types and intensity of interactions between the selected countries.

TABLE II:

ECONOMIC, POLITICAL AND MILITARY RELATIONS

(AVERAGE ANNUAL COOPERATION AND CONFLICT BETWEEN THE US AND THE USSR AND EGYPT, ISRAEL AND SAUDI ARABIA)

| | | USA → Egypt | | | | | | USSR → Egypt | | | | | |
| | | COOPERATION | | | CONFLICT | | | COOPERATION | | | CONFLICT | | |
	YEARS	Econ.	Pol.	Mil.	Econ.	Pol.	Mil.	Econ.	Pol.	Mil.	Econ.	Pol.	Mil.
I	1950–56	61	73	12	40	40	25	63	41	31	3	12	4
II	57–62	182	98	2	27	25	13	113	43	55	0	34	0
III	63–67	76	46	16	66	85	31	135	82	70	0	4	6
IV	68–73	23	72	7	0	26	43	85	127	140	3	17	26
V	74–78	189	196	76	4	17	8	14	73	45	3	74	26

| | | Egypt → USA | | | | | | Egypt → USSR | | | | | |
	YEARS	Econ.	Pol.	Mil.	Econ.	Pol.	Mil.	Econ.	Pol.	Mil.	Econ.	Pol.	Mil.
I	1950–56	50	64	15	15	91	33	47	32	26	0	12	0
II	57–62	106	50	7	40	95	10	67	65	57	0	21	3
III	63–67	56	40	10	36	198	138	90	64	43	0	8	4
IV	68–73	15	81	15	25	184	91	70	162	63	0	53	39
V	74–78	93	261	30	8	31	11	33	85	18	31	142	52

| | | USA → Israel | | | | | | USSR → Israel | | | | | |
	YEARS	Econ.	Pol.	Mil.	Econ.	Pol.	Mil.	Econ.	Pol.	Mil.	Econ.	Pol.	Mil.
I	1950–56	91	59	25	17	42	20	12	5	0	0	48	9
II	57–62	113	58	24	4	56	7	0	7	0	0	45	11
III	63–67	81	34	63	6	29	20	5	7	0	0	152	15
IV	68–73	43	131	181	11	63	15	5	29	1	3	186	52
V	74–78	74	231	202	27	104	59	2	18	4	0	63	0

| | | Israel → USA | | | | | | Israel → USSR | | | | | |
	YEARS	Econ.	Pol.	Mil.	Econ.	Pol.	Mil.	Econ.	Pol.	Mil.	Econ.	Pol.	Mil.
I	1950–56	91	79	49	3	53	55	14	11	3	1	29	36
II	57–62	50	65	32	0	47	23	2	4	1	8	26	19
III	63–67	47	30	36	3	18	23	5	8	8	0	37	31
IV	68–73	27	106	80	1	65	33	6	13	4	12	58	107
V	74–78	37	196	39	2	113	51	0	17	0	3	9	36

| | | USA → Saudi Arabia | | | | | | USSR → Saudi Arabia | | | | | |
	YEARS	Econ.	Pol.	Mil.	Econ.	Pol.	Mil.	Econ.	Pol.	Mil.	Econ.	Pol.	Mil.
I	1950–56	12	11	23	5	0	2	0	3	4	0	0	0
II	57–62	1	43	41	0	3	3	1	0	5	0	0	0
III	63–67	38	28	73	0	5	8	0	0	0	0	3	0
IV	68–73	20	14	28	1	1	1	0	0	0	0	1	0
V	74–78	56	59	108	3	1	13	1	7	12	0	10	3

| | | Saudi Arabia → USA | | | | | | Saudi Arabia → USSR | | | | | |
	YEARS	Econ.	Pol.	Mil.	Econ.	Pol.	Mil.	Econ.	Pol.	Mil.	Econ.	Pol.	Mil.
I	1950–56	1	24	11	2	12	5	0	1	1	0	3	2
II	57–62	6	35	17	0	26	29	0	1	0	0	1	0
III	63–67	16	22	37	0	30	0	0	4	0	0	0	3
IV	68–73	23	25	10	14	47	1	5	2	0	0	3	0
V	74–78	72	76	18	27	25	0	0	0	0	0	1	0

The data permits some broad generalizations about US and USSR behavior toward Egypt, Israel, and Saudi Arabia and vice versa. For example, only during the sixties did the USSR begin to have a pronounced role in Egypt and this of course did not last very long. The Saudi-Soviet relationship is virtually non-existent. The period after 1974 ushered in serious disasters for Soviet policy in Egypt, Israel and throughout the Middle East although this is not documented in Table II but is found elsewhere in the COPDAB files.

It is interesting, however, that Soviet interactions with Egypt (and some other regional actors) tended to be progressively better until the early 1970s. Economic, political, and military cooperation improved substantially and conflict or disagreements over the same issues were relatively limited and tolerable. After the October war, however, cooperation on all dimensions dropped approximately 65 percent while conflict over the same issues increased approximately 115 percent. By comparison, US cooperative interactions with Egypt increased about 625 percent over the period preceding the October war, and conflict dropped to a negligible level, about 40 percent lower than in the preceding period.

In the substantive data in COPDAB, one discovers that the fortunes of the Soviet Union in the Middle East in the seventies cannot be envied. In the 1960s, it looked as if the USSR was making rapid headway in the Middle East, especially because the US pursued a relatively lower profile towards the Arabs of the region. However, the USSR soon discovered that there is much more to deepening a relationship with the peoples of the Middle East than simply building upon disenchantment with the behavior and policies of the West in general and the US in particular.

By the time the USSR was ousted from Sudan and Egypt, it had acquired the image of an incompetent friend. The USSR was pictured as incapable of providing the needed goods and services that had been promised to the region. It was charged with unwillingness to meet the developmental aspirations of the Middle East. Providing arms did not satisfy the needs of the region. More recently, attacks on the Soviet Union, especially in Egypt, speak of an impe-

5

rial USSR that tried to exploit economic and military weaknesses instead of helping to build the social and political system.

Generally speaking, there appears to be a symmetrical reactive pattern in the interactions, except that the level of activity with the US is almost always significantly higher than that with the USSR. Relations with Israel, however, did exhibit some differences. Both cooperation and conflict between the US and Israel increased substantially after the October war, especially political conflict. Israeli-Soviet relations decreased dramatically with respect to both cooperation (such as it was!) and conflict. United States-Israeli military cooperation during the period 1974-78 cooled in spite of US military support for Israel. As Egyptian, and especially Saudi, military cooperation with the US has increased since 1974, US-Israeli military cooperation recorded a major shift between 1968 and 1973.

United States-Saudi relations have also experienced significant shifts in 1974 and have grown more cooperative on all dimensions, especially militarily. Saudi-Soviet relations are so insignificant they are not worth discussion at this point.

These quantitative descriptors are interesting because they indicate that, despite the negative images, the US has a much better chance in the Middle East than the Soviet Union does. They tell us that the US, despite the past, has a chance to win over the Middle East to its side. The US ought not to waste this chance by relying on military arrangements alone and neglecting the comprehensive developmental and peace aspirations of the people of the region.

SUBSTANTIVE DISCUSSION OF US-MIDDLE EAST RELATIONS SINCE WORLD WAR TWO

BACKGROUND

Following World War Two, US involvement in the Middle East

started to grow, albeit very slowly, until about a decade ago. Illustrating this point is Table III: US Assistance to the Middle East, 1946-78, based on data provided by the Agency for International Development and Table IV: US Yearly Interactions with Middle Eastern States 1948-78. Both Table III and IV show that US involvement in the Middle East increased far more in the last eight years than ever before.

TABLE III:

US ASSISTANCE TO SELECTED MIDDLE EASTERN STATES
IN MILLIONS OF US$ (ROUNDED OFF) 1946–78

Country	1946–52	1953–61	1962–73	1974	1975	1976	1977	1978	Total Loans + Grants 1946–78[b]
ISRAEL									
Economic[a]	87	507	662	52	353	714	742	792	4,009
Loans	—	248	535	—	9	239	252	267	1,553
Grants	87	259	127	52	345	475	490	525	2,456
Military[c]	—	1	1,429	2,483	300	1,500	1,000	1,000	7,904
Credit	—	1	1,429	136	200	750	500	500	4,454
Grants	—	—	—	1,500	100	750	500	500	3,450
Other[d]	135	58	279	47	62	105	1	5	511
EGYPT									
Economic	12	302	583	22	370	464	908	943	4,169
Loans	11	131	454	10	299	352	797	797	3,314
Grants	2	171	129	12	71	113	111	146	855
Other	7	31	39	9	38	8	—	1	124
JORDAN									
Economic	5	275	451	65	99	62	84	103	1,249
Loans	—	5	39	16	25	19	30	54	216
Grants	5	271	429	49	74	43	53	49	1,034
Military	—	16	236	46	105	138	132	127	806
Credit	—	—	69	—	30	83	75	71	328
Grants	—	16	168	46	75	56	57	56	463
Other	—	—	17	8	—	—	—	—	25
LEBANON									
Economic	4	96	32	6	3	—	30	33	181
Loans	2	18	14	—	—	—	7	8	33
Grants	2	78	18	6	3	—	23	25	148
Military	—	8	27	—	—	—	25	1	50
Credit	—	—	20	—	—	—	25	—	34
Grants	—	8	7	—	—	—	—	1	16
Other	—	2	14	6	60	—	—	—	231
SYRIA									
Economic	—	45	45	—	105	35	100	105	481
Loans	—	24	29	—	99	33	89	93	414
Grants	—	21	16	—	5	2	11	12	67

SOURCE: Agency for International Development, US Overseas Loans and Grants and Assistance from *International Organization*, July 1, 1945–September 30, 1978

a) Categories under countries where assistance was given. Egypt received no military aid 1946–76.

b) Figures are rounded and may not add up to cumulative totals found here or in original source after computation.

c) Military aid total includes the foreign Assistance Act credit sales and grant programs, transfers from excess stock, other grants and loans under special programs.

d) Some grants under $500,000.

TABLE IV:

US INTERACTIONS WITH
SELECTED MIDDLE EASTERN STATES FROM 1948 TO 1978

US towards	Egypt	Syria	Lebanon	Jordan	Israel	TOTAL	US Towards Israel as % of TOTAL
1948	105	22	54	16	150	347	43
1949	161	74	0	24	276	536	52
1950	79	12	0	0	237	328	72
1951	173	73	72	93	301	648	47
1952	166	30	10	37	224	467	48
1953	326	18	108	229	518	1,199	43
1954	253	49	82	192	257	833	31
1955	494	94	88	62	445	1,183	38
1956	653	160	110	51	419	1,393	30
1957	796	611	226	434	788	2,855	28
1958	410	107	1,098	464	289	2,368	12
1959	289	31	60	318	152	850	18
1960	422	222	149	369	256	1,418	18
1961	273	118	34	103	140	668	21
1962	219	78	100	211	328	936	35
1963	546	49	43	261	212	1,111	19
1964	164	49	6	91	183	493	37
1965	327	24	151	478	189	1,169	16
1966	420	97	140	156	392	1,205	33
1967	933	160	167	540	620	2,420	26
1968	79	27	95	588	378	1,167	32
1969	52	46	27	134	289	548	53
1970	154	38	41	359	500	1,092	46
1971	285	53	59	165	463	1,025	45
1972	161	86	40	201	498	986	51
1973	457	173	91	161	945	1,827	52
1974	787	288	42	234	805	2,153	38
1975	404	125	31	195	570	1,325	43
1976	543	141	227	249	651	1,811	36
1977	890	169	201	382	1,024	2,666	38
1978	542	145	90	93	833	1,703	49

AVERAGE OF % 37

SOURCE AND METHODOLOGY: Derived from data in Edward E. Azar's Conflict and Peace Data Bank (COPDAB). The above quantities are yearly averages computed by the author according to a procedure which multiplies yearly frequencies of political, economic, military and cultural-technological-scientific events times their respective intensities. These quantities provide the researcher with a yearly measure of the total of conflictive and cooperative relations directed by one country towards another.

These tables do not show much activity between Iraq, Libya, South Yemen, Kuwait, Algeria and the US. On the other hand, Israel, Jordan, Turkey, Egypt, Iran and even the small states of Lebanon and Tunisia have had active links to the US.

In the early fifties, the US conceived of the region, except for Israel, as a largely British and French domain, and the US more or less went along with the Middle East policies of its European friends. Following the Suez war of 1956, US policy toward the Middle East developed more independently as the US began to pick up the pieces the British were leaving behind. Toward the end of the sixties and early seventies, matters began to change and the Middle East began to look like a very crucial piece of real estate with vast oil resources which the West had to have.

How to ensure a secure, cheap supply of oil and ensure Israel's security have been the most important factors in US activity in the Middle East.[10] Other concerns such as blocking Soviet expansion, combating radical activity, cooperating with and aiding Egypt, and establishing military and political alliances are but parts of the equation which must guarantee the uninterrupted flow of oil from the Middle East to the industrialized West while increasing Israel's security. Stability, peace and the reduction of Soviet influence are certainly not incompatible with the security of the most important strategic/economic concern, namely oil. Of course, positive and attractive mechanisms that would encourage the rich OAPEC (Organization of Arab Petroleum Exporting Countries) to invest its financial resources in the US are also of great concern. Unfortunately, however, the United States has had to struggle against historical relationships of its own making.

The US strategic and security role in the Middle East as reflected by US official doctrines and policy statements appears to be primarily reactive to perceived Soviet goals and behavior. Originally in the US overall view of the world, the Middle East formed a boundary which separated very vital American allies in Europe from important but much less vital regions in Asia and Africa.[11] In recent years, however, oil and Israel have introduced changes in the way the US views the Middle East so that much of it is included in the area considered vital to American security. However, since there is no comprehensive US view which takes the Middle East as a vital human and economic resource and ally, and since US defense commitments do not really encompass the whole Middle East in any credible way, United States policies, initiatives and statements appear to be disconnected, impromptu, and more recently, not highly credible.

The past three decades have witnessed different emphases in US doctrines and policy on the Middle East. The 1950s were primarily military/strategic and anti-Soviet in focus and attention. The 1960s were characterized by economic/diplomatic efforts and benign neglect for most of the decade at least. The 1970s saw more military/economic, diplomatic, and regionally-oriented policies, although these were more confusing than many realize.

THE 1950s: THE DECADE OF STRATEGIC/MILITARY INITIATIVES

After World War II, the USSR delayed withdrawing from Iran, made demands on Turkey, and appeared to be instigating civil war in Greece. As a reaction, and because of other US goals and objectives, the Truman Doctrine of March 1947 stated that the United States was willing to support states that resist Soviet pressures. Starting in 1950, the US tried to create security systems in the Middle East jointly with European powers. The Tripartite Declaration of May 25, 1950, was intended to govern the flow of armaments into the region and to prevent changes in the status quo or frontiers and armistice lines between Arabs and Israelis. [12]

The Tripartite Declaration was a partial reaction to the Arab-Israeli war of 1948. It also made good political sense for the incumbent Democratic President, Harry Truman. On a more speculative note, it was an important device for the US to gain time in order to understand the Middle East. It was valuable for some Arab countries and others in the area because of its reference to the balance of armament which meant, if fully implemented, that the status quo between the Arab states and Israel would be maintained.

Following this, the US and the United Kingdom began a campaign to engage local governments in security pacts designed to stop Soviet expansionist schemes and stabilize the region (i.e., maintain the status quo). To this end, a plan called the Middle East Defense Organization (MEDO) was proposed in 1951.[13] But the West failed to convince Egypt to play a role in the proposed MEDO. Egyptian nationalists resented the British military presence on Egyptian soil and did not think the Soviets were the immediate threat the US and UK made them out to be.

After the 1952 revolution in Egypt, the US launched a friendship campaign toward the new regime, but this did not last very long. The Egyptian agenda included British military withdrawal, Egyptian-Sudanese relations and the reconstruction of Egypt's military and economy. Close association with Britain did not help the cause of the United States in the Middle East of the post World War II period.

The US was not able to capitalize on the benefits of its assistance to Egypt after the British withdrawal in 1954. The US seemed to perceive that the Soviets had a design for gaining control of the region but lacked a comparable vision spelling out a US design beyond containment. This preoccupation with establishing military alliances and pacts with countries and people it did not really know well, or even like or trust, is rather odd. The US appeared not to have a long-term view of the future of the region, Egypt's role in it, or its own role. American containment of Soviet expansion, support of the state of Israel, and the several attempts by American officials to advance Arab-Israeli peace may have been, to some, the equivalent of a crisp and overall approach. Perhaps the failure of these initiatives can explain why the military alliances approach became a central focus!

In 1955, by pursuing the Baghdad Pact in the same manner as the US had done with the NATO Pact in Europe, the US government displayed a limited knowledge of the forces at play in the Middle East. United States approaches to the short-lived security pacts in the area stem from the concept that the external environment shapes the region and that the domestic setting is of limited importance. This concept is fallacious.

The idea of linking Turkey, Iran, Iraq and Pakistan in a pact as a safety zone against the USSR looks good on paper and may have been of some military use for several years, but it did not take into account the sources of instability in the Middle East, particularly domestic social and economic underdevelopment, inequalities, and the deeply felt resentment of foreign cultural and military influence and control. The American economic aid programs were helpful, but could not ameliorate these basic sources of instability.[14]

In one sense, the Baghdad Pact, which was supposed to form part of a *Cordon Sanitaire* against the Soviets, ended up doing just the opposite. It became a legitimizing focus for new military arrangements and arms deals between the Soviets and those Arabs who felt threatened by the Pact. In order to counterattack, the Soviets moved in to help Egypt both economically (e.g., the Aswan Dam) and militarily by modernizing the Egyptian armed forces. While the Soviets were doing this, the US was forced to take steps against Egypt (with the exception of US actions in 1956-57 in opposition to the British, French and Israeli attack on Suez). Again, the impressive US role in terminating the consequences of the Suez attack did not pay off as much as it should have vis-à-vis Egypt and the other Arabs, mostly because of the US's fragmented and narrow Middle East policy at the time. In any case, instead of the US reaping the benefits of the good and forceful work of 1956-57, the Soviets appeared to be the true beneficiaries. It was the USSR, not the US, that was seen as the major factor behind actions to terminate the 1956 Suez crisis. Because of apparent US inconsistencies in dealing with Egypt and the region as a whole, the elites in the area were puzzled by US words and deeds.

The way the US reacted to Nasser after its involvement in the settlement of the 1956 war is very instructive. On January 5, 1957,

Eisenhower addressed a joint session of Congress and outlined what later became the Eisenhower Doctrine.[15] He stressed the predatory nature of international Communism and called upon Congress to adopt a resolution providing him with the authority to give military and economic aid to those countries or groups of countries that desired such aid, and to use the armed forces of the United States to protect the territorial integrity and political independence of nations requesting military help when endangered by the overt armed aggression of international Communism. The Eisenhower Doctrine can be considered an extension of the Truman Doctrine. Both were aimed at containing the USSR north and east of the Middle East and preserving the status quo. The Doctrine also represented Secretary Dulles' concept of building up the Northern Tier states in the Middle East as a bulwark against the danger of Soviet expansion. Under the Doctrine, the US was prepared to contain the radicalism symbolized by Nasser.

The Eisenhower Doctrine was put to test in the cases of Jordan in 1957 and Lebanon in 1958. In the first case, Eisenhower, faced with apparent destabilization of the regime, announced on April 24, 1957, that the US regarded the independence and integrity of Jordan as vital. The British also responded to the situation by sending paratroopers to Amman. On July 15, 1958 (one day after the overthrow of the monarchy in pro-West Iraq) Eisenhower ordered 14,000 American marines to land in Lebanon to preserve the sovereignty and independence of that country against armed rebellion and Communist agitation. The UN of course pressed for the early withdrawal of British and American forces from the Middle East, and in both instances the forces were withdrawn after a short stay. In the case of Lebanon, for example, the US ended up helping some opposition leaders (i.e., the so-called rebels and agitators!) to come to power and share in the governance of Lebanon. Why then had the US gone to all the expense and trouble to land marines in Lebanon? To answer this question is to deal with the basic critique of US Middle East policies since World War II.

Much US activity in the region appeared to be discontinuous, off-the-cuff and reactive. The doctrines and initiatives were viewed as having limited value in terms of their development impact, military modernization and assistance, and redressing the injustice and dislocation precipitated by the Arab-Israeli war of 1948 and the Suez war of 1956.

THE 1960s: THE DECADE OF PARTIAL NEGLECT

Except for initiating limited military sales to Israel in 1962, the first half of the sixties was a time when the US pursued a very low profile in the Middle East. In 1959, of course, the US initiated agreements with Iran, Pakistan and Turkey now allied together in CENTO (the Central Treaty Organization), which came into being after the collapse of the Baghdad Pact (when Iraq withdrew from the latter). Both the Kennedy and Johnson administrations repeatedly pledged their support to Israel and started experimenting with policies of limited economic development in selected countries in the area. Pro-US states received some US weapons. After the 1967 war, the US began what later became a very deep involvement in Middle East affairs without much coordination with Britain.

The US role at the UN, the support for Israel during and after the 1967 war and the Rogers' Plan of 1969, represented some of America's objectives in the region. Initiatives taken during the last years of the sixties had the effect of legitimizing even the limited role of the USSR in peacemaking in the area. And, although many continued to see the Soviets as a nuisance in the region, the US had in fact neutralized its own past anti-Soviet role in the Middle East by pursuing several initiatives in cooperation or in prior arrangement with the USSR. The UN 242 Resolution, talks leading up to the Rogers' Plan, the Nixon idea of four-power talks in 1969, and so on, legitimized a Soviet role in the region. Thus, despite all the setbacks, the USSR gained for itself a role (albeit undefined now) in future Middle East settlements and international politics.

THE 1970s: THE DECADE
OF FRAGMENTED BUT DEEP
INVOLVEMENT FOR THE US

In the early seventies, the United States began an active campaign to secure its objectives in the region, with a special focus on Israel, Egypt, Iran and Saudi Arabia. Egyptian acceptance of the Rogers' initiatives, the Jordan war against the PLO, Nasser's death in 1970, and the emergence of Sadat were very important turning points in US-Middle East relations. These were followed by the purge of pro-Moscow Egyptians, the expulsion of the Soviets from Sudan and Egypt, and the October war of 1973. But while the US was concentrating on these states, the USSR was working to improve and consolidate relations with South Yemen, Iraq, Syria, Libya and the PLO. The Soviets and Iraq signed a Treaty of Cooperation and Friendship in 1972 and at the same time the USSR increased its naval presence in the Indian Ocean. The seventies, however, were not the good years the Soviets had bargained for.[16]

Both the United States and the Arab states exploited the October War to begin the process of disengagement, shuttle diplomacy, diplomatic and economic realignments, and the building of long-term relations. The US appears to have benefited from moving quickly after the 1973 war. In the seventies, the USSR, while pursuing linkages with some Arab states, appeared to be too slow for its own good. The Soviets showed indecisiveness and reluctance except in the cases of the Southern tip of the Red Sea, Sudan, post October War rearmament, and more recently Afghanistan. As far as the Middle East proper is concerned, the United States was better able to pursue a very active role. It is noteworthy that the US did not act quickly after the 1967 war although she could have done so, partly because the consequences of failure to act were less clear then. However, the US was reluctant, even in the early seventies, to do much about the process of conflict resolution in the region, other than to help Israel militarily and diplomatically. This may have led Israel unwisely to focus its policy on US-Israeli cooperation.[17]

The middle and late seventies were much different. Developments in the area have increased the hope that the United States will have a long agenda for the region. Sadat's visit to Jerusalem in November 1977, and the peace treaty in 1979 proved to be a step towards a more active (and financially costly) role for the US. Also, the Iranian revolution and the anti-American sentiments there, along with the Soviet invasion of Afghanistan, provided further evidence that the role of the US in the region will continue to increase rather than decrease as long as US objectives remain the ones listed above. The US response under Nixon (i.e., shuttle diplomacy, disengagement and the preservation of peace between the confrontation states on the Arab-Israeli borders in part using US personnel) and under Carter (the Camp David agreements and the Rapid Deployment Force for the protection of the uninterrupted flow of oil from the Persian Gulf) have added to American responsibilities. United States success in gaining naval, air and resupply facilities in Oman, Kenya, Egypt, Somalia and Bahrain have also added to the list of US responsibilities commensurate with the new privileges. American involvement in the Middle East is now very deep.

THE PRESENT
MIDDLE EAST SETTING AND
THE US CHOICES AND ROLE

INTRODUCTION

The seemingly disconnected military and political bilateral linkages which the United States has established with several Middle

Eastern regimes in the past three decades may be among the most difficult constraints on the future of US flexibility in policymaking or initiative-taking in the region.

United States options in the eighties are dependent on these past activities, on the present conditions in the region, on the goals and actions of the superpowers, and upon the strength of the West itself technologically, spiritually, economically and politically. It is dependent on US ability to manage war and peace in the world in general as well as the region in particular.

Considering all these factors, and more, how can we generate enough courage to assess and identify Middle East options that serve the American national interest? The answer resides in further understanding the role of two clusters of problems that dominate the Middle East itself, and in figuring out how the US might respond to these problems as part of its overall plan for the region. These core issues have the most important spillover effect on the destiny of the Middle East. They are:

(1) *Conflict* and its management where protracted social conflicts are dominant and ever present. Here the Arab-Israeli protracted social conflict is primary.
(2) *Development* (economic, technological, socioeconomic) is essential to a stable Middle East, the peace process and a pro-US region. The development process in the Middle East has been failing and the problems are mounting.

Peace and development are in America's best interest in the Middle East. These are guarantees of better US relations and greater stability in the area so as to block any Soviet penetration in the region.

ETHNICITY AND PROTRACTED CONFLICTS

Many conflicts in the Middle East resemble those in other parts of the Third World, in that they tend to be societally-based, intractable, and protracted. Protracted social conflicts (PSCs) remain dormant at times thus deceiving observers or crisis managers as to their end-point or termination.[18] Empirical evidence shows, however, that these conflicts break out from time to time in very violent warfare.

These conflicts involve whole societies and affect definitions of the scope of national identity and social solidarity. Although protracted conflicts manifest themselves internally, they spill over into regional and international arenas as well. Therefore, they sometimes become strategic interactions that overlap with domestic conflict, thus mak-ing it difficult to establish meaningful causality. Such protracted conflicts show no clear and distinct termination point.

Protracted social conflicts tend to become sources rather than out-comes of policy. They tend to have a distorting impact on the govern-mental machinery and lead to severe social disintegration.

PSCs are not to be confused with class conflicts. These conflicts mean something to everyone in the society and they are the determi-nants of meaning and value for almost all aspects of a social setting. Their objective is the redress of perceived inequalities that deter-mine in this instance the access of ethnic groups to economic resources, especially in the highly politicized systems of the Middle East. One's position in relation to these conflicts provides persons with an an-choring system and an identification, thus making them very basic to the generation of action.

Protracted social conflicts are hard to reverse because of three complex problems common to them all:

(a) Security vs. vulnerability;
(b) Acceptance vs. rejection; and
(c) Social interaction vs. official contacts.[19]

For the parties to a PSC, *security* is more than the ability to win particular fights. It involves the perception of continued personal safety and the avoidance of those situations that can break out into open hostilities.

Security is not increased by simply purchasing and stockpiling arms. It involves arrangements for the maintenance of law and order and, simultaneously, initiatives and programs aimed at reducing the sources of social, political, and economic vulnerability of groups and states. In these cases, increased security for one group is often tantamount to an increase in the security of others.

Acceptance vs. rejection is another complex issue. Cases studied show that the rejection of the other party's right to exist or to have a claim for participation in the conflict is a powerful tool in conflict maintenance both psychologically and politically.[20] Acceptance, on the other hand, requires a level of rehabilitation and integration among parties to a conflict that makes it hard to reverse the process. Because acceptance requires major transformations in the affect levels of people and groups in a conflict setting, and because it is about social integration and the transformation of familiar symbols and behavior in relation to objective elements, it remains a sore point in matters of war and peace.

Interaction in a PSC setting is generally limited in scope. It tends to be skewed toward verbal and physical hostilities. Reversing this process and expanding the scope of the interaction map between parties to a conflict means going beyond intergovernmental or inter-elite actions.

Socially-based interactions have to be rewarding and complementary. They have to involve situations of sharing and positive reinforcement. Thus the movement away from inter-elite or intergovernmental relations to more social interaction is a complex and often cumbersome matter requiring major shifts in habits, attitudes, and organizational perceptions.

ETHNIC CONFLICTS IN THE MIDDLE EAST

Conflicts in the Middle East possess certain characteristics that make them intractable. How and why?

Conflict in the Middle East, on the whole, has tended to focus on the problem of ethnic, religious, or national identity. Although some conflicts in that region have been about material grievances and appear to have a solution, most contemporary conflicts have been about some "indivisible good." Whether it is conflict between Arabs and Jews, Moslems and Christians, Kurds and Iraqis, Baluchistanis and Bakhtiaris, Sunnis and Shiites, or Druzes and the Syrian central authorities, the properties of these conflicts and their ability to escalate, spill over, and destabilize the region is very high.

Ethnic conflicts in the Middle East (intra- and inter-state) have been on the increase since the mid-forties. Moreover, they have accelerated in frequency and intensity during the last ten years to such a degree that they have become a major source of instability in the region and the world.

Some of the more important reasons for the intensification of ethnic conflicts in the past forty years are found in the social history of, and in new social forces at work in, the Middle East. The legacy of the Ottoman and pre-Ottoman social organization of the region, the intolerance of the Arab unionist movement for pluralism and national diversity, the establishment of the Jewish state of Israel in 1948, and the direction of socioeconomic change in the highly politicized systems of the region are some examples. Quarrels over access to power, security, recognition and acceptance between minorities and factions in the Middle East predate the Ottoman Empire. These deeply rooted hostilities seem to reemerge every now and then due to several triggers.

After World War II, Israel was created on ethnic lines as a Jewish state. The response of the Arabs was ethnic in nature, stressing Arab oneness and the identity of Arab Palestine. In this case, the classical conflict over access to resources and power has been "overdetermined" by ethnic identities.

Socioeconomic processes of change in the Middle East, the extensive role of the state in these processes and the spillover effect of the Arab-Israeli conflict within the internal regimes of most Arab countries, have made violent conflict intractable.

After World War II, most Middle East states gained formal independence. Nationalist regimes came to power in Egypt, Iraq, Syria, etc. with a deep concern for solving the problems of underdevelopment and poverty through a variety of programs. This led to the takeover of the economy by the state. The strong identification of the ruling elites with a policy of nationalism, Arabism, and concomitantly, Islamic unity has helped the process of statism and the high tone of ethnic (i.e. Moslem Arab) pride and identification. Minorities in the Middle East such as the Iraqi Kurds, Egyptian Copts, Sudanese Christians, etc. who have traditionally played a role in the private sector of the economy and in the political arena, were threatened by the new wave of Islamic Arab identification in the post World War II period. However, in the first stages of development and in the euphoria of independence, the ethnic conflict was muted or absent. High rates of economic growth in the beginnings of the development programs and the populist trends of these regimes in their early stages curbed, for a while, ethnic rivalries and seemed to strengthen the shaky beginnings of nation-building in this part of the world.

However, the potentials of the type of development policies adopted, known as "import substitution," were soon exhausted and an acute phase of economic crisis threatened most of the populist policies of the ruling nationalists. This state of affairs coupled with the complete defeat of the Arab armies in 1967 led to the collapse of the Nasserist ideology which dominated the Arabs from 1956 to 1967.

The breakdown of the nationalist-populist ideology, military defeat at the hands of Israel, and the failure of the development programs created a generalized political and ideological crisis and set the stage for a new sense of loss and disorientation.

The past ten years have intensified the sense of insecurity and despair among Arabs. The crisis of the fragmented Arab nations has become real with the split of Egypt from the rest of the Arab coalition through the process of normalization of relations with Israel and with the emergence of very wealthy Arab states due to the boom in oil prices. Egypt, which had been viewed as the political leader of the Arabs, was the first to defect amidst a campaign against Arabism that stressed the specificity of Egypt. On the other hand, the oil wealth resulted in vast migration trends from the poorer countries, especially Egypt and Jordan, to the oil-rich Arab states. As we shall discuss in the following section, these two major events sharpened ethnic identification in a more pronounced unequal system of stratification—economically, politically, and socially in the whole region.

Threatened by the loss of a unified Arab nationalist or a unified Moslem ideology, most Arabs, especially the underprivileged and those hit hardest by the effects of the economic crisis, turned to Islam under the banner of "revivalism." Islamic revivalism in the Middle East, therefore, is not a doctrinal or theological movement in terms of its efficient cause; it is a form of political protest. It is a protest caused by perception of an embattled Islam, threatened from outside (i.e. Israel, the West, and the USSR) and from within (increasingly deformed Moslem Arab economies, polities, societies and values). Because Islam and Arabism have been so closely intertwined in the minds of most Arabs, the search for solutions to the problems of the Middle East in the post World War Two period was located precisely in those two domains. In the early periods of independence, Arabism was perceived as the key to the complex questions of development and security, with Islam tagging along. With the failure of the Arab nationalist-populist solutions to the issues of war and development, the search shifted focus. Now Islam is perceived as a solution to the same problems and Arabism merely tags along. The implication of this change for non-Arabs and non-Moslems in the Middle East is serious. These minorities tend to be regarded as peripheral and distrusted.

The new trend of Islamic revivalism is built specifically on the idea of the cultural and moral superiority of Islam and derivatively of the Arab people.[21] Non-Moslems and non-Arabs are the first to witness the intensity and implications of the crisis of identity in the Middle East. The examples of Lebanon, Egypt, and Iraq are but a few contemporary ones. Syria may become one at any moment.

However, Islamic identity and Arabism are often employed as a political method to impose the hegemony of a state or a regime over the region. Egyptians conceive of Arab nationalism and Islam only under the banner of Egyptian leadership. The Iraqis make a similar claim. The Saudis, with their newfound wealth are less prone to adopt the Egyptian or other Arab approaches. Although they seek power, influence and authority in the Arab world, they prefer the "low-key" approach. The Saudis, with all their wealth, have not been as enthusiastic as the Egyptians and Syrians in attempting to bring the Arab world together under their own hegemony. The Saudis have a high status in the region and the world but they have shied away from the strategy followed by Arab nationalist-populist countries of yesterday. Saudi demography, institutional incapacity and infrastructural weaknesses do not qualify them for any larger role than the one they have pursued in the past ten years.

In summary, a new wave of ethnic identification as Egyptians or Syrians is veiled under the call for Islamic solidarity and revival. This trend is an ideology of hegemony for certain groups such as the Egyptians or Syrians, while it is a defensive policy of pacification for others such as Saudi Arabia.

The intensification of inter- and intra-state ethnic conflicts in the area is a major threat to its peace and security. It is largely generated by deepening economic inequalities, increased levels of absolute poverty in the midst of unprecedented wealth and the collapse of the nationalist and populist ideology that was partly the result of the general defeat of the Arabs in wars with Israel.

THE ARAB-ISRAELI CONFLICT

Of all the conflicts in the Middle East, the Arab-Israeli (and especially Palestinian-Israeli) aspect of the conflict is the most critical. Other conflicts are exacerbated by the general and all-pervasive Arab and Palestinian conflicts with Israel. Of course, there are many important elements of the conflict that need careful examination by those trying to help Arabs and Israelis strike a historical compromise.

However, this paper will only draw attention to one of the most complicated elements of the conflict, namely, the quarrel over the right of self-determination and identity.

Through the many years of hostilities during the struggles of both Arabs and Jews for identity and nationhood, the parties to the Middle East conflict have developed images of one another built upon skewed interactions. No "normal" political or social interactions have taken place; each side has "learned" about the other only through hostile encounters. The elites on each side have written about their counterparts with arrogance and disdain. Most of the research has been done "at a distance" and has tended to serve only war objectives. This conflict environment has provided ample but skewed data to those who have studied the "enemy" and it is to this body of distorted experience and information that one may attribute many of the offensive stereotypes and mechanisms of deception that have helped render the Middle East conflict so intractable.

The problem of Middle Eastern underdevelopment is an integral part of the conflict that has been neglected. The continued failure to ascertain the kind of development that could facilitate peace in the area can sabotage the stability of any proposed strategic or political arrangements that the US is presently contemplating and pursuing.

Structural inequalities and relative poverty existed in the Middle East much before 1948 and have persisted since. The increasingly repressive character of the situation in the Middle East that the Arab-Israeli conflict situation has affected has proved dysfunctional to the development process. *All* the states in the region have for some period of time succeeded in oppressing some or most of their citizens in order to do what they have defined as "redressing grievances." Since 1948, both Arab and Israeli ruling elites have defended increased government circumscription of the freedoms of individuals and groups in the name of national security and national liberation.[22]

The Arab-Israeli conflict has hindered development, not only by contributing to state interference in the affairs of groups and individuals, but also by absorbing almost all available attention and resources. Israeli and Arab rulers have had little time to invest in assessing alternatives to war.

Both Israelis and Arabs have tried (albeit at times unsuccessfully) to shelve intra-party disputes in favor of unified support for (the desirability of) waging war on the enemy. Not surprisingly in such a climate, very little has been done about social, institutional and political development. Even the more acute problems of underdevelopment have been attacked only in those situations in which the cumulative effects of economic and political decay have already placed the stability of a regime in jeopardy.

The preoccupation of Middle Eastern governments with conflict has clearly precluded sufficient emphasis on development. Development, however, is essential to peace. It remains, then, to determine the kind of development that might allow for a final resolution of the Arab-Israeli conflict.

DEVELOPMENT AND ECONOMIC RELATIONS IN THE MIDDLE EAST

Development is the structuring of economic, political, social, and technological happenings within an environment *for some purpose*. And, for Third World countries that *purpose* cannot be mere "growth," which will increase hardship and poverty for many. Unless development is aimed toward reducing socioeconomic gaps within and between nations, then stability and order will not be served. Development can work to reduce the potential for violence and therefore augment diplomacy and law in world affairs. In this sense, development is an arm of diplomacy that works towards promoting pride, good citizenship, and justice instead of submissiveness and potential disorder.

Development should be viewed as the most effective form of diplomacy, especially vis-à-vis the Third World which has been experiencing severe levels of protracted social conflict. *Development Diplomacy* is a label for conjoining diplomacy and development in the pursuit of conflict resolution and crisis management in the world.

Development diplomacy goes a long way toward explaining how to contain and ultimately reduce conflict and violence between groups and nation-states. It does so by focusing on those strategies, programs, forms of assistance, alliances, linkages, etc. which would reduce the severe stress on the states and the system as a whole. And by focusing on structural factors, (e.g. dysfunctional concentrations of wealth, poverty, exponential population growth, ethnic hate and injustice, brain drain), development diplomacy points out the areas of potential instability that can lead to violence. Most importantly, development diplomacy can serve as a conceptual framework for US foreign policy in the Middle East.

In order to understand how the US might address the matter of development diplomacy in the Middle East, it is necessary to know what has been taking place on the economic and social development fronts in that region. Thus, we have chosen to address ourselves below to two major issues which provide important challenges for the US and the regional elites. First, there is the increasing gap between the oil wealthy Arab states and the oil hungry ones and the negative consequences of this phenomenon on cooperation in the region. Second, there is the negative impact of massive migrant labor on oil exporting Arab countries as well as on the labor exporting countries in the region. We are witnessing an increase in disintegration among the Arab states as a function of precisely those factors that once were thought to be integrative, namely massive wealth and the economic interactions betweem mass and elite.[23] The Arab subsystem is the focus in this section because it would be artificial to include Israel, Iran, or Turkey with whom very little joint development or regional integration has ever been sought.

DEVELOPMENT AND RELATED ECONOMIC CONSIDERATIONS: ARAB SUBSYSTEM PROBLEMS

In recent years, Arab states have become a classic case for the urgent need to reformulate the concept of development.[24] From the standpoint of political science, one has to consider the whole system of feedbacks between various social processes. In a purely developmental context, economic actions can contribute solutions or partial solutions to certain problems of a national or transnational society. On the other hand, these actions reinforce the problems and distortions incurred by the whole social structure. And, to examine the Middle East in this manner is to better interpret the dramatic increase in capital surpluses accumulated by the OAPEC.

Although accumulated wealth should provide a momentum to Arab efforts towards development and economic integration, one discovers that oil surpluses have split the Arabs into two categories—the rich and the poor states.

Theoretically, one would expect mobility and coordinated policies that combine financial surpluses of the low population density states with labor surpluses of the capital hungry states as an effective approach to economic development. One would also expect that such an economic regional integration trend would appear to be in the interest of all concerned—the Middle East, the US and the West. Why?

(a) Because regional economic integration would increase potentialities of the combined OAPEC and other Arab markets for commodity exports and joint ventures of the subsidiaries of Western-based multi-national corporations; and
(b) Because it guarantees a supply of oil as a result of increased dependence on oil revenues for the coordinated plans in the Middle East.

Regional economic integration, however, is facing difficulties that need speedy attention in a developmental context. To understand these difficulties, let us examine three forms of oil-related Middle East economic transaction. These are:

(1) Migratory labor;
(2) Financial aid; and
(3) Joint ventures.

Migratory labor: Migratory labor is a mode of interdependence that could have had a substantial effect on the economic development and integration in the region. Migratory labor is not only the most significant form of economic transaction between rich and poor Arab states, but it has proved also to be the most durable. What are its spillover effects on inter-Arab integration?

Remittances of the nationals working in the oil-rich states represent a significant source of foreign exchange for countries like Egypt, Syria, North Yemen, Jordan, and the Palestinians. Meanwhile, migratory workers constitute a major source of employed labor, amounting to 43 percent for Saudi Arabia, 43 percent for Libya, 70 percent for Kuwait and 85 percent for UAE. Most of these laborers come from the Arab states, especially Egypt.[25]

The dominant analysis of labor migration has focused traditionally on its positive effects, economically and politically. This analysis derives from the logic of classical economics where equilibrium in the labor market made possible by labor mobility guarantees not only the highest wage rates, but also the highest productivity for the exporting and importing states as well. This is not the case with most underdeveloped societies where the labor market is sectorially distorted and generally inflexible. Emigration of labor takes place in the most vital and scarce branches of work-skills: such as professionals, technical workers, artisans, maintenance workers, and others. The labor exporting economy loses not only the initial costs of education and training, but also the precious managerial and technical skills necessary for maintaining and raising productivity levels. The wage structure, consequently, becomes severely deformed. A sharp increase in the cost of labor occurs in the sensitive skills, thus producing inflationary pressures from the supply side. Meanwhile, the traditional constraints and the overall inelasticity of the labor market prevent the diversion of labor from one area to another. Accordingly, inequalities which are already substantial become ever more flagrant.

Moreover, the claimed benefits derived from the remittances of migrant workers are not without limits. In the first place, patterns of investment are generally skewed in favor of speculative activity, especially in real estate which normally increases inflation. Second, these remittances tend to be associated with conspicuous consumption patterns amidst extreme poverty. Not only is that consumption overwhelmingly composed of imported commodities, but it also favors commercial over productive activities in investment patterns.

Egypt's case is a pronounced example of all these harmful effects of the economy where artificial demands sustained mainly by remittances have considerable inimical spinoff effects.

The impact of migratory labor in the recipient states may generally be more positive economically in the short run. However, the social dynamics suffer a lot. Especially important in this context is the culturally demoralizing impact of the vertical and asymmetric integration of expatriate labor in the local economy. The citizens of OAPEC states often regard the supervisory top administrative and managerial jobs as their own ascriptive privilege. The outcome is the emergence of a special patriarchic class of indigenous administrators who are related to each other by extensive patron-client networks, and who look disdainfully at physical and mental work. The degradation of the work ethic causes serious human losses in potential development as well as a distortion in the popular understanding of economic capabilities and skills.

This factor explains particularly why conflicts between Arab states have gone beyond the official level, and acquired a social root. The migrant workers, especially from Egypt, Yemen, Palestine, Jordan, Syria and Lebanon are not only integrated on an unequal basis in the economies of Saudi Arabia, UAR, Kuwait, Qatar, etc. but they are socially alienated and deprived of several economic and social rights and, most glaringly, the potential to move upward in the organization. They know but dislike the limits placed upon them and they become second class non-citizens (underdogs) in the labor market of the host countries. This social disparity which is exhibited in almost every mode of social communication is juxtaposed with the increasing inequalities between the states themselves.

Financial aid: Financial aid offered by the rich to the poorer states in the area was a part of the *modus vivendi* which dominated Arab politics in the period 1967-75. The initial aim of these transfers was to support the military efforts of both Egypt and Syria against Israel. It has been estimated that several billion dollars were granted to Egypt and Syria by Saudi Arabia, Kuwait and UAE. The practice of capital transfers, however, has been broadened to include financing development efforts. During the period of 1967-75, the poorer states of the Arab world received about half of the total of $11.6 billion in aid and soft loans from the oil exporters. Equity and investment loans were much less important, amounting to less than 10 percent of the total offered by rich states of the area.

Capital transfers are not by themselves, however, vehicles of economic integration since they represent unilateral operations that are justified by a one-way dependence of the poor on the rich.

Joint Ventures: Instead of pooling the resources of the various states of the region in order to (effectively and collectively) negotiate the integrated industrialization of the region, the Western countries motivated by both short-term interests and an unwillingness to deal with the regional problems of the Arab states, have found better ways of absorbing Arab oil profits by dealing with the states of the region on a bilateral basis. The very high propensity for importation among OAPEC states enabled the West to benefit from the complete recycling of oil surpluses without having to support real integrative or developmental programs. However, this is worrisome for those who understand the developments in the Middle East because this short-term gain forebodes a very dangerous accumulation of long-term destabilizing aftereffects.

Although many of the big OPEC states are not Arab, the Arab states have actually realized a more sizeable surplus than the others. The surpluses realized by the richer members of OAPEC are not only absorbed in conspicuous importation, but also through various channels for recycling funds to the Western economies. The implication of this factor, together with the quite limited flow of capital to the other Arab states, is the apparent failure of the present institutions of integration in the Arab world. And it has helped produce the huge debt problem of many of the developing states and, hence, a potential crisis for the banking system and liquidity.

WHERE DO WE GO FROM HERE?

Now that we have identified the problems of the Middle East analytically and empirically, where do we go from here?

First, it is important for US analysts to know that the leaders of the region with whom we have had intensive interviews feel that the problems of development, order, and Arab-Israeli (especially Palestinian-Israeli) peace are intertwined.

Second, the region is undergoing rapid change without any serious effort at reducing the inequalities between and within states of the region. Thus, anxieties about the future are high and disorienting. Violent ethnic conflict and protracted instability are around the corner for more of the states of the region than the ones engaged in them now.

Third, the US serves its own interests best by designing an integrated and comprehensive view for dealing with the region, as well as a clear picture of its own national objectives.

It has been argued here that the US approach to the Middle East in the past three decades has been limited in scope. It has been based on negatives and incremental dyadic linkages. This needs to be changed in the eighties.

Recent concerns about US credibility stem from several sources. The most important, from the point of view of the regional elites we have interviewed, is that the United States is not sincere about its pronounced concerns towards Middle East development and peace with justice. The majority of the Arab elites (including two foreign ministers and several national security specialists and advisers) we have interviewed appeared to be disappointed with the recent US preoccupation with the Soviet threat as the primary threat in the region. One foreign minister told me, "I do not like the Soviets one bit but I am not threatened by them. The only threat for me is next door," meaning Israel and Syria! American preoccupation with the Rapid Deployment Force, power projection, protection of the oil fields, security consensus, and strategic allies is confusing. These US concerns reflect the view that the US has defined the region as a US-USSR conflict arena. Regional states have to fit into this conflict and competition model.

A number of important intellectuals and journalists stated during our interviews that the United States is going back to its policies of the 1950s by overemphasizing the military option as opposed to designing a well thought out and comprehensive approach to the region and its future. And, just like the policies of the 1950s, the present ones will not work.

The contribution made by this paper is to argue in favor of a US Middle East policy, an American Comprehensive Regional Policy for the Middle East (CRPME). To shift from the present purely dyadic to a regional perspective will add realism to dealing with the Soviets and the intra-regional conflicts. A CRPME would make these issues more manageable. The United States would not have to think primarily about the USSR should it pursue this approach. The Soviets would become, in a sense, secondary, because their presence and influence would be diminished and neutralized. A CRPME will make more clear in US minds what things can and cannot effectively be undertaken and what things the US can effectively influence.

Directly, the United States cannot do much about ethnic hostility. The US can do very little *directly* about corruption, fanaticism, inequality and such other ills found in the Middle East or the world over.

However, the United States does have a large measure of competence in doing something about many of these problems *indirectly*. Indirectly, and through an enlightened regional approach, the US can help ameliorate these conditions. The US can do a great deal by influencing regional elites to work out programs which would attack the basic problems of ethnic inequality and hostility, corruption, repression and general instability. The US has ample leverage in world affairs and especially with a number of countries in the area. America can exercise this positive influence in three ways:

(a) Power and advice (the carrot and stick approach);

(b) Informal contacts between governmental and nongovernmental (e.g., academic) organizations or individual elites; and

(c) The US as role model.

All in all, if the US were to project the image of a partner in regional terms, a relationship could develop based on mutual advantage and eventually even respect. This approach should be more fruitful than an inter-state military arrangement which can be overturned overnight as Iraq did on July 14, 1958, with the Baghdad Pact. A regional approach will enhance overall Israeli security and the continuous flow of oil at a much lower cost than a purely military approach; it will reduce any Soviet threat to the area; and it will help the countries of the Middle East to develop in peace.

NOTES

1. Neither the Carter Camp David approach nor Reagan's so-called Jordanian Option approach of August 1982 addresses the twin sides of the Middle East dilemma, namely that peace and development must go together. Diplomatic and security arrangements that do not incorporate the structural development needs of the region will not serve the long term interests of a stable Middle East.

2. See Herman Kahn: *On Escalation: Metaphors and Scenarios* (New York: Prayer, 1965), W.W. Kaufman, ed. *Military Policy and National Security.* Princeton, N.J.: Princeton Univ. Press, 1956; Bruce Russett, "The Columbus of Deterrence" *Journal of Conflict Resolution*, VII, (1963), pp. 97-109; Morton Kaplan and Richard Quandt, "Theoretical Analysis of the 'Balance of

Power'," *Behavioral Science*, Vol. V, No. 3, July 1960, pp. 240-52; Kenneth Boulding, *Conflict and Defense*, (New York: Harper and Brothers, 1962).

3. See Edward H. Carr, *The Twenty Years' Crisis*, 1919-1939, 2nd ed. (New York: Harper & Row, 1964). H. Morgenthau, *Truth and Power*, (New York, Praeger; 1970); Anatol Rapoport, *The Big Two*, (New York, Pegasus, 1971); and G. Schwarzenberger, *Power Politics*, (3rd ed. 1964).

4. See Ray S. Cline, *World Power Trends and US Foreign Policy for the 1980s*, (Boulder, Co.: Westview, 1980). Richard Rosecrance, *Action and Reaction in World Politics*, (Boston: Little Brown and Co., 1963); H. Morgenthau, *Politics Armory Nations*, (New York: Alfred A. Knopf, 1956); J.E. Mueller, "Deterrence, Number and History," *Security Studies Paper*, No. 12, Univ. of California, Los Angeles, 1968); and J.G. Stoessinger, *Why Nations Go to War*, (New York: St. Martin's Press, 1974).

5. See H. Chenery, *et al.*, *Redistribution with Growth: An Approach to Policy*. (New York: Oxford University Press, 1974); R. Rubohson, E. Azar, "Peace Amidst Development," *International Interactions*, Vol. 6, No. 2, (1979), pp. 123-143; F.H. Cardoso and F. Faletto, *Dependency and Development in Latin America*, (Berkeley: UC Press, 1979); R. Repetto, *Economic Equality and Fertility in Developing Countries*, published for Resources for the Future, (Baltimore: Johns Hopkins Univ. Press, 1979); E. Azar and Nadia Farah, "The Political Dimensions of Conflict," in Nazli Choucri, ed., *Population and Conflict*, 1983.

6. See H. Field Haviland, Jr., *The Formulation and Administration of United States Foreign Policy*, Washington, DC: Brookings Institution, 1960); B.C. Cohen, *The Influence of Non-Governmental Groups on Foreign Policy-Making*, (Boston: World Peace Foundation, 1960); C. Wright Mills, *The Power Elite*, (New York: O.U.P., 1956); M. Kaplan, *System and Process in International Politics*, (N.Y.: J. Wiley and Sons, Inc., 1957); S.P. Tillman, *The US in the Middle East*, (Bloomington, Indiana:

Indiana University Press, 1982); J.P. Rubinson and R. Meadow, *Polls Apart*, (Cabin John, Md.: Seven Lock Press, 1982); Richard Nixon, *The Memoirs of Richard Nixon*, (New York: Grosset and Dunlap, 1978).

7. S. Rosen and H. Shaked, "Arms and the Saudi Connection," *Commentary*, 65, 6 (June 1978), pp. 33-38; R.D. McLaurin and J.M. Price, "OPEC Current Account Surpluses: Assistance to the Arab Front-Line States," *Oriente Moderno* 58, 11 (November 1978), pp. 533-46; T.N. Dupuy, *Elusive Victory: The Arab-Israeli Wars*, 1947-1974, (New York: Harper & Row, 1978); R. Brodkey and J. Horgen, *Americans in the Gulf*, (Washington, DC: A.I.R., 1975).

8. N.Z. Alcok and K.W. Lowe, "The Vietnam War as a Richardson Process," *Peace Research*, 6:2 (1969), pp. 105-113; D.A. Zinnes, *Contemporary Research in International Relations* (New York: Free Press, 1976), L.F. Richardson, *Arms and Insecurity*, edited by N. Rashevsky and E. Trucco (Chicago: Quadrangle Books, Inc., 1960), P. Smoker, "A Mathematical Study of the Present Arms Race," *General Systems*, 1963, pp. 51-60; A. Rapoport, *Fights, Games and Debates*, Ann Arbor, Michigan: Univ. of Michigan Press, 1960; E. Azar, et. al., "Steps Towards Forecasting International Interactions," *The Papers of the Peace Science Society* (International), No. 23, 1974; J.H. Dixon, "The Evolution of the Arms Race Research Program," in J.H. Dixon, ed., *Readings in Quantitative Methods* (West Point, NY, USMA, 1979).

9. E. Azar, R. McLaurin, P. Jureidini, "Protracted Social Conflict in the Middle East," *Journal of Palestine Studies*, Autumn 1978, pp. 41-69; E. Azar and S.P. Cohen, "Peace or Crisis and War as Status Quo," *International Interactions*, Vol. 6, No. 2, 1980, pp. 159-184; E. Azar and N. Farah, "The Structure of Inequalities and Protracted Social Conflict," *International Interactions*, Vol. 7, No. 4, pp. 317-335.

10. E. Azar, "The Conflict and Peace Data Bank (COPDAB)

Project," *Journal of Conflict Resolution*, Vol. 24, No. 1, March 1980, pp. 143-152.

11. A good source of US preferences in international relations can be found in the US political parties platforms, US Congressional debates and positions advocated by several officials including, but not restricted to, the Department of State. Recent memoirs of former US presidents, secretaries of state and national advisers are rich sources for researchers on US international goods.

12. J.A. Nathan and J.K. Oliver, *United States Foreign Policy and World Order* (Boston: Little Brown and Co., [2nd ed.] 1981), J.S. Szyliowiez and B.F. O'Neill, eds., *The Energy Crisis and US Foreign Policy* (New York: Praeger, 1975).

13. G. Lenczowski, ed., *US Interests in the Middle East* (Washington, DC: American Enterprise Institute, 1968), R.H. Magnus, ed., *Documents on the Middle East*, (Washington, DC: A.E.I., 1969).

14. R.H. Magnus, ed., *ibid.*; Congressional Quarterly, Inc., *The Middle East*, 4th ed., Washington, DC, 1979; W. Quandt, *Decades of Decisions* (Berkeley: Univ. of California Press, 1977).

15. N. Safran, *Israel the Embattled Ally*, (Cambridge, Ma.: Harvard Univ. Press, 1978). T. Robertson, *Crisis* (London: Hutchinson & Co., 1964); I.L. Gendzier, ed., *A Middle East Reader*, (New York: Pegasus, 1969); P. Groisser, *The US and the Middle East*, (Albany, N.Y.: SUNY Press, 1982).

16. Y. Evron, *The Middle East*, (New York: Praeger, 1973); G. Lenczowski, *The Middle East in World Affairs*, 4th ed., (Ithaca: Cornell Univ. Press, 1980).

17. E. Azar, "The USSR, China and the Middle East," *Problems of Communism*, May, June 1979, pp. 18-30.

18. The Israeli-PLO war in Lebanon during the summer of 1982 has changed some aspects of the US-Israeli relationship.

19. W. Eckhardt and E. Azar, "Major World Conflicts and Interventions, 1945 to 1975," *International Interactions*, Vol. 5, No. 1 (1978), pp. 75-110; S.P. Cohen and E. Azar, "The Transition from War to Peace Between Israel and Egypt," *Journal*

of Conflict Resolution, Vol. 25, No. 1, March 1981, pp. 87-114; E. Azar and A. Almashat, "Contradictions and Skepticism: How Egyptian Students View the Peace Process," *International Interactions*, Vol. 7, No. 4, 1981, pp. 379-398.

20. H. Cantril, *The Psychology of Social Movements*, (New York: Wiley and Sons, 1941); S. Cohen, H. Kelman, F. Miller and B. Smith, "Evolving Intergroup Techniques for Conflict Resolution," *Journal of Social Issues*, Vol. 33, 1977; L.W. Doob, *Patriotism and Nationalism*, (New Haven: Yale Univ. Press, 1964), M. Deutsch, "Trust and Suspicion," *Journal of Conflict Resolution*, Vol. 23, 1958; J.W. Burton, *Conflict and Communication* (London: McMillan, 1969).

21. S.E. Ibrahim, "Anatomy of Egypt's Militant Islamic Groups," Paper presented at the Middle East Studies Association meetings, Washington, DC, November 6-9, 1980; R.S. Humphray, "Islam and Political Values in Saudi Arabia, Egypt and Syria," *Middle East Journal*, Vol. 33, No. I (Winter, 1979); I. Altman, "Islamic Movements in Egypt," *The Jerusalem Quarterly*, No. 10 (Winter, 1979), pp. 87-108; H. Dekmejian, "The Anatomy of Islamic Revival and the Search for Islamic Alternatives," *Middle East Journal*, Vol. 34 (Winter 1980), pp. 1-12; B. Lewis, "The Return of Islam," *Commentary* (January, 1976), pp. 39-49; E. Azar and C. Moon, "The Many Faces of Islamic Revivalism," in R. Rubenstein, ed., *Worldwide Impact of Religion on Contemporary Politics*, (Washington, DC: Washington Institute, forthcoming, 1984).

22. Ian Lustick, "Arabs in the Jewish State: Study of Effective Control of Minority Population," Ph.D. dissertation, Univ. of California, Berkeley, 1976; P. Jureidini and R. McLaurin, *Beyond Camp David* (Syracuse: Syracuse Univ. Press, 1981).

23. See Hazem el Beblawi, "The Predicament of the Arab Gulf Oil States: Individual Gains and Collective Losses" in M.H. Kerr and S. Yassin, eds. *Rich and Poor States in the Middle East* (Boulder: Westview Press, 1982), pp. 165-224.

24. See R.W. Baker, *Egypt's Uncertain Revolution under Nasser*

and Sadat (Cambridge: Harvard Univ. Press, 1978); M.L. Kerr and S. Yassin, eds. and Nadia Farah, *Religious Strife in Egypt: Crisis and Ideological Conflict in the Seventies* (a monograph published by the Center for International Development, University of Maryland College Park, 1983, mimeo).

25. See Saad Eddin Ibrahim, "Oil, Migration and the New Arab Social Order" in M.L. Kerr and S. Yassin, eds., *op. cit.*, pp. 17-70.

REAGAN IN ASIA: AN ASSESSMENT

By
TETSUYA KATAOKA

The first year has passed since the inauguration of the Reagan administration, with its pledge to restore the country to robust economic health and to a position of military strength with a margin of superiority over its major adversary. The time span has been sufficient to take the measure of the Reagan administration and to make a preliminary assessment of Reagan's Asian policy.

What is Reagan's Asian policy? Is there a coherent policy? Some skeptics doubt this. Even if not, what has the United States done in Asia? Is Mr. Reagan seen to be succeeding in what he is doing? What should he do to succeed if he is not now succeeding?

Ronald Reagan came into power riding the wave of a new consciousness in America that the country was in an ever worsening crisis caused by the decline of its power. Since public awareness of a problem is part of the solution in a democracy, President Reagan was and perhaps still is in an enviable position to mobilize the na-

Tetsuya Kataoka is Professor of Policy Science at the Graduate School of Policy Science, Saitama University, Japan.

tional resources to cope with the crisis. The decline of American power can be characterized in two mutually related ways: economic and politico-strategic.

Perhaps more than other nations, America is thought to depend on material foundations for its power, including the productive power of its factories, the vastness of domestic natural resources, and the technical skills and organization of its people. "The Imperial Republic" and its hegemony over the postwar world would have been unthinkable without, for instance, that enormous and expendable fleet of jeeps produced by American factories. The economic power of the United States has slowed down, thus causing it to decline relative to other countries. The decline of economic power has had quite direct strategic consequences. The Reagan administration has correctly perceived the politico-strategic implications of America's economic decline and sought to address the problem squarely.

If the rise of Japan symbolized the relative decline of American economic power, that of the Soviet Union in pursuit of hegemony was achieved directly at the expense of American military prestige. Unlike his predecessor, President Reagan holds that "world order" depends on the stability of the US-Soviet balance of power which in turn depends first and foremost on unilateral American efforts under the present circumstances.

Reagan's stress on unilateral American efforts, both strategic and economic, has dual meanings: on the one hand, it is meant to be a springboard for a renewed American activism that draws on the lore of America as "Number One." The content of this drive is hegemonic. Will to power is a precondition for attaining it, and in the nature of the case it is unilateral.

On the other hand, Reagan's stress on unilateralism is not merely inspirational but represents a critical and negative appraisal of a strategic concept upheld by his predecessor. Former President Carter's retrenchment of American power rested on the assumption that local or regional balances of power can substitute for the decline of American power in the central balance against the Soviet Union. The conceptual delinking of the central from the local-regional balance has its origin in the internal war theory that came into vogue during the latter days of the war in Vietnam. The internal war theory purported to replace the falling domino theory by maintaining in essence that wars of national liberation in the third world have their causes in the social structure of the 'afflicted regions. Such wars, the theory implied, being indigenous in origin, are both unstoppable by outside intervention and benign.

One need not go to the other extreme of arguing that every trouble spot in the world is caused, instigated, or abetted by the Soviet Union. One need only acknowledge the fact that the Soviet Union's interests and outreach have become global in the decade of the 1970s. The Kremlin has received US sanction and blessing for its attainment of superpower status during detente in the form of the SALT I treaty, which recognized Soviet parity with America in strategic weapons.

But far from being content with its newly acquired status, the Kremlin continued to expand its military power and political influence abroad. It kept up its relentless efforts at strategic and theater military buildups and extended its influence into peripheral areas from which it had hitherto abstained. In these latter efforts, the Soviet Union has successfully enlisted Cuban and East German proxies, and has utilized its worldwide airlift and sealift capabilities.

The United States is for the time being the only country that has the will to compete with the Soviet Union worldwide. The Chinese word for that will, hegemonism, is probably the closest approximation to the underlying motivation. There is naturally a large dose of anxiety about what might happen if the United States refuses to be drawn into one-on-one competition with the Soviets: and the failure of the Kremlin to exercise self-restraint in Angola, Afghanistan, South Yemen, etc. are cited as proof of its lack of will.

Although the United States is inclined as well as compelled to act unilaterally vis-à-vis the Soviet Union, it must nonetheless at least pay lip-service to and accommodate multilateralism vis-à-vis the allies that are fast becoming America's full equals in every respect save strategic. Complete unilateralism on the part of the United States would call for a hierarchical inter-allied relationship, whose prototype was the Cold War bloc. If, furthermore, the United States could tax its allies for their protection as empires have taxed their territories in the past, the nagging problem of "burden sharing" would disappear. But then, one must note, the allies would have turned into protectorates.

Or, again speaking theoretically, the task of coping with the Soviet Union worldwide can be much more multilateralized than heretofore and shared in common by a "Directorate" made up of the United States, Japan, West Germany, Britain and France, as proposed by David Watt, et al., in *Western Security*. But if the idea of American unilateralism, born of the peculiar post-war circumstances, is now outmoded, that of a Directorate is like the Aesopian fable about mice trying to put a bell on the cat's collar: it is a good idea but there seems to be no means of getting it done. America is too used to dominating, its allies are too used to being protected by America, and they are all interdependent with each other. Without falling into the cynical fatalism of saying that an international system built through the crucible of a great war cannot be changed without another war, one is justified in admitting the sheer weight of a past that lasted for thirty-seven years. For now, both the United States and its allies are required to proceed on two tracks by finding and striking a balance between American unilateralism and multilateralism.

Without foreclosing other options for the future, we must find a viable division of labor among the allies for now. And that means defining the minimum functions of an anti-Soviet balance for which the United States' unilateral efforts are both necessary and insufficient. Central to the strategic balance is an American military capability that matches and deters the Soviet strategic offensive capability with land, sea, and air weapon systems. Britain, France, Japan, and West Germany—if and when the latter two go nuclear—can only augment but not displace the US strategic capability. None of the US allies is endowed with adequate resources or geographic position (30-minute warning time against Soviet ICBM attack) to maintain a stable balance of mutual deterrence in this area. In any event, the United States is firmly opposed to nuclear armament by Japan and

West Germany, thus obliging itself to be their only nuclear umbrella.

The other function of an anti-Soviet balance for which the United States is indispensable is in the area of conventional forces. Generally speaking the role of US conventional forces in defense of allied territories in Asia and Europe ought to be that of the sword, a strategic reserve, that delivers a counter-blow to Soviet ground forces if they challenge the shield maintained by native allies. Some minimum US forces may remain deployed in these forward areas to serve as hostage or tripwire, but the main reserve need not remain in forward positions.

This is the idea embodied in former CIA director Stanfield Turner's article in the New York *Times* magazine recently. The latest *Report to Congress* by Secretary of Defense Casper Weinberger also assigns to US forces the role of strategic retaliation at places of their choosing, which seems to call for their move back from theater fronts to a central position. While Turner made no mention of Asia, it is, ironically, in Asia itself that the idea has been put to practice already.

The United States maintains one army division in South Korea, one marine division in Okinawa, and the 7th Fleet and the Fifth Air Force in Japan. The marine division and the 7th Fleet are earmarked for deployment in the Persian Gulf. In the event of a conflict in the Gulf, only the Korean contingent and the 5th Air Force will be stationary. Therefore, East Asia may be said to be the first to be readied for the application of the swing strategy.

However, the swing strategy is at best a palliative that papers over the fact that American defense commitments are stretched beyond limit around the world, and that something has to give somewhere. Beyond a rational division of labor that relieves the United States from non-strategic missions, there is the problem of whether it is financially capable of performing the bedrock role in the central balance. Mr. Reagan was certainly correct in trying to increase unilaterally the supply of American power. But his solution to the problem, namely Reaganomics, is running into a crisis of confidence both at home and in allied capitals. The spillover effect of declining American economic power to the defense area was demonstrated graphically and disastrously in the outcome of the MX basing decision. Candidate Reagan's outcry against the alleged "Minuteman vulnerability" or the "opening of the window of vulnerability" naturally seemed the most concentrated expression of his all too well justified call to reverse the US strategic decline. Nothing could be worse, therefore, than his own decision—after all the hue and cry—to scale down the number of MX to be deployed from 200 to 40 and to base them in the old Minuteman silos and without any hardening to boot. To America's friends and allies who took Reagan seriously, the decision was much more discouraging than the failure of Carter's attempted rescue of the hostages in Iran.

In one stroke, the Reagan administration has undercut itself in one of two ways: having played up the alleged need to close the "window of vulnerability" but having failed to act on it, the administration suggests that the "window" was not really open. Or the "window" is still open but the United States cannot afford to close it. Since neither implication can be owned up to, the Reagan administration seemed to revert quietly from a nuclear war fighting strategy to MAD (Mutual Assured Destruction). At least this was the impression created by the flap over limited nuclear war in Europe broached by Alexander Haig but denied by Caspar Weinberger. To make matters worse, the Defense Secretary's 1982 *Report to Congress* has reaffirmed the nuclear war fighting doctrine, but the 1983 budget that provides a fiscal prop to it is now under serious questioning in Congress as to its feasibility.

The Economist of London was perhaps a bit too indulgent with Mr. Reagan when it reacted to the hobbled MX decision thus: "Unlimited US capacity to pull surprises." Together with America's unsatisfactory economic performance, the MX decision seems to symbolize the disturbing gap between American aspirations and reality. Will the American people then good-naturedly shrug their shoulders, accept the rhetoric as mere rhetoric, and go back to business as usual? The decibel level of the attacks on the allegedly unfaithful, self-interested allies of the US is too high for this. One therefore cannot dismiss the dark foreboding that somehow the American system is working itself up to a towering outrage at the intractable world, an outrage so shattering in its impact that the only exit from it would be a retreat to isolationism.

As of this writing the United States and Japan seem headed for a major collision over a combination of defense and trade issues, which translate into a question over the distributive justice of current defense burden sharing between the two countries. Because there is so much that Japan should be doing both in defense and trade but is not, a mistaken assumption prevails in the United States that it is simply a victim of Japanese selfishness. Relief from the burden of defense is thought to give Japan its legendary competitive edge in trade and manufacture. If Japan were then to be asked to double this year's defense budget of a slightly over $10 billion to $20 billion, a figure frequently mentioned as one of the upper targets the US Department of Defense considers amply adequate, the additional tax cost per capita would be a mere $100, which could hardly be a drag on Japanese economic performance. The ease with which Japan could double its defense outlay is naturally an argument for doing so at the earliest possible opportunity, but it is not one that will assuage America's concern about its loss of competitiveness.

In addition, Japan's arms manufacturers, who are lobbying with increasing intensity to have the ban on the sale of arms abroad removed, may get in on the band wagon of general arms expansion, with the result that Japan will join the international arms market with its cost effective hardware. Though this eventuality is unavoidable in the long run, it does constitute for the moment that "other side of the coin" which should be taken into account by Japan's allies. All in all, Japan's "free ride," an indisputable and objective fact, should be dealt with on its own terms rather than as a means of achieving extraneous objectives. There is, in short, no substitute for restoring America's internal economic strength and therewith its self-confidence.

The friction between Japan and the United States may be said to stem from the fact that they are both consciously pursuing a status quo policy that preserves in some way their respective political position that resulted from World War II while their actual power is shifting almost in spite of themselves—that of Japan upward, that of the United States downward. The United States must face up to the fact that its efforts to end Japan's dependent status on matters of defense is not an economic but a political problem with great long range consequences. What is needed today is not a search for a means of preserving the status of "Imperial America" by levying a "security tax" on Japan but a soul-searching dialogue on a gradual devolution of power, political and strategic, to Japan.

The United States must also realize that even if Japan were to demand or accept a great devolution of power, an unlikely event in the foreseeable future, America's leading or hegemonic role will not nor cannot be impaired because this is a geographic and historical imperative as long as Japan remains a free and democratic country. There is, in other words, a certain international role that history has assigned to the United States only. This is a privilege as well as a duty, which it cannot share with others, and the performance of which does not constitute an act of generosity to others less fortunately endowed than it. "Burden sharing," America must realize, is a euphemism that contains an irreducible minimum of inequality that favors it in political privilege but that favors its allies in economic terms. There has never been greatness that was cost free.

The foregoing constitutes a review of Reagan's overall conduct of foreign policy and a preliminary to a discussion of his Asian policy in particular. To be honest, Mr. Reagan did not have much of an Asian policy while he was on the campaign trail, and, after his first year in office, Asia remained an area of only occasional interest to him even though the TNF negotiations in Europe, for instance, are bound to involve Japan ultimately. The Reagan administration conveys an unmistakeable impression that it is not, at least in its upper echelons, very knowledgeable about Asia. The Assistant Secretaries and Under Secretaries of State are heavily oriented toward Europe and those who deal regularly with Asia at State seem to be Carter carryovers. Mr. Mike Mansfield still sits in Tokyo as US ambassador. The Heritage Foundation's *Mandate for Leadership*, on which the new administration has avowedly drawn for guidance, deals with Japan in a mere 8 pages out of 1093.

Mr. Reagan's campaign rhetoric concerning Asia consisted mostly of criticism of President Carter's retreat from South Korea and Taiwan; he said next to nothing on Japan or China—even though his support for Taiwan, in the nature of the case, would have an immediate repercussion on the China connection.

United States policy toward China, "One China but not now," was established by President Nixon in the Shanghai communiqué, and every president since has promised to honor the policy and uphold the strategic rationale behind it. But there has been a considerable shift in emphasis within the framework established by the Shanghai communiqué. As detente evaporated and US-Soviet antagonism came to the fore, Washington and the Kremlin lost room for maneuver and initiative in the triangular relationship with Peking. Peking's position was correspondingly enhanced because it alone was in a position to pit the other parties against each other without fear of their combining against itself. This accounts for the fact that the triangular relationship is yielding not a "China card" for America but an "America card" for China.

To be sure, China seems to be under Soviet pressure avowedly designed to counteract its enlistment in the so-called Washington-Tokyo-Peking axis. But the net increase in pressure since the demise of detente is a psychological one in the form of the Moscow-Hanoi treaty of alliance, and in any case the treaty's major objective was to challenge US control of the western Pacific and the Indian Ocean by providing the Soviets with major base facilities near the Malacca strait. To what extent the considerable Soviet presence on the land frontier of the Northeast is perceived as a threat to Peking can be fathomed by the fact that Chinese defense spending has been decreasing lately.

Nonetheless, it has been in the Chinese interest to get maximum credit from Washington for its policies against the Soviet Union or its proxy, as it did during the Carter administration when Deng Hsiao-p'ing announced a punitive action against Hanoi during his visit to Washington and carried it out subsequently. Chinese skill in theatrics was demonstrated yet again when in 1980 Peking raised a chorus of protest against Japan concerning the allegedly inadequate planning involved in major plant export projects from Japan, many of which, it was maintained, had to be cancelled or scaled down. After the good-natured Japanese were thrown sufficiently off balance, Peking asked for and managed to get refinancing loans. The government of Ohira Masaoshi silenced the grumblings among Japanese business and paid up nearly in full.

All this is not to suggest that the strategic rationale behind the Shanghai communiqué has become invalid or useless. The United States and Japan need to preserve the alignment and configuration in the three-way relationship laid down in the Shanghai communiqué for the global balance against the Soviet Union. But the "semi-allied" relationship of China to the United States is the closest approximation in today's world to the traditional offensive alliance of rather predatory character. An element of opportunism cannot be eliminated on either side without deviating from the Shanghai framework. Yet a desire to eliminate Chinese opportunism was clearly discernible as a major motive of the Carter administration's China policy, both dovish (Vance) and hawkish (Brzezinski). To suppose that a communist state can enter into an alliance with a democracy for more than transient interests, however, would only encourage China to up the ante and do the opposite of what is desired.

Candidate Reagan's criticism of the Carter China policy, therefore, could have paved the way toward a more balanced policy in keeping with the original Shanghai design. But Mr. Reagan erred in insisting on form (upgrading US relationship with Taiwan) and not insisting enough on substance (Taiwan's security). The former goes clearly against the "One China, but not now" principle, but the sale of arms to Taiwan accords with it. The United States is morally responsible for the prevention of forcible integration of Taiwan with the mainland, and in exchange for US recognition of Peking, President Carter is reported to have secured a Chinese consent to America's right to help Taiwan preserve an ability to defend itself against such an attempt. That is the correct implementation of the "not now" formula.

China's threat to downgrade its relationship with Washington unless the latter desisted from the sale of arms to Taiwan might or might not have been a bluff. But it was not justified because it contravenes the Shanghai principle. The United States should have majestically brushed aside China's protest and let the onus, for whatever consequence, fall on it. Instead the Reagan administration caved in at the last minute to the Chinese bluff and imposed a kind of voluntary restraint. But then appeasement of China is perhaps no worse than appeasement of Saudi Arabia over the AWACS issue let alone the appeasement of the Soviet Union over the Polish crisis.

One bright spot in the Reagan administration's Asian policy is the US-South Korean relationship. Not only has the United States done well by South Korea but there have been valuable spillover effects on Japan. The White House invitation to President Chun Doo Hwan as the first state guest of the new administration was executed swiftly and smartly, creating an indelible impression that Carter's policy toward South Korea has been reversed. Confident of US support and buoyed by the coming of the Olympic games, the Chun government has even made some progress in the human rights area as well by sweeping away corruption. Washington must consult the South Korean government closely on what to do with the overture from Pyongyang for a US connection. If the unification of the South and North Korean governments is out of the question, we should not be remiss in seeking their mutual accommodation according to the German model.

With Washington's quiet encouragement, the ROK government has lobbed a salvo at Japan: a demand for six billion dollars in payment for Korea's role as Japan's outer defense. Traditionally the Japanese are easily unnerved when they are sandwiched by a united front of continental and Pacific powers, and the latest envelopment has worked its desired effect. Japan is now contemplating economic assistance to South Korea, although for less than the Koreans had asked for.

Indochina happens to be the only area in the world where the US policy of containing communism is implemented effectively with local self-help and where it enjoys broad Third World and United

Nations support. China and the ASEAN countries are the major actors in containing Vietnam and its agent in Cambodia, the Heng Samrin regime. Aside from its small military assistance to Thailand, the United States confines itself to low-key diplomatic efforts to support ASEAN in order to frustrate Hanoi's dream of unifying all of Indochina under its aegis. However, containment in Cambodia consists of an indefinite stalemate and low-level fighting. The independent forces in Cambodia, even including Pol Pot's Khmer Rouge, seem destined to be an appendage of ASEAN and to subsist on the latter's handouts. Because of severe deterioration in its economy— caused in large measure by its invasion of Cambodia—Hanoi cannot bring its intervention to a decisive conclusion. However, because some ASEAN members, notably Indonesia, are more fearful of Chinese design than of Vietnamese expansionism, the Chinese-ASEAN united front suffers from built-in limitations.

Critical to the stalemate is the Chinese and Vietnamese will to support their respective clients in Cambodia, and US influence over them seems marginal. There is no doubt that Hanoi is interested in rapprochment with the United States and Japan as a precondition for receiving aid, and such aid may act as a countervailing force to Soviet influence in Hanoi. But it seems impossible for Hanoi to give up Cambodia to the Chinese in exchange for aid and recognition from the United States.

The Japan problem is central to US foreign policy problems not only in Asia but globally. This is because the new world strategic balance demands a greater reorientation by Japan and such a change is rapidly coming within the realm of possibility. Japanese politics is shifting to the right, and if orchestrated properly, the move can upgrade Japan into an ally and a bastion of democracy in the Orient. The outcome will depend critically on Washington's skill, vision, and understanding.

United States policy toward Japan received full articulation in the Suzuki-Reagan joint communiqué of May 1981, and it represents in the main a continuation of the Carter administration's policy as it was reformulated after the invasion of Afghanistan, the enunciation of the Carter Doctrine, and the formation of the Rapid Deployment Force to protect allied interests in the Persian Gulf. In the area of defense, the American policy, according to the joint communiqué, is to see to it that "Japan, on its own initiative and in accordance with its Constitution and basic defense policy, will seek to make even greater efforts for improving its defense capabilities in its surrounding sea and air space, and for further alleviating the financial burden of US forces in Japan."

There is a curiously half-baked character about this policy indicating that it represents an unsatisfactory compromise between Japan's domestic political constraints and its unavoidably global role. While deferring formally to Japan's constitutional straitjacket, Washington insists nonetheless that the constitutionally-derived injunction, "defensive defense" or territorial defense, be ignored in coping with the protection of sea-lanes.

The "basic defense policy" of Japan lays down 1% of GNP as the upper limit of defense expenditure and "even greater efforts" to reach that limit. Under unprecedented pressure from Washington, the Suzuki government has appropriated a 7.75% increase in real terms for the 1982 defense budget. This represents an increase from 0.91 to 0.93% of GNP. At this rate Japan will reach the 1% of GNP mark by the end of this decade.

Inextricably wound up with defense and also central to US concern worldwide is Japan's trade policy since the first oil crisis in 1974. In the first instance the Japanese government justifies its huge surplus in balance of payments with the principle of free trade pure and simple: Japanese goods are competitive in price, excellent in quality, and should have access to whoever is willing to buy them. Secondarily, it concedes the principle of reciprocity in a multilateral balance, which means that bilateral and temporary trade imbalance with a particular trading partner is of no account. To uphold the reciprocity principle, Japan has been rapidly eliminating tariff barriers to foreign imports over the years, and today has one of the most access-free economies in the world. Still, Japan's feisty export sector is chalking up earnings in excess of imports, and by the beginning of 1981 the world owed Japan $4.7 billion in current account. When it comes to the bilateral trade account, the United States is in debt to Japan to the tune of $18 billion in 1981. And this at a time when the United States is in thrall to the severest recession since World War II and yet spending an unprecedented sum for defense.

For the umpteenth time, though with the greatest animus yet, the outcry is heard in America and Europe that Japan is exporting unemployment, or that it is following a "beggar thy neighbor" policy. The suggested solution this time was drastic elimination of non-tariff barriers at first, but it escalated rapidly to a demand that once again Japan become the locomotive of the world economy through fiscal stimulation of domestic demand. But the Suzuki government is reluctant to do this at a time when it is carrying out fiscal retrenchment to get rid of deficits caused in part by past external pressure.

Japan's declaratory policy of multilateral reciprocity with the qualification that countries in acute distress in bilateral trade with Japan should receive special consideration seems to be an economically rational one. But the issue between Japan and its trading partners in the industrialized world is as much political as economic. Neither at present nor back in 1978-79, when the charge of "free ride" was also raised, would Japan move of its own accord to honor its own self-proclaimed principle. Instead, even when it is in its obvious and enlightened interests to act first, it waits for external pressure to build up, so as to use that pressure for leverage in arranging the required domestic response. It gives the appearance of being niggardly, lethargic, and indifferent to the plight of other people. One suspects that something intrinsic to the nature of the Japanese political system makes it prone to be a sort of money-changer at the temple.

Japan's tardiness in responding to the grievances of its partners has built up a dangerous pressure. While the Japanese government and people should bear a major share of the blame for bringing about this state of affairs, the United States cannot escape a share of responsibility for indirectly causing Japan to be what it is today inasmuch as the Japanese polity is still shaped today by the original occupation design. Most importantly, the US deliberately kept Japan in a status of military dependency, and it can play only a minor supporting role for basically unilateral American defense commitments.

In testifying before the Solarz Subcommittee of the House Foreign Affairs Committee on March 1, 1982, John H. Holdridge, Assistant Secretary of State for East Asian and Pacific Affairs, remarked that he expected Japanese policy to be "consistent with our views on the need for a credible but still strictly defensive Japanese military posture." In order to hold Japan in this posture, the United States government pays regular lip service to the restrictions imposed by Japan's constitution while conniving with those Japanese who take extreme liberty in interpreting Article IX. "The no-war clause of the constitution," said Mr. Holdridge, "is broadly supported, although it has been interpreted to permit just about all the improvements in Japan's self defense posture likely to be required in the foreseeable future."

All the shrill voices demanding the end of Japan's defense free ride must be understood in the context of this decisive ceiling imposed by the United States as a matter of active policy today. The fact that many Japanese are inclined to live with the constitution provides a convenient cover to conceal the US motive in controlling Japan. It creates a dangerous illusion in the United States that the Japanese reluctance to rearm is solely Japanese, not American in origin, and hence that pressure and bluster will overcome it. It does not occur to America that a policy of demanding increased defense efforts by Japan is basically at odds with its policy of controlling Japan. Nor does it occur to America that the Japanese are reluctant to rearm because they are not really asked to defend their own land but merely to increase their supporting contribution to an otherwise American show. The Japanese are a proud nation with a distinct culture. Can they be expected to take seriously the demand that they "make even greater efforts" to serve a foreign army?

The Americans suspect a causal linkage between Japan's economic prowess and its defense posture; in this view the two are opportunity costs with respect to each other, so that where there is more of one, there is less of the other, and vice versa. Thus, Mr. Holdridge simultaneously calls on Japan to assume an economic responsibility consonant with its global interests and a military role that is even less than regional. He fails to see that there is another kind of linkage: Japan is seemingly insensitive to the economic plight of its friends precisely because it need not be sensitive about its own security. Thus the US policy of keeping Japan in the position of a protectorate may be said to be the cause of Japan's indulgent trade policy.

This is not to suggest that Japan can be forced by the United States to be self-reliant militarily without impairing the vital bilateral relationship. But since no initiative for a changed military posture is forthcoming from Tokyo, Washington must commence a dialogue by enlisting those in Japan who are willing to take up the case for greater military self-reliance on their own. A movement is underway in Japan which seeks to revise the existing Security Treaty to make the rights and obligations of the signatories completely equal and truly mutual. While keeping on good terms with the government in Japan, the Reagan administration can encourage private American citizens to collaborate with this movement and can act to bring it into the limelight.

To conclude, the United States seems to be heading into trouble in Asia over the mid-term future because internal developments in the US and Japan are becoming increasingly incompatible with the alliance structure. Everything else in Asia palls in significance. Unless the United States can restore its economic health, and unless Japan is more forthcoming in defense and in efforts to maintain free trade, the US-Japan alliance, the foundation of American foreign policy in Asia, will be undone.

United States Foreign Policy and The China Problem

By
MORTON A. KAPLAN

The opening to China of the Nixon administration that produced the Shanghai Communiqué was received with a great deal of euphoria in the United States and much fear in the Soviet Union, where initially it was perceived as an encircling move. Although official circles within the Soviet Union soon saw the significant limitations of the relationship between the United States and mainland China, many in the United States still perceive the relationship with Communist China as an important link in the American defense system.

Although "normal" relations between the Peoples' Republic of China and the United States certainly are to be desired, the defense link concept is extraordinarily weak. In the first place, China is not a significant military power. It had difficulty in mounting a sustained offensive against Communist Vietnam. Communist China is in no position militarily to threaten the Soviet Union. As the mainland authorities themselves openly state, the Chinese military forces have outdated military equipment and are incapable of mounting any kind of serious offensive against a modern force. Their main purpose is to make an invasion of China so costly that the Soviet Union, facing NATO to the west, will not make the effort.

Whether China actually diverts Soviet forces from the West is open to question. It is likely that Soviet forces on the Chinese border have as their chief purpose the intimidation of the Peoples' Republic of China. However, even if China does divert forces that otherwise might be arrayed against NATO, that is a product of the geographic proximity of the two nations and not of cooperation between the Peoples' Republic and the United States.

Although it is in the American interest for the Peoples' Republic not to feel so isolated that it believes itself forced to accommodate to Soviet policy, that result is not likely in any event; and the United States need not pay any significant price to achieve it. On the other hand, excessively hostile policies by the United States or excessive military weakness in the United States might produce that kind of temporary accommodation.

The Peoples' Republic of China can be depended upon to pursue those policies that are in its own interests. Under most circumstances, it would be in the interest of the Peoples' Republic to equidistance itself from the United States and the Soviet Union. The degree of public antipathy the regime faces may incline it to some partial accommodation with the Soviet Union. But there is no reason to believe that the United States can change this or that it should do so at the expense of the Chinese people if it could.

The greatest deterrent to a move to the center by the Peoples' Republic lies in the encircling activities of the Soviet Union, including its ventures in Afghanistan and its presence in Vietnam. The same intransigence that prevents the Soviet Union from returning the northern islands to Japan also prevents the Soviet Union from making the minor border adjustments that would ease a rapprochement with Communist China.

On the other hand, the Peoples' Republic can be counted upon to follow policies parallel to the United States if Soviet activities threaten Thailand, Malaysia, or Indonesia because its interests will require this. It will not do this out of friendship for the United States or for the nations under threat. In 1934, for example, Hitler warned the Poles that he would divide Poland with Russia if they did not cooperate with him. And the day after Munich, Potemkin, the number two man in the Soviet foreign office told Coulandre, the French ambassador, "Ah, my poor friend, this means the fourth partition of Poland." Nonetheless, Britain and France refused to believe that Communist Russia and Nazi Germany would follow parallel policies because they focused on their hostility rather than on their temporarily parallel interests. The current policy of the United States that placates the mainland regime is not required to achieve parallel Chinese activities when mainland interests facilitate them and is insufficient to do this if mainland interests do not. The current Chinese moderation on wars of liberation fits into this picture. Support for these wars is likely to resume if and when the local situation makes it advantageous quite apart from American policy on arms to Taiwan. Although it cannot be excluded that the United States might be able to influence the timing and degree of such support, that influence is likely to be marginal, transient, and not necessarily related to policy toward the Republic of China. Similarly, Chinese moderation on the issue of South Korea is likely to be affected more by the Chinese/Soviet rivalry for influence in North Korea and by Chinese trade with South Korea than by American policy on the Republic of China. Any marginal—and hypothetical—gain that might follow from concessions to the mainland on this issue will be overbalanced by heavy costs both in terms of strategic considerations and American values.

The late Senator Henry Jackson's fear that if we do not accommodate the Peoples' Republic, there will be a Sino/Soviet pact equivalent to the Nazi-Soviet pact is based on a complete misreading of the latter. The Soviet Union would not have fought on the side of the West if there had been a war over Czechoslovakia. Among other factors, neither Rumania nor Poland would have given them transit rights; and for good reasons. However, if the West had stood up at Munich either Hitler would have been overthrown by the army or the good Czech army and the Czech military glacis would have functioned on the allied side while German rearmament was still in its early stages.

When Czechoslovakia was thrown away and the West supported Poland, General Gamelin promised the Poles that France would remain firm in support behind the Maginot line. If Russia had not made the Pact, it feared Hitler would have continued to march East. Russia would not have had half of Poland for defensive purposes and it would have lost important time to recover from its own army purges and economic weaknesses. Moreover, misunderstanding the weakness of France, Stalin thought the war would be a stalemate in the West.

No possible parallel exists in the present situation. China needs to play on the US/Soviet conflict. Russia is not deliberately moving to war. And, if it were, China would seek some way to divert it to us. In the meantime, the only threat to it is Russian encirclement.

Contrary to much poor history, Stalin knew that he was under threat from Nazi Germany, and the Pact was an expedient to divert or to delay attack. Friendly gestures or concessions from the West could not have changed his policies. Only effective anti-Nazi policies could have done so. If there is a parallel at all, the advice of Senator Jackson is irrelevant. China some day will move closer to the Soviet Union to balance against the West, because this will serve its interests. But it will not be foolish enough to cooperate in Soviet plans against us except to divert attack from itself. And then it will not matter whether or not we have betrayed the Republic of China.

Furthermore, it is not in the American interest that relations between China and the Soviet Union become critically strained. The threat of war between those two powers would confront the United States with uncomfortable alternatives. The United States would be most unlikely to come to the military assistance of China, although it might provide economic assistance and perhaps even military equipment. Certainly the United States has no interest in a war that might result either in a puppet regime in North China, thus enhancing Soviet power in the Pacific, or the embarrassment resulting from American unwillingness or inability to do anything substantial to help the Chinese.

Far more important than a quasi-alliance with the Peoples' Republic is the defense triangle: Japan, South Korea, and the Republic of China. This defense triangle, which is based on common interests and relatively common values, protects both the East Asian rimland, including the Philippines and Southeast Asia. Whereas the threat of Chinese subversion or even armed pressure might increase if the Soviet presence in Southeast Asia is reduced, this defense triangle is a dependable asset because it is based on relatively permanent common interests.

As strong as this confluence of interests is, it would not justify an American effort to interfere with the unification of China if this occurred consonantly with the wishes of the inhabitants of both of the areas. The strategic risks that such unification would invoke necessarily would take second place to American interests in a principled international order. Furthermore, given the legitimate nationalism of the Chinese people, such interference would give rise to risks of still an additional character. However, the current American policy, including President Reagan's three letters to Beijing are a form of low comedy; for they sacrifice vital strategic interests of the United States and at the same time are contrary both to American ideals and to its interests in a just international order. The amateur Machiavellians of the State and Defense departments who are the architects of this policy are both unprincipled and foolish.

Inasmuch as the United States has overvalued the importance of a quasi-alliance with the Peoples' Republic, there is every incentive for the United States to follow a principled policy with respect to the Peoples' Republic and the Republic of China. The United States should follow a consistent policy with respect to the three divided states of Germany, Korea, and China. The United States should favor the eventual unification of these states and make clear that it will do nothing to inhibit such reunification as long as that occurs in the absence of force, or the threat of force, and according to the freely-expressed wishes of the peoples of both of the divided areas. In principle, the United States should enter into diplomatic relations with both the contending governments of each divided state. Of course, western Germany should take precedence in Germany because it is the larger entity and has the willing acquiescence of its people, whereas the East German regime is maintained only by force and Soviet military support. In the case of Korea, clearly the government of South Korea has the greater popular support, a larger territory, and more population. In the case of China, the mainland regime takes precedence on all counts except voluntary acquiescence of the population, and this justifies the fact that the Peoples' Republic holds the China seat in the Security Council of the United Nations. On the other hand, it is quite inconsistent that the United States maintains no formal relations with the Republic of China because of the diplomatic threats of the Peoples' Republic. Moreover, in a world in which not genuinely independent governments such as those of Byelorussia and the Ukraine hold seats in the United Nations, it is a disgrace that the Republic of China is not represented in the General Assembly of the United Nations.

According to well-established principles of international law, if there is a revolt within a state, recognition remains with the established legitimate government. However, if the war continues for a long time, if the revolutionary forces acquire territory of significance, if they have the acquiescence of the population within that territory, they acquire rights of belligerence and even have some rights of normal intercourse with respect to other states, even while the civil war continues. In China, the civil war has ceased. As in Germany and Korea, two regimes with claims to the whole state have become part of a peaceful international order.

One might have argued in late 1949 or 1950 that the Peoples' Republic had won the civil war and that relations should be broken with the Republic of China. However, thirty years later, that argument no longer has force. The Republic of China is a stable regime, it has the support of the population, and it is in control of its territory. In a bipolar system in which an attempt to reestablish by force the unity of a divided state might well initiate a destabilizing and spreading war, it is in the interest of all states that these issues no longer be settled by force and that each of the contending parties acquire status within the international system without prejudice to the eventual reunification of the states.

If the position of the Republic of China is threatened, there likely would be an internal coup that establishes an independent government of Taiwan: for almost no one in the Republic wants any part of mainland rule. If this occurs, the same American sympathies that produced the Taiwan Relations Act likely would lead to its recognition. Thus may come about the two Chinas that both Chinese regimes profess to oppose. The fact that mainland policy produces this risk knowingly is an indication that its leaders place personal, factional, and ideological considerations above Chinese nationalism. The force of Chinese nationalism, however, likely would prod them into adventurous policies if this occurs; and therein lies a very dangerous aspect of the policies of the United States and of the Peoples' Republic.

Recognition by the United States that there is only one China and that Taiwan is part of China does not in and of itself constitute recognition by the United States of any authority on the part of the mainland regime with respect to the Republic of China. Both the Republic of China and the Peoples' Republic recognize that the state of China includes both the mainland areas and Taiwan. There are two contending regimes and each has acquired certain legitimate rights under contemporary international law.

Therefore, even apart from the Taiwan Relations Act, there is no reason why the United States should not supply weapons to the Republic of China. This is not interference in the internal affairs of China; to the contrary, negotiation of this issue with the mainland regime constitutes interference in the affairs of the Republic of China. Furthermore, were the United States to acquiesce in such demands by the mainland regime, what would prevent that regime at some future date from asserting that trade with the Republic of China comes within the framework of the sovereign power of the mainland and that each shipment must pass through mainland customs? How indeed would Communist China react if South Korea asserted that military aid to North Korea constituted interference in the internal affairs of Korea? Suppose West Germany argues that nations that have diplomatic relations with East Germany are interfering in the internal affairs of Germany? One can easily see the type of disruption that would occur in the international community if such principles were accepted. There is no basis in logic or law to support the demands of the mainland regime. If it wishes to rupture or to reduce relations with the United States as a consequence of the shipment of arms to the Republic of China, that, of course, is its privilege. But it would pay a high price for exercising that privilege, and it would do so on the basis of no understandable principle.

There are no important practical reasons for the United States to succumb to this type of diplomatic blackmail by the Peoples' Republic. There are additional important practical reasons to resist it. Among other reasons, it would ease the task of the Soviet government in securing the acquiescence of the Russian people to the harsh conditions they must endure to maintain such a large military force. The Soviet government is a dictatorship and an unpopular one that must force production out of an otherwise unwilling population. Furthermore, dissent and internal sabotage are increasing because the conditions of life in the Soviet Union are growing worse. The latest estimates concerning growth in manufacturing industries in the Soviet Union place it barely over one percent. Longevity is on the decline and infant mortality is way up. To the extent that the population still strives loyally to produce war material for the Soviet military regime, this shows the patriotism of the Russian people. That patriotism is fed by the brinksmanlike talk of the Reagan administration and by racial fear of China. There is much talk of a "yellow peril" by intellectuals in the Soviet Union. Among European Russians, fear of China runs very deep.

Although the Soviet leadership does not fear China or an attack from Europe, the Russian people are aroused by the argument that there is an aggressive alliance between the United States and the Peoples' Republic. Any appearance of coordination of policy between the United States and China can be used successfully by the Soviet regime to feed this fear and to support the Soviet policy of military strength.

Not only is American responsiveness to Chinese mainland demands on this issue counterproductive in terms of its policy toward the Soviet Union, but it is counterproductive in other important terms. For instance, an additional betrayal of its friends by the United States will further reduce the credibility of the United States and its value as an alliance partner. No matter how much Communist China wishes the United States to betray the Republic of China, even it will begin to consider the United States a paper tiger if it does so. Furthermore, such a betrayal would be destructive of the principles for which the United States stands. A democracy that is not true to its principles will soon corrupt its policy process and undermine popular support for policy.

In any event, the mainland regime does not really believe that in supplying weapons to the Republic of China the United States is following a two-Chinas policy. It makes its demands for three reasons. In the first place, they are useful ideologically in the internal struggle for power in the Peoples' Republic. In the second place, accession by the United States to these demands would further delegitimize the Republic of China, open up the United States to additional demands at a later time of the kind already indicated, and weaken survivability of the Republic of China. However, third, and most important, the demands are being made because the mainland regime has only very limited legitimacy. Their own journals and newspapers acknowledge that even within the Chinese Communist Party there are demands for a multi-party system, a return to economic rationality, and freedom of speech and inquiry. The mainland journals admit that party members, as well as many in the general population, point to the superior economic performance of the Republic of China and ask why the mainland regime is not doing better.

Acceptance of its demands with respect to the Republic of China by the United States would reinforce the legitimacy of the mainland regime both by means of this recognition and as a harbinger of unification, which is an essential aspect of legitimacy in China. Certainly this is not something that we owe them or to which they have any right. If they can point out that the United States recognizes their suzerainty over the Republic of China, the discouragement of the democratic forces on the mainland would be profound.

The position of the United States should be that all states, divided and undivided, should be insulated as much as the international system permits from external intervention. In particular, the future of the two Chinese governments is a matter primarily for the Chinese people. If, however, in the case of China, unlike the case with respect to Germany and Korea, the United States accepts the demands of the Peoples' Republic, it will be interfering in that free choice. Moreover, the leader of the free world, the United States, would be saying in effect that the contest between democracy and dictatorship in China—not of the military civil war that ended in 1950 but of the contest of ideas as exemplified in two competing political and economic systems—had ended and that it recognized the system on the mainland as the legitimate system for all of China. This would be a betrayal not merely of the Chinese people but of the United States and of the principles for which the American republic stands.

Subject to the proviso that the United States does not allow itself to be coerced into accepting the *dictat* of the mainland regime, friendly relations are certainly to be desired. If the mainland regime is threatened externally, prudent assistance would be in accordance with American interests. It is also in the interest of the United States that the present hostile relationship between the Peoples' Republic and the Soviet Union be ameliorated. Although the United States certainly does not wish to see a revival of the former alliance between the Peoples' Republic and the Soviet Union, it has no interest in conditions that produce the threat of war or coercion by the Soviet Union.

Furthermore, the United States should support reasonable relations between the two Chinese regimes. Both regimes should subscribe to the non-use of force or the threat of force against each other. Both should recognize that they are in contention for the hearts and minds of the Chinese people and that each should strive to produce a regime and conditions of life that would persuade the people of the other regime to accept unity. Both should agree to assist the other if it is attacked by an external power. They should agree to trade under reasonable conditions. Perhaps the Republic of China might even be persuaded to assist in the economic development of the mainland and the mainland regime to sponsor the reentry of the Republic of China in the United Nations. Occasional meetings between officials of the two regimes under conditions of equality should take place. These conditions are illustrative only and are not intended to be either exhaustive or definitive in their present formulation.

The agreement that the United States reached on August 17, 1982, with the Peoples' Republic of China is wrong in principle. In the first place, the United States negotiated an agreement concerning the Republic of China without any participation by that nation. This follows the unfortunate practice of Henry Kissinger with respect to the Republic of Vietnam. The Soviet Union would never show such disrespect to states with which it has been associated; and for good practical reasons.

In the second place, the agreement binds the Peoples' Republic of China to absolutely nothing. The PRC does not commit itself to peaceful measures. Nor does it even define what is meant by peaceful measures. It merely reaffirms that its current fundamental policy is to reunify China by peaceful means. It has stated many times that it will use force if peaceful means fail.

On the other hand, although the United States claims that it has stated that its restraint on arms sales is conditional upon the maintenance of the Chinese position on peaceful means—the communiqué says less than this: "having in mind the foregoing statements of both sides"—it will in fact limit and decrease its arms sales to the Republic of China in the intervening period, thereby reducing the defensibility and confidence of the Republic of China. Moreover, its statement "leading over a period of time to a final resolution" appears to confirm the Chinese claim that the United States has agreed to phase out arms sales.

In the third place, the United States has virtually affirmed the legitimacy of the Chinese mainland position with respect to the Republic of China. It has redefined that Shanghai Communiqué to the further detriment of the Republic of China. Thereby, it tends to legitimize other "peaceful" measures that the mainland Chinese may insist upon and that in time conceivably could involve control over commerce, visits, and other important matters. It was unnecessary, unwise, and unprincipled for the United States to place itself in this position.

Although some in the State Department argue that the position of the current leadership in the Peoples' Republic of China would be weakened if the United States did not make at least this much of a concession, so much remains unknown about the internal politics of China and its likely development that this game would be unwise even if it were advisable on other grounds.

There are forces inside the Chinese army that would like to modify the position of the Peoples' Republic with respect to the Soviet Union. In fact, it may not be entirely bad for the Chinese to move closer toward a middle position between the United States and the Soviet Union. In any event, that is likely to be the position the Peoples' Republic will take provided that the Soviet posture permits this.

Finally, it is a mistake to base external policy upon such considerations. In the Soviet Union, for instance, Malenkov was overthrown by Khrushchev and the "anti-party" clique with the support of the military on the grounds that he favored increased civilian production and believed that a nuclear war could not be won. Khrushchev then won dominance over the "anti-party" clique by means of similar alliances and arguments. Brezhnev secured the support of the military against Khrushchev on similar grounds. In office, they all changed positions.

It is very likely the case that the policies of administrations in power are constrained by factors distinctly different from those that lead to the formation of cliques designed to replace the current power holders. The attempts by the State Department to use arguments of this kind to support devious policies would be ill-advised if its record has been better with respect to predictions concerning the policies of new foreign regimes. Given the fact that department bureaucrats appear to have had worse than chance records in these matters, this makes even worse what would be a bad basis for policy on other grounds.

It can only be concluded that Assistant Secretary of State for East Asian affairs John Holdridge has hoodwinked an inexperienced president into accepting a policy position the implications of which the president does not understand. I have even heard that some on the China desk have stated that Taiwan will fall eventually and that there is no point in delaying this. A more recent version of this position is that mainland China can conquer Taiwan if and when it is willing to pay the price. Examined, however, this argument is weak, for this is precisely where US policy can play a role. China is a huge country with vigorous internal feuds and extensive internal opposition. The costlier the attempt to conquer or to destabilize Taiwan, the weaker the mainland's ability to maintain control and to assure its security vis-à-vis the Soviet Union. The more we assist Taiwan with arms and the greater the likelihood of our naval intervention if mainland China threatens to interdict maritime trade, the less likely this outcome. This is precisely why the recent joint communiqué went too far. The president accepted policy cunningly designed to weaken the Republic of China by China desk people who, like the former assistant-secretary, Richard Holbrook, are positively hostile to the non-Communist states of East Asia.

Let us remember that friendly relations depend on both parties. We don't have to be the ones that bend all the time. We have more to offer than the mainland regime has to offer us because what they offer, for the most part, they cannot withhold. I suppose they might get rid of our intelligence base, but that would hurt them too. They need that intelligence. They need their forces on the Soviet border. They are not going to remove them to spite us. The things we would withhold would not hurt us either, on the whole. The administration has shown both lack of character and lack of firmness—and also some lack of understanding of the reality in the situation—by concluding the recent agreement with the mainland regime. Despite the explanation the State Department has given, the Chinese did not agree to anything; they merely stated their fundamental policy to unify China by peaceful means. Now we have the experts telling us what the word *peace* really means. We ought to read the Chinese news agency which on August 20, 1982 reiterated that China has not given up the right to resort to force if Taiwan does not accede peacefully. The Chinese made a unilateral statement. Keeping both of the foregoing statements in mind, our position doesn't amount to much: we agreed to decrease our arms sales, but why?

The smaller Chinese state needs qualitative superiority. We have undermined Taiwan's resolve and we have also undermined or done damage to its business prospects. The former Dean of the School of Business at the University of Chicago happens to be on the board of directors of a company conducting over half of its business with Taiwan. The day after the communiqué was published, he attended a meeting of its board of directors, and this is what happened: These are people friendly to Taiwan and they agreed that they would now invest on the mainland, so that when the PRC took over Taiwan, perhaps their company would not be expropriated. It is incorrect to assume that nothing has changed and that these are ambiguous statements.

The Shanghai Communiqué was bad enough, but the Reagan administration succeeded in redefining it for the worse. It appears the Department of State wants to keep Deng in power. If we undermine him now on the issue of Taiwan, then, the desk people say, those favoring the Cultural Revolution will take over—or, they say, there are people in the Chinese Army who would like closer relations with the Soviet Union. Those people are politically very naive. They would soon discover several things. The Soviet Union would not modernize the Chinese army, and the reasons for this are obvious. Nor would it substantially reduce Soviet forces on the border.

Are we playing the game of who takes over after what? Some arguments are used to get power and other arguments are used to keep it. We are not experts at estimating this or even in knowing what it might mean if the radical side took over in China. In the first place, the radicals are probably unable to take over. No one there really wants to go back to the Cultural Revolution or wants to tear down the industrial system. Even if they did, who was the most anti-Russian in China? Mao.

If a change occurs, will relations with the United States worsen? I don't know, and the State Department doesn't either. Arguments are thrown around to justify their policy the way some of us use footnotes to support a position.

In short, if there is a single good reason to support what the administration has done with respect to its China policy, I have not yet heard it.

COMMENTARY

By
DOUGLAS MACARTHUR II

I agree with much of Morton A. Kaplan's thoughtful and provocative paper on "United States Foreign Policy and the China Problem." It has background and balance in its description of the problem to enable those not familiar with all the details of US policy with respect to China since the late 1940s to grasp the essential elements of this very important problem.

At the same time, there are several points on which our conclusions (Kaplan's and mine) seem to differ, at least in emphasis or nuance where a bit more amplification might be useful.

For example, both mainland China and Taiwan are governed by gerontocracies that will not be in place in a few short years. Dr. Kaplan rightly points out that the policies of the Peoples' Republic of China (PRC) will be governed only by the PRC's perception of its own interests and that this perception may change substantially at some future time with respect to both Taiwan and Southeast Asia to

---

Douglas MacArthur II is a former United States Assistant Secretary of State and Ambassador who has worked within the American foreign policy establishment for over 40 years.

the detriment of important American interests. But surely when the old men presently governing mainland China are replaced by a younger group, the chances of policy changes hostile to US interests should be somewhat less if relations between the US and the PRC are on a reasonably friendly and stable basis which the PRC leadership at that time perceives to be more in its interests than a hostile United States.

Dr. Kaplan's paper would seem to suggest that we re-recognize the Government of the Republic of China on Taiwan (GRC). In my judgement this is a total non-starter. People can honestly differ on whether it was wise or necessary or in our own interest to withdraw recognition from the GRC on Taiwan. But that was done and to now re-recognize it would not only rupture our present relationship with the PRC, but also make us look even sillier in the eyes of most nations throughout the world—both friends and allies as well as those in the Third World.

Insofar as supplying military weapons and equipment to Taiwan is concerned, the recent "US-China Joint Communiqué" of August 17, 1982, when taken with the Presidential statement of the same day, has not jeopardized the security of Taiwan. Although it is true that the communiqué says that the US intends "to reduce gradually its sale of arms to Taiwan, leading over a period of time to a final resolution":

a) It is a reduction from the level supplied "in recent years" (which includes the year 1980 when I understand roughly $800 million worth of arms and equipment were supplied). Since no rate of reduction is specified there is a lot of room to work with.

b) There is no terminal date for the cut-off.

c) Paragraph 6 of the August 17, 1982, US-China Joint Communiqué states that US arms sales to Taiwan will be reduced gradually "leading over a period of time to a final resolution." Since both Taiwan and the mainland agree that there cannot be two Chinas, a "final resolution" in the US view is the *peaceful reunification* of China which the US and the PRC maintain is the objective.

d) Should the PRC abandon its stated intent for peaceful reunification, the US is bound by nothing in the Joint Communiqué from supplying Taiwan with whatever weapons we deem necessary.

e) As Dr. Kaplan points out, "the Chinese military forces have outdated military equipment and are incapable of mounting any kind of serious offensive against a modern force." Taiwan has not only a first-class modern force well equipped with modern weapons but also as an island, separated from the mainland by a large body of water, occupies a defensive position that would require a major and sophisticated amphibious landing operation by a modern and highly trained force with the most sophisticated weaponry. Every military expert with whom I have talked says that it will be years before the PRC has such a capability.

I do not concur with the view that current American policy sacrifices "vital strategic interests of the US." As pointed out above, it seems to me that the present arrangements (except in one contingency set forth below) provide adequate safeguards for Taiwan until such time as peaceful unification of China may occur or until current US policy undergoes major change. At the same time the present arrangements allow for the maintenance and possible improvement of relations with the PRC which is important to our overall strategic position.

I am at a loss as to the basis for the statement that current US policy is contrary to both American ideals and interests in a just international order. While there is much to criticize with respect to the PRC, whose regime is both undemocratic and dictatorial, alas, this is an imperfect world and we find similar shortcomings in varying degrees in other countries (in our own hemisphere and elsewhere) with whom we have normal relations.

Kaplan points out, and I agree, that should an international coup occur in Taiwan that established an independent government, the American sympathies that produced the Taiwan Relations Act might eventually lead to its recognition and thus might come about the "two Chinas" that both Chinese regimes profess to oppose. Such a development would indeed place the greatest strains on our relations with mainland China to say the least. However for the present, I see no acceptable way that the risk of such a development can be avoided. Again let me repeat, this is an imperfect world and there are no policies that can safeguard against all risks that the US or any power is subject to. All that can be done is to balance risks against advantages in developing policies.

COMMENTARY

By
SMITH HEMPSTONE

It is singularly appropriate that, on the tenth anniversary of President Richard Nixon's watershed visit to the Peoples' Republic of China, we should be considering Morton Kaplan's excellent paper on the problems that have grown out of that initiative.

I find little to criticize in Kaplan's paper, but I could expand on much that he has written.

It is, for instance, true that the PRC is, despite its size, "extraordinarily weak" as a military power. Although the PRC can muster 9 armored divisions, 93 main force divisions and 69 militia-type divisions, these troops are poorly equipped and, as the Vietnam border war showed, lacking in an adequate command and control structure. Peking's navy, despite some recent advances—it has 11 post-World War II destroyers and 3 more under construction—is essentially a coastal defense force. The air force, while it has a large number of combat planes, is largely lacking in the advance avionics necessary to give it an all-weather and night-fighting capability. Its

---

Smith Hempstone is Executive Editor of the Washington Times *and a nationally syndicated columnist.*

nuclear capability is primitive compared to that of the Soviet Union.

Thus Kaplan is correct when he asserts that "Communist China is in no position militarily to threaten the Soviet Union." What the PRC does have is the strategic depth and the manpower to make any Soviet incursion into China both difficult and expensive.

The quarrel between Moscow and Peking predates Nixon's visit to China a decade ago and has deep ideological, racial and historical roots. As Kaplan states, PRC policy toward the Soviet Union—like the Soviet Union's policy toward the PRC—springs from the Chinese leadership's perception of their state and party interest. This is so whether the area in question is Northeast Asia, Southeast Asia or Tibet. Thus in reality it was the PRC that played the America card, not the United States that played the China card, ten years ago. That remains the case today.

In the unlikely event of a major conflict between the Soviet Union and the PRC—I say unlikely because the self-interest of neither nation would be served by such a conflict—the US while it might tilt toward China, would have no major interest in the outcome.

Kaplan predicts that "China some day will move closer to the Soviet Union to balance against the West." Although some improvement in relations between Moscow and Peking can be anticipated—if only because relations are so bad at present and leadership changes in both countries are in the offing—both logic and history would seem to suggest a continuing rivalry between these two nations. Although the US remains in Chinese eyes a potentially hostile nation, the Soviet Union is by far the nearer and the more dangerous of the two devils. Nevertheless, it is difficult to see how improving the military might of the PRC is in the interest of the US.

In contrast, as Kaplan points out, the US shares greater common interests and common values with the defensive triangle formed by Japan, South Korea, and the Republic of China. I would enlarge that triangle to a quadrilateral, extending it southward to include the Philippines.

Permit me at this time to clarify my own view on the matter of US relations with the two Chinas. I have never felt that the policy of non-recognition of the PRC pursued by John Foster Dulles made much sense. Indeed, I spoke openly in favor of diplomatic recognition of the PRC as long ago as 1953, at which time that was not a popular or even safe public stance to assume.

I argued against non-recognition of the PRC then for much the same reasons as I oppose derecognition of the Republic of China on Taiwan today.

Diplomatic recognition has nothing to do with approval of a regime: prior to 1979, we recognized regimes far more criminal and oppressive than that of the PRC; we have continued since then to recognize states infinitely more brutal and unfriendly than the Republic of China. Recognition relates to control of territory and population, and to the possession of recognizable governmental institutions and structures. Both Chinas exhibit these characteristics.

Thus I had no quarrel with President Carter's decision to extend diplomatic recognition to the PRC in 1979. What I did and do take issue with is the terms upon which this was accomplished: the derecognition of the Republic of China on Taiwan, a loyal ally and a nation inoffensive by contemporary standards. In so doing, the US sacrificed principle and made itself an object of contempt to friend and foe alike, without receiving any tangible benefit in return. It is, as Kaplan states, "a disgrace" that fictional nations such as Byelorussia and the Ukraine should be represented in the General Assembly of the United Nations while the Republic of China is not.

Even in terms of greed—of trade and markets—the switch makes little sense. The fabulous "China trade" hinted at by advocates of recognition of Peking at any price has proved to be a chimera. Little Taiwan, with 18 million inhabitants, continues to do twice as much trade with us—an exchange of $13 billion makes it our sixth largest trading partner—as the mainland, with a population of nearly 1 billion.

Although it is easy to see what we have surrendered to the PRC, it is more difficult to ascertain what has been gained. Peking has remained silent on Poland. It has denounced the US role in El Salvador, sided with Argentina in the Falklands dispute, and had little to say about the Soviet occupation of Afghanistan.

Enemies of the Republic of China point to the continued existence of martial law on Taiwan as evidence of the undemocratic nature of President Chiang Ching-kuo's regime. It is true that the ROC is not a Jeffersonian democracy. It is equally true that it is moving on the local and provincial level toward democracy, and that it is an infinitely freer country than the PRC, where something like freedom exists only for the party elite. (In this respect, the similarities between the PRC and the Soviet Union are startling, given the stark differences between their social, political, and religious histories.) There is no evidence of any desire for merger with the mainland on the PRC's terms among either native Taiwanese or mainlanders resident on the island. There are, of course, differences between the two groups over who should exercise political control, but not more than 1% of either group in the population wants to associate with the PRC. Not only is there substantially more freedom in the Republic of China, there is greater prosperity: the annual income is about $1,600 compared with the PRC's $200.

As to the question of arms sales to the Republic of China, I fail to see why the US should agree—as Assistant Secretary of State John Holdridge said—"to engage in prior consultations with Beijing" on the issue. This would appear to be a violation of the spirit—if not the words—of the Taiwan Relations Act, and amounts to giving the PRC a veto over the formulation and conduct of American foreign policy. This is an issue that goes far beyond the capability or intention of the PRC to launch an attack on Taiwan *at this time*. Neither exists *now*; no one can say what the situation may be ten years down the road, particularly if the ROC, a group of 18 million people facing nearly a billion, is denied the sophisticated weapons they need to exert air control over the straits. I also wonder if Ambassador MacArthur is correct that $800 million worth of arms and equipment were supplied to Taiwan in 1980. My recollection is that they received a lot less. Given the spiraling price of arms and the effect of inflation, within a few years the ROC will be lucky to get a case of rifles out of us.

As we ought to have learned long ago, sacrifices of principle are made at a real and terrible price in men's lives. Although the hour is late, it is still not too late to turn back from the dangerous path this country has followed in its China policy since 1979.

THE UNITED STATES AND CENTRAL AMERICA: POLICY OPTIONS IN THE 80s

By

ROLANDO BONACHEA

As the decade of the 1980s unfolds, the events in Central America reinforce the urgency and necessity for a clear definition of United States interests in and foreign policy strategy toward this troubled region. As Morton A. Kaplan emphasizes in his analysis of American foreign policy, a coherent global strategy must not be superseded by regionalism, but rather a global approach should dictate the overall framework within which regional considerations are approached. With the aforementioned premise in mind, this chapter seeks to assess US policy options in the context of regional conditions and

Rolando Bonachea is Associate Professor of Latin American History and Dean of the College of Arts and Sciences at St. Louis University. The author wishes to acknowledge Ms. Emma Easteppe who provided invaluable research assistance, and expresses his gratitude to Nancy Efferson-Bonachea who assisted as editor, researcher and critic.

long-range US strategic interests.

United States involvement in the Central American region at the turn of the century firmly established the geographical strategic importance of the area for US national security interests. The Monroe Doctrine clearly indicated that European or foreign encroachment in the Americas was impermissible. The rising US power developed at a time in which an important trait of European global politics had been the acquisition and preservation of colonial empires. In the case of the United States, perhaps due to national ideology, as perceived by US policymakers, empire building was anathema, and security interests and humanitarian motives dictated a posture of assuring on the one hand "a sphere of influence" and on the other a policy of fostering law, order, stable governments and prosperous economies in an area that already, at the turn of the century, had a long history of internal strife. These policy objectives, the US assumed, would be attained if America helped the tiny nations establish civilian governments to carry out elections, instill the values of due process and democracy, and establish sound economic policies and fiscal accountability. Roosevelt's good neighbor policy, Kennedy's Alliance for Progress, and more recently Reagan's Caribbean Basin Initiative have confirmed the lofty ideals of US policy toward the area. However, in Central America itself the military organizations before and since the turn of the century have ousted presidents, staged hundreds of coups, closed legislative assemblies, established martial law, and amended or abolished constitutions. The internal dynamics of the area have been—like US foreign policy—consistent, but not conducive to stability. The revolutionary theme, namely the advocacy of socioeconomic reforms to meet the needs of the people, is not new. Indeed, the socioeconomic conditions that the US found in the area at the end of the 19th century continue to plague the nations of Central America today. In fact, the brief period of economic prosperity which Central America witnessed from 1950 to 1978[1] contributed to and augmented the socioeconomic problems facing this region, as Barber and Ronning contend in their analysis of this "peace and prosperity" period:

A period of economic development helped to produce the conditions of insurgency—population explosions, urbanization, contact with other parts of the world, and better communications within a country. Yet during the same period, the institutional props capable of facing a major challenge (political parties and independent labor unions) were not developed. Furthermore, the economic prosperity reached only a small minority.[2]

The socioeconomic pressures resulting from population growth (currently at 3 percent per annum), urbanization, land distribution patterns, and rural and urban unemployment have increasingly placed demands on governments to address the basic needs of its citizens in the areas of education, public health, housing, employment, and land reform. The inability, and in some cases unwillingness, of established governments to satisfy the needs of their people have fostered political movements committed to overthrowing existing political institutions and implementing a new political order more responsive to socioeconomic equities.

What has been a new development in the course of the 20th century has been the rise of revolutionary movements bent on redressing these grievances, and, in some cases—Mexico, Bolivia, Cuba—carrying out successful revolutions. Further, in the 1960s a new development of importance to US policy occurred when many of the revolutionary movements openly declared a Marxist ideological affiliation. The radicalization of the revolutionary movements in the area, which followed on the heels of Castro's revolution and Cuban-Soviet ties, triggered on the part of the US a more dramatic emphasis on what was increasingly seen as an East-West conflict. Whereas US policy responses to the revolutions in Mexico and Bolivia demonstrated the possibility of successful negotiations and reconciliation even when US economic interests were adversely affected, US policy seems to have hardened whenever the possibility of Soviet-proxy and/or communist-oriented movements in the US sphere of influence has loomed on the horizon. This East-West emphasis was exhibited when, in 1960, the incoming Democratic administration of John F. Kennedy chose to inherit the policies of the outgoing Republican administration of Dwight Eisenhower toward the reformist-nationalist provisional revolutionary government of Cuba, and, twenty years later, when Republican Ronald Reagan inherited the policies of the outgoing Democratic administration of Jimmy Carter toward the reformist-nationalist Sandinist government of Nicaragua and toward a leftist-centrist insurgency in El Salvador. In each of these cases the new administration opted for continuity, namely, a posture of confrontation regarding the revolutionary governments and insurgency movements in Central America and the Caribbean.

Although the Central American nations share a common colonial Spanish legacy and several developmental characteristics, it is evident that these nations cannot be placed into a general category and labeled, as they have been in the past, with a stereotypical title such as the "banana republics." For example, Costa Rica, the most stable and democratic country of the area, stands in marked contrast to all of its sister-nations. On the other hand, El Salvador's military has, in the past, been the advocate of social reform. Further, moderate and conservative parties, powerful economic pressure groups, leftist and right-wing organizations and the Roman Catholic Church comprise important variables whose role and influence must be analyzed within the context of a given Central American nation. These aforementioned examples merely illustrate the importance of a US foreign policy which addresses the national realities of this region.

It is against this historical-political background that President Reagan has tried to frame a US policy toward Central America and the Caribbean which is comprised of a) a lessened emphasis on human rights; b) a militant anti-communism and emphasis on the East-West conflict; c) a renewed emphasis on military assistance; and d) a development plan as envisioned by the Caribbean Basin Initiative. The analysis that follows seeks to assess the effectiveness of the Reagan policy, the prospects and possible options for the remainder of the 1980s.

In Europe the administration's new military emphasis was not welcome, and in Latin America, except for the most hardened right-wing military governments, the prospects of US intervention in Central America were not well received. Countries like Venezuela and Mexico, who support opposite sides in the conflict in El Salvador, favor a political solution and continue to be opposed to US military intervention. The emphasis on communist subversion as the cause for violence in Central America was considered by many a simplistic approach. Indeed US long-range policy planning must take into account the indigenous causes and forces in the conflict. When Alexander Haig said in February 1981 that the US would "go to the source" of the aggression, he should have added and to the *source* of the causes of the insurrection: political repression, social and economic inequities and injustices.

The Reagan administration's emphasis on the military aspect in more recent months has been counterbalanced by underlining the need for social reform. In the months preceding the elections of March 1982, President Reagan spoke about the agrarian reform of President Jose Napolean Duarte, and Ambassador Deane Hinton referred to it as "the most revolutionary ... "[3] On both counts, President Reagan conveyed the message that a tough stance against communism is not necessarily correlated with opposition to social justice. Very few disputed the assessment that President Duarte represented the best option to act as an anti-communist stalwart and carry out reforms, thus serving legitimate US interests in El Salvador.

But because of the untimely implementation of the US policy emphasis on elections, the United States now finds itself faced with a democratically elected government in El Salvador that is unresponsive to social reforms.

In January of 1981, the Reagan administration inherited President Carter's policy toward El Salvador, and it is in El Salvador where the Reagan administration has chosen to "draw the line."

The US presidential rhetorical campaign persuaded the Nicaraguans, Cubans and the guerrillas of El Salvador that the election of Ronald Reagan would lead to policies designed to overthrow the Sandinista government and to a military solution in El Salvador. During the last months of 1980 the arms flow to the FDR from Nicaragua intensified, and a decision was reached by the guerrillas to launch a final military offensive and to call for a general strike in January 1981. President Carter responded by resuming "non-lethal" military assistance to the Duarte junta. The guerrilla military offensive failed, and the Salvadorans failed to heed the call for a general worker-peasant strike. The opposition's failure to mobilize the masses indicated a lack of legitimacy, whereas Duarte's failure to capitalize on the defeat also indicated the ambiguous feelings of many Salvadorans toward the Duarte junta.

This stalemate situation in January of 1981 presented Reagan with a unique opportunity to explore a political solution. However, when President Reagan dismissed Ambassador Robert White in January of 1981, a signal was sent that the new US administration might opt for a harder military line.

In fact, the State Department produced a document containing evidence of the flow of arms from communist nations through Cuba to the Salvadoran guerrillas.[4] The document concluded that "over the past year the insurgency in El Salvador has been progressively transposed into a textbook case of indirect armed aggression by Communist powers through Cuba." The Reagan administration proceeded to request increased military assistance for Duarte's government, to support socioeconomic reforms, and to prevent the opposition from gaining a military victory.

President Reagan's position on El Salvador might have been intended to regain the confidence of European allies, warn Cuba and the USSR, and continue to harness support among conservative constituents in the United States. Regardless of US motives for the hardline on El Salvador, emphasis was placed on the East-West conflict as an adequate interpretation of the turmoil in Central America and USSR-Cuban sponsored subversion as the cause of this violence. The message sent from Washington was one of military reliance. On both counts this initial approach was wrong.

The dynamics of Salvadoran national politics are complex, and it is questionable whether a policy that seeks a military solution will best serve the strategic interests of the US in El Salvador. A brief synopsis of the recent events in El Salvador reinforces the questionable nature of a military solution.

Jose Napoleon Duarte, a democrat and moderate of the Christian Democratic Party, came to power under trying circumstances. In 1972, Duarte had won the elections for the presidency with his vice-presidential running mate, Guillermo Ungo, a Social Democrat who, like Duarte, had a well-established reputation as a democrat and advocate of reforms.[5] The military abolished the elections, imprisoned, tortured and exiled Duarte, and established a military dictatorship headed by General Carlos Romero. The unrest and agitation triggered by the coup (October 15, 1979) led the military to allow political participation by civilian members, among them Ungo, as a way of compromise. This experiment collapsed when, several months later, the civilian members resigned, citing government unwillingness to implement reforms and complicity in repression and human rights violations. Ungo then joined the opposition, and the military, no doubt under pressure from the Carter administration, invited Duarte to head the new junta formed on January 9, 1980.

The incoming Reagan administration began a consistent effort in Congress to increase economic and military assistance. Duarte's agrarian reforms proposal was launched, and the US placed its confidence with the junta. The dilemma for Duarte was how to sway the military in practice to implement reforms in spite of the powerful land-holding and commercial pressure groups who had been assisting right-wing paramilitary terrorist organizations. For Ungo, on the other hand, the dilemma lay in how to achieve a united front among the opposition, comprised of Christian Democrats, Social Democrats, church activist groups, professional organizations, and the Marxist-Leninist Augustin Faribundo Marti movement, and to insure a democratic future for El Salvador. Whereas the united front has been achieved, it is not certain that the democratic forces of the FDR could prevail in a post-war period over the Faribundo Marti movement, since this latter group is the military backbone of the FDR. Unfortunately, Ungo is as captive of the Marxist-Leninist guerrillas as Duarte had been of the military, and more recently, Alvaro Magaña of the extreme right wing.

The pressure the US brought to bear on Duarte and the military to undertake elections in March of 1982, although no doubt geared to gain legitimacy, was premature and a miscalculation. Premature because Duarte's social reform policies had not had time to prove their effectiveness, and a miscalculation of the great power of El Salvador's extreme right wing elements which have consistently blocked reforms for over a century and have gained political power in adroit ways.

The election results placed former Major D'Aubuisson in power, along with other extreme right conservatives who have isolated Duarte and the Christian Democrats. Further, the new government has begun to dismantle the agrarian reform program which Duarte[6] and the US were backing to generate peasant support.[7] Moreover, subsequent US expressions of support, and promises of increased military assistance continue to embolden right wing elements, making it increasingly difficult for moderates, such as Duarte, and the United States to move El Salvador toward reform. The right has consistently opposed reform over the years, and there is no objective reason to believe they will undermine their own economic position now that they control the legislature and administration, and when the US has placed its prestige on the line by militarily backing the El Salvadoran government against the opposition.

Since the pursuit of a military solution has already emboldened the government of El Salvador and begun to undermine the agrarian reform supported by the US during the Duarte administration, other reforms are likely to be overturned. The course of the present El Salvadoran regime will only serve to increase the grievances and alienation of the peasantry and the middle class of the country.

But of equal concern to US policymakers is a recognition of a continuing pattern of human rights violations in El Salvador, in spite of the clear position of the US Congress on this matter. Moreover, the Reagan administration must adopt an unequivocal position in support of human rights in Central America. Our commitment to fostering democratic government should not be contradicted by our support of governments which do not abide by a basic respect for human rights. To do so is to betray our traditional values as well as to alienate democratic elements in Central America who have ideologically respected and admired our long-standing respect for the basic rights of man. Ambassador Jeane Kirkpatrick's academic discussion of the subtleties between repression from the left or the right provides little solace to those who struggle for open and pluralistic societies, and therefore should be unacceptable. The fostering of democratic governments and human rights are in our national security interest, and anything that makes us depart from that position will contribute to undermining our long-range strategic interests in the region.

In brief, we do not serve our national interests by the presence of administration officials seeking human rights certification before the Senate and going through long-winded rationalizations that fly in the face of continuous reports of assassinations and massacres.

It could be argued that a continued and increased military assistance program could give the Salvadoran military the massive firepower wanted by the Salvadoran government. Yet, massive military assistance, as Vietnam showed, is not necessarily the key to a successful anti-guerrilla war. It is also expected that Cuba, Nicaragua and other parties would increase their military assistance to the guerrillas proportionately to US aid to the El Salvadoran government.

As long as US policy toward Cuba and Nicaragua is one of isolation and destabilization, it is to be expected that these countries will continue to support the guerrilla movement in El Salvador, and there will be little Washington can do if we and our Salvadoran allies prove incapable, as in the past, of preventing the arms flow. Indeed, if we are to believe the State Department reports, enough arms and munitions may have entered the area to sustain the guerrillas, assuming that a more effective program of arms interdiction is not undertaken. [8]

Although the armed forces of El Salvador were considered at one time a highly disciplined and well-trained force, [9] it is not certain that this is the case today. The enormous supply of US military weaponry to El Salvador and the effort at rapidly training Salvadoran troops in the US seems to indicate that the armed forces are not prepared to undertake an effective counterinsurgency campaign.[10]

The above considerations point toward a protracted war with disastrous consequences for the people of El Salvador and for US policy in Central America. As a result, political stability and socioeconomic development may become elusive objectives. It is precisely these objectives, as well as the pursuit of just reforms, that should move the US to seek a politically-negotiated solution to the conflict.

The exploration of the feasibility of such negotiations entails a reassessment of our perceptions concerning the political forces in El Salvador. First, the US must recognize that the FDR is an indigenous movement comprised of several movements ranging from Marxist-Leninists to Social Democrats. For example, many of the Christian Democratic Party and church activists are members of the FDR rank and file.

Second, while it is irrefutable that the FDR has received assistance in the heat of the conflict from communist countries, or for that matter from anyone willing to help, this fact in itself should not lead the United States to conclude that the FDR is a satellite of either Havana or Moscow. Individuals like Manuel Ungo, among others whose democratic trajectory is irrefutable, are not bound to become marionettes of foreign governments.

Third, there must be a recognition that the grievances of the opposition are rooted in many years of social injustice, political repression and economic deprivation. The disaffected includes not only peasants and workers, but professionals and intellectuals. The Catholic Church, as well as other Christian churches, have joined in their condemnation of governmental abuses. It is precisely this broad-based disaffection that has enabled the FDR, through typical guerrilla strategy, to meet the military offensives of the government.

Fourth, rather than reject or give a cool reception to mediation efforts, the US should recognize that countries like Mexico, Venezuela and Costa Rica have legitimate concerns in Central America. Nor should the United States discard the potential positive contributions of France, West Germany, or international movements of prestige and influence in Latin America, such as the Christian Democratic Party based in West Germany and the Socialist International (Social Democrats) based in Geneva.

Fifth, a negotiated solution in El Salvador should lead the United States to reconsider US policy toward Cuba and Nicaragua.

How then can the contending parties be brought to a dialogue? Who in the international arena can invest its prestige in a peaceful solution to the conflict, and who in the international community has the capability for successfully undertaking a peaceful resolution?

The US will have to exercize its considerable amount of influence to persuade the military and the conservative government coalition to come to the peace table. West Germany and the European Christian Democratic parties could influence Duarte and his Christian Democratic followers to support the effort at dialogue. President François Mitterand of France and the newly-elected President Miguel de Madrid of Mexico, two leaders who have already recognized the opposition in El Salvador, could bring their governments' influence to bear on the FDR. The Socialist International, of which Ungo is a member, could exercise its influence on the FDR for a negotiation effort as well. It is also possible that Venezuela and Peru could play constructive roles in using their considerable prestige in Latin America to encourage the political opposition parties in El Salvador to engage in a dialogue with the government.

Rather than specifics, the negotiations should deal with a broad range of socioeconomic and political issues that will determine the future of El Salvador by Salvadorans. As a precondition for negotiations, a cease-fire must be in place, and the above-mentioned countries could provide representatives to supervise a cease-fire. Certainly, a cease-fire agreement must be preceded by a halt to military deliveries from the US, Cuba, Nicaragua, and any other country supplying arms to the guerrillas. It should also be noted that Mexico, which for over twenty years has supported the Cuban regime, had no difficulty in reaching Fidel Castro during this year's mediation attempt; and given reassurances by the US of our determination to seek a peaceful settlement, Mexico should be willing to use its diplomatic skills in extracting a commitment from Castro to halt arms deliveries to El Salvador. In addition, Venezuela, which has been approached to sell oil to Cuba, thus reducing the considerable expense of transporting oil from the Soviet Union, may very well have an incentive to offer Castro for his cooperation in the effort toward peace and stability in the Central American region.

As an initial step to signal the El Salvadoran government of a US policy reassessment, and the seriousness with which this policy will be pursued, the United States should put some distance between Washington and El Salvador. It is highly predictable that the partisans of D'Aubuisson will unleash an anti-American rhetorical campaign, but this will allow the United States to signal its dissatisfaction with the undoing of land and banking reforms, disregard for human rights, as well as emphasize the posture that there are limits to US involvement in an internal civil war. There are limits because, in the final analysis, only the Salvadorans can come to an understanding that will bring to an end the anarchy and violence.

Were US policymakers to view the conflict for what it is rather than an East-West conflict, the door could be open to foster an understanding among Salvadorans, upon whose will the closure of the violence and anarchy that have enveloped this unfortunate nation ultimately depends.

If Fidel Castro were to cooperate in this international effort regarding El Salvador, the US should reappraise its policy toward Cuba. Fidel Castro has survived six US presidential administrations, including the Bay of Pigs invasion of 1961, economic embargoes, diplomatic sanction, travel prohibition, and US threats. The pattern of the last two decades illustrates that the US has not served its interests well by posturing threats it could not or was not willing to carry out to their final conclusion. Kennedy's promise to return the Invasion Brigade flag to a free Havana, Carter's disregarded demand for the withdrawal of a Soviet Brigade from Cuba, and Haig's most recent statement that "we will deal with it at the source" are a few examples that have led Havana to dismiss lightly statements issued from Washington. Further, there is also a pattern of Castro's initiatives in fostering insurrections whenever any of the last seven US presidents, including Reagan, has adopted a hostile position. Castro's guerrilla adventurism in the 1960s in Latin America and Africa in the 1970s, and more recently in Central America, are cases in point. This is not to underestimate Castro's own self-perceived role as a messianic leader of revolutionary movements in the Third World, a role which has not always been viewed with sympathy by Moscow. But this being as it may, a reappraisal of US-Cuban relations should lead to focus on the issues that have separated the countries for the last two decades.

If the US is to achieve its aim for long-range stability in Central America and a decrease of international tension in this area, the US-Cuban policy should be reappraised. While insuring our legitimate concerns in the area, the president of the United States should break the deadlock on US-Cuban relations and regain flexibility in its posture toward Castro's Cuba. First, the status quo has repeatedly afforded Castro the opportunity to blame the US for Cuba's inefficient economic system. Secondly, a rapprochement is worth exploring if it would lead to a constructive decrease in tensions between the two countries and in the Central American-Caribbean Basin area. Thirdly, the political changes that have taken place since the 1959 Cuban Revolution in the Latin American international scene have affected the original positions of the US and Cuba, both adversely and favorably.

For example, Castro's attempt at exporting revolution in the 1960s was defeated throughout Latin America, culminating in the ill-fated Che Guevara expedition to Bolivia.[11]

Castro's subsequent retreat from support of revolutionary movements led to denunciations of Castro by Peruvian guerrilla leaders[12] and others, which underlined Castro's pragmatism even at the expense of other "liberation" movements. Castro's inconsistency toward "struggling" revolutionary movements is best exemplified by Castro's successful efforts in the 1970s at re-establishing diplomatic and economic ties with Latin American countries (Panama, Peru, Ecuador, Barbados, Guyana, Jamaica, Trinidad, Tobago, and

Venezuela, among others) regardless of their political and economic systems. [13] It is true that one can argue that in the past Castro has been willing to assist anyone who was confronting the US. Yet this argument does not necessarily explain the signing of an economic agreement with a military junta considered to be one of the most repressive in Latin America.

The changes in Cuban-Latin American bilateral relations have been reflected in the Organization of American States (OAS). The OAS, which imposed sanctions against Cuba in 1964, is now divided over the issue of lifting the sanctions. Though Cuban adventurism in Africa, and most recently in Central America, may have cooled off the pro-Cuba movement, it is highly possible that in the 1980s the OAS will end its sanctons, most of which were only symbolic in 1982.

As for Washington and Havana, the signing of the 1972 anti-hijacking agreement, Ford's authorization of US companies abroad to trade with Cuba, and Carter's lifting of travel restrictions to Cuba [14] illustrate modest progress, but the two countries have remained basically locked into their own preconditions for negotiation and normalization of relations.

The years 1974-1975 seemed to indicate a willingness on the part of Washington and Havana for direct negotiations. The US decision to allow US subsidiary firms abroad to trade with Cuba signalled a partial lifting of the economic embargo. In 1975, Cuban support of the Popular Movement for the Liberation of Angola (MPLA) and Puerto Rico's pro-independence movement cooled the rapprochement. In addition, the bombing of a Cuban airline plane and Castro's repudiation of the anti-hijacking agreement stalemated the possibility of negotiations until 1977.

Carter ordered the State Department to allow US citizens to travel to Cuba, suspended reconnaissance flights over the island, and allowed some Cuban technicians to travel to the US. Cuba reciprocated by granting visas to tourists and businessmen, allowed a US volleyball team to visit Havana, and released a dozen political prisoners.

In the spring of 1976 direct negotiations resulted in an agreement on fishing rights and boundaries and the establishment of "interest actions" in Havana and Washington. In 1978, Cuba's intervention in the Ethiopian-Somali War and its growing involvement in Angola prompted Washington to again freeze the rapprochement. More recently, there have been indications that President Reagan sought to explore the feasibility of direct negotiations with the Cuban regime but with little success. For example, Haig met with Rodriguez in December 1981 in Mexico and General Vernon Walters with Castro in Havana in March 1982. Yet these meetings were only preliminary attempts, and there was no follow-up to undertake serious negotiations.[15]

Castro over a period of years has raised what he considered his "preconditions" for resumption of relations. One could anticipate that from the Cuban side, the lifting of the economic embargo, the future of the Guantanamo Naval Base and finally diplomatic recognition of the Cuban revolution would be objectives for Castro to pursue. From Washington's viewpoint, compensation for American property nationalized by the revolution and Cuba's support and involvement with guerrilla movements in the Third World would be of paramount importance to the long-range strategic interests of the United States. The economic advantages and disadvantages of resumption of relations between the two countries have been explored by Mesa-Lago.[16] The strategic value of Guantanamo could be assessed in the context of larger and more sophisticated naval bases in Puerto Rico, but regardless of the conclusion, President Reagan is right in placing a freeze on negotiations as long as Castro continues his policy of military intervention abroad.

It is clear that economic trade between Havana and Washington could enhance Castro's independence from the Soviet Union. It is true that the relations between the USSR and Cuba have at times been shaky and that Castro has at times asserted his nationalist line in spite of the Soviet Union. Yet Castro's anti-Americanism and his own self-perception as the savior of the Third World may be too deep, thus preventing him from trading the obvious economic advantages for the Cuban people in renewed relations with the US for a promise to cease interfering in the internal affairs of other countries. Since the 1960s, Castro has established a pattern of subversion in the Latin American countries that more recently includes Central America, as well as his military intervention in the African continent. Less significant, but also to be noted, is Cuban military involvement in Syria and South Yemen which was reported in the mid-1970s.

The United States, on the one hand, could choose to ignore Castro's Cuba and concentrate on stamping out the revolutionary movements in Central America. This approach would not resolve the causes of friction between the two countries, nor will it discourage Castro from continuing his support of revolutionary organizations in the Central American isthmus. The United States could, on the other hand, approach Cuba with a willingness to discuss Cuba's legitimate concerns and grievances, many of which were at the source of the break in diplomatic relations between the two countries in January 1961. A reappraisal of US-Cuban relations, if pursued in a framework of equality and mutual respect, could yield positive results.

Nicaragua adds yet another case study of US foreign policy gone awry. A policy of economic embargoes and clandestine operations aimed at destabilizing the Nicaraguan junta will not serve the long-range interests of the United States in the Central American region. Furthermore, Reagan's policy toward the Sandinista junta has striking similarities to the United States-Cuban policy between 1959-61, which only succeeded in isolating the Cubans and moving them closer to the Soviet camp.

Following the departure of Anastasio Somoza on July 17, 1979, and his appointed successor, Francisco Urcuyo, twenty-four hours later, the Sandinistas seized control of the Nicaraguan government. Faced with a war-torn country, the revolutionary junta, composed of two FSLN members, a member of the Group of Twelve, and two right-of-center representatives, enacted immediate measures to consolidate power and secure foreign aid to rebuild Nicaragua. With the country's agricultural crops virtually ruined for 1979 and facing a deficit left by the Somoza government of $1.4 billion, the Sandinistas appealed to foreign governments for relief supplies to aid the Nicaraguan people. Cuba quickly responded, sending $5 million between July and August 1979, while the US hesitated until the end of October to send $35 million in emergency supplies.[17] Likewise, the Brazilians quickly forwarded emergency goods to Nicaragua and granted a $30 million line of credit. To date, the Brazilians have granted more economic loans than the USSR to the Nicaraguan government and seem to a certain extent to be "filling the vacuum left by the United States."[18] Yet, one must not conclude that the Soviets are not interested in future developments and cooperative relations with the Nicaraguan government. In addition, Mexico, Venezuela, France and Sweden, among others, have granted loans to the Nicaraguans.

Since assuming control of the government in July of 1979, the Sandinistas have nationalized as much as 50 percent of the farmland, currently managed by the Instituto Nacional de Reforma Agraria (INRA), along with banking, mining, and many commercial areas of the economy. As a result of the ever increasing preference given state-owned businesses, many independent businessmen, who supported the Sandinistas during the insurrection, have publicly criticized government policies.[19]

Internally, the new government took immediate steps to counter any attack from different opposition groups by placing FSLN veterans in key positions to replace the former National Guard (EPS), creating a separate police and state security force, forming a citizen reserve corps (MPS), and Sandinista Defense Committees (CDS). The Nicaraguan government initially opted for 200 Cuban advisers, which have increased to approximately 1,500,[20] rather than the US offer to provide training for the EPS, and within a year the citizen reserve ranks had risen to a force of over 100,000.[21]

As an internal security organization, the CDS is developing along lines similar to the Cuban model. The CDS functions through neighborhood political units involved in civil projects and vigilance against "counterrevolutionaries" at the local level. Moreover, the government's increasing concern over national security threats by exile groups attacking from Honduras, resistance by the Miskito Indians in the northeastern region, and exiles in Florida, who, the Nicaraguan government claims, are advised by the US, has led increasingly to a crackdown on public criticism and the postponement of elections until 1985. *La Prensa*, the leading newspaper and the only remaining opposition paper, has been repeatedly shut down, along with several radio programs. In fact, a recent Watch Report noted censorship and sanctions against critical publications, along with the forced relocation of the Miskito Indians as the two major concerns of the committee. For several months Amnesty International has charged that hundreds of Miskito Indians had been rounded up by the Sandinista government for political dissent. Recently 69 Indians were tried on subversion charges and received prison sentences of four to sixteen years.[22] One of the report's authors, Juan E. Mendez, stated, "We think that there is a very strong potential for a deterioration in the human rights situation."[23] During the last year, more than 85,000 Indians have been uprooted from their homes near the Atlantic coast and relocated to Susha, Nicaragua.[24]

The leftist political coalition, the National Patriotic Front (FPN), was dissolved in late 1979 because it was no longer needed for mass support. At the present time, the centrist Broad Opposition Front (FAO) remains in existence as the largest political coalition following the Sandinist victory. However, the token representation given the non-leftists in the Nicaraguan government soon became apparent, leading to the resignation of Alfonso Robelo and Violeta Barrios de Chamorro from the junta, and Arturo Cruz as Nicaraguan Ambassador to the United States in April of 1980.[25] Moreover, Eden Pastora (known as Comandante Zero—who led the Sandinistas to victory) fled Nicaragua in early 1981, denouncing the Sandinista government's ties with communist governments.[26] All of these internal developments, combined with US concern over Soviet and Cuban involvement in Nicaragua, have led to deteriorating US-Nicaraguan relations.

Adding to US concerns over the military buildup and radicalization of the revolution has been the Nicaraguan involvement with the Salvadoran guerrillas. The training of Salvadoran guerrillas in Nicaragua and the shipment of arms through Nicaragua to El Salvador prompted US policy to shift from a wait-and-see attitude toward the Sandinista government to a policy of suspension of all aid. In addition, US influence has been used to press European allies to cooperate in a military-economic embargo.[27] However, the French announced in January 1982 that they had agreed to sell non-offensive military equipment to the new government, expressing their view that such aid would lead the Nicaraguans to be less dependent on the USSR. Prior to resuming aid, the United States' main prerequisites were that the Sandinistas limit their military buildup, resume the original goals and objectives of the revolution (i.e. pluralistic governments, elections) and cessation of support to Salvadoran guerrillas. With regard to the US emphasis on the original objectives of the revolution, it has been reported that one of the reasons for the US opposition to a negotiated settlement in El Salvador is the perception that the Sandinistas had previously agreed to a pluralistic government and early elections and then changed their policy once in control of the government.[28]

As the previous discussion has indicated, the Nicaraguan government faces a precarious future, both internally and externally. Although the Sandinista government has been able to secure some foreign loans, the economic situation continues to be very precarious. To the disappointment of the Sandinistas, Daniel Ortega's recent trip to Moscow resulted in a much smaller economic aid package ($166 million over 5 years) than had been anticipated. However, the Nicaraguans hope that their recent support for the Argentines in the Falkland Islands crisis may lead to future loans from the Inter-American Development Bank, provided that they receive Latin American endorsement over US vetoes.[29] Given the recent announcements of the Argentine withdrawal of advisers from Honduras-based Nicaraguan exile camps, and Argentina's offer of 700 tons of wheat as emergency aid due to recent flooding in Nicaragua, the Nicaraguan expectation may be valid. In contrast, the US embassy sent $25,000 and 44 tons of rice, flour, salt, cooking oil and soap, while Washington considers sending further aid.[30]

A rapprochement between the US and Nicaragua does not appear to be in sight at the present time. Although the Nicaraguans expressed some willingness to discuss issues with the US, the US did not agree to the Nicaraguan condition that Mexico act as host and witness to such discussions.[31] Yet the vacuum created by the US suspension of economic aid has not been filled by the USSR. Although the USSR has granted military assistance to the new government, the Soviets may not be willing to commit substantial economic resources on a long-range basis, as they did in the case of socialist Cuba.

Given the current domestic situation in Nicaragua and the Central American region, it would be advantageous for the United States to encourage a pluralistic society in Nicaragua. At the present time, the internal developments within Nicaragua, particularly with regard to censorship and political participation in the government by non-leftist segments of the society, do not indicate a future for pluralism. The continued isolation of Nicaragua by the United States has heightened both the economic crisis and the threat of intervention thereby providing the Sandinist government with justification for postponing elections, increasing the size of the military, imposing censorship and other restrictions to suppress the opposition. Those elements within the opposition who favor democracy and free enterprise in the private sector face a dismal future without the resumption of United States aid to Nicaragua. Rather than condition US resumption of aid on domestic developments within Nicaragua and cessation of aid to El Salvadoran guerrillas, the US would be in a better position to reach agreement with the Nicaraguans by emphasizing only the cessation of Nicaraguan intervention in Central America as the US precondition for aid and with the expectation that a pluralistic society may evolve. Internal events in Nicaragua, though important to the United States, should not be pursued to the detriment of our primary interest in interdicting aid to the Salvadoran rebels and in preventing Nicaragua from forming closer ties to the Soviet Union.

The Nicaraguan government's recent rejection of AID aid ($5.1 million) to encourage the private sector in that country illustrates the suspicion and tension which persists between Managua and Washington. Yet, in view of the Nicaraguan accusations of US attempts to "destabilize the revolutionary government" through such aid, the Sandinistas also reiterated their desire to resume negotiations with the United States.[32] Likewise, the warning by Daniel Ortega Saavedra, the Sandinist junta leader, of an impending war with Honduras over US advised anti-Sandinists based along the Honduran border, was followed by stressing the desire to negotiate.[33]

A persistent destabilization program will continue to drive the Nicaraguan junta into a greater alliance with Havana, as well as to intensify its support for guerrilla movements in the area, that if successful, may be sympathetic to Managua. Since Nicaragua has expressed a willingness to talk to the United States, the differences should be explored. For Washington not to do so is ultimately to risk a Sandinist government which will be driven into the socialist bloc, thus defeating our national strategic interests. Finally, a willingness to talk to Managua will signal Havana of our willingness to create an environment conducive to discussions.

Guatemala, the largest of the Central American nations, poses a challenge to United States policy. Since 1954 when Washington successfully helped finance and organize the overthrow of Jacobo Arbenz, the country has been engaged in a cycle of violence. There are twice as many US business investments in Guatemala as in El Salvador, and Guatemala has oil reserves estimated at over 2 billion barrels.

In 1979 Carter suspended military aid because of the government's human rights violation and atrocities, and pressed the government, as in the case of El Salvador, to hold elections.

The last two decades of civil war in Guatemala have, according to most observers, eroded the position of moderate elements in the political spectrum. In the 1960s the Castro government earmarked assistance for the ill-fated Revolutionary Armed Forces (FAR). More recently, there have been allegations of Cuban involvement with the Guerrilla Army of the Poor (EGP). Right-wing paramilitary organizations, as in El Salvador, have also engaged in terrorist acts, at times condoned by the military governments. Many of these moderate elements were driven to join the guerrillas. It has been estimated that since 1954 there have been 30,000 political assassinations, 3,000 in 1980, and that they continue to take place at the rate of 50 to 60 per day.[34] The US State Department estimated that assassinations rose from 70 to 100 per month in 1980 to 250 to 300 per month in 1981[35] and many moderate Christian Democrats who chose to remain working toward a peaceful democratic solution continue to be assassinated. In 1981, two hundred Christian Democrats and two of their town mayors were assassinated by unidentified gunmen.[36]

On February 10, 1982, against this backdrop of violence and on the eve of the presidential elections encouraged by the United States, the four guerrilla organizations established a united front called the Guatemalan Committee of Patriotic Unity (CGUP)[37] to pursue their aim of establishing a Marxist government.

The alleged winner of the fraudulent March 7, 1982 presidential election was quickly overthrown by General Efrain Rios Montt*, a born-again Christian who quickly won the support of the Reagan administration.[38] The Reagan administration was no doubt impressed by the fact that the three pro-private enterprise parties supported the coup, and by General Rios Montt's speedy firing of four junta members and dismissal of several members of the disreputable Secret Police. Further, in the recent months after the coup there seems to have been an improvement in the human rights situation in the urban areas.[39] A month after the coup, the United States announced it was ending the freeze on arms sales imposed by Carter and that $4 million in spare parts for helicopters were being approved along with at least $250,000 for military training in fiscal 1983.[40]

Thus, the US government has now invested its prestige in supporting General Rios Montt, a member of the Christian Church of the World, a fundamentalist group that began proselytizing in Guatemala in 1976. The General, who believes his authority to rule comes from God, takes his inspiration to govern from the Bible,[41] and has said he wishes to establish a communitarian society where human

*Since this writing, General Rios Montt was overthrown in a military coup— Publisher.

relations do not come from communism or democracy but from the family (i.e., the sharing of everything) and in which fundamentalist missionaries would assist in building model villages.[42] It is not clear whether General Rios Montt envisions a democracy, theocracy or simply a military dictatorship. He has been more precise in admitting that government forces continue to violate human rights.[43] Indeed, violations of human rights have increased in the countryside as the government intensifies its counterinsurgency campaign.[44] The United States should continue to use its influence to make the government accountable for abuses in the countryside and should abide by the Senate's resolution not to support regimes that are persistent violators of human rights.

In Guatemala, the best long-range option may be in strengthening progressive elements within the military and supporting the remaining members of groups of a centrist persuasion such as the Christian Democrats. Rios Montt has promised elections, and the US should encourage democratic elections that will provide guarantees to the moderate and opposition parties.

The challenge for the US lies in identifying those within the military, business and professional sectors who have a genuine commitment to social reform. While Rios Montt has initiated some limited measures that may give hope for greater prosecution of human rights violations, he has done nothing for the implementation of socioeconomic reforms; and the violence in the countryside, which claims the lives of civilians, peasants, and Indians, overshadows the decreased urban violence.

Moreover, 55 percent of Guatemala's population are Indians who have only recently joined the ranks of the opposition.[45] The potential for increased turmoil and bloodshed can only be defused by immediate, extensive, and equitable socioeconomic reforms.

HONDURAS

In 1981, the military-backed government of Paz Garcia conducted elections, and civilian President Roberto Suazo Cordova of the Liberal party assumed office. Suazo Cordova's opponent in the presidential race, Nationalist party leader Ricardo Zunigo, emphasized the communist threat and had the support of the military. In the opinion of many, this issue did not attract a majority of the votes.

Although many of the older military officers who surrounded Paz Garcia are due to retire from the military and their political offices, some observers have expressed concern that many of the younger generation (a group of approximately five to eight colonels) are expected to remain in key positions within the army to ensure that the liberals do not enact any radical reforms.[46] Relatively speaking, the political situation in Honduras continues to be one of the most stable, yet fragile, in Central America. Apart from the terrorist activities of the Revolutionary Popular Forces Lorenzo Zelaya and Juan Rayo Guerrilla group, and most recently those of the Cinchonero Popular Liberation Movement, the civilian government has remained unchallenged.[47]

The large percentage of landowning farmers, and the exercise of press freedom through newspapers such as *El Tiempo* are partially responsible for this stability.[48]

However, the recent influx of Nicaraguan counterrevolutionaries and El Salvadoran and Guatemalan guerrillas threaten the stability of this Central American country. In 1982, the United States granted $10 million in military and $48 million in economic aid to assist the Honduran government in its border patrols and to improve the country's economic condition. From the US perspective, behind the current political stability lies a fragile and helpless country which, given the political realities in Nicaragua and El Salvador, could follow suit in the region's recent civil wars. Therefore, in addition to military aid, the United States has upgraded its embassy staff (from a Class 4 to Class 2 post) and has increased the number of US military advisers to 97.[49] It is highly possible that the Sandinistas will seek to expand their military assistance to revolutionary groups in Honduras, following the same pattern of assistance they have granted to the guerrillas in El Salvador.

As long as Central America remains vulnerable to leftist guerrillas, the Hondurans require United States military assistance to defend its borders. The increased US economic package is also vital to protect the Honduran domestic situation from deteriorating. Washington's emphasis on democratic government may prevent the army from undertaking a coup, provided that the current government does not arouse military concerns over Honduras' future policies.

Deteriorating Honduran-Nicaraguan relations have not been helped by the United States' attitude toward Nicaragua, and US support for counterrevolutionaries in Honduras. At the present time, this situation poses a potential long-range dispute between Nicaragua and Honduras.

PANAMA

After the military coup in 1968, the country has slowly and steadily advanced toward democratic rule. After the indirect election of President Royo in 1978, the political parties have been allowed to undertake normal activities and restrictions to freedom of expression have been lifted. There is intense political activity regarding the oncoming general elections scheduled for June 1984. The Democratic Revolutionary Party, which is the government party, appears to be the favorite in the electoral process of 1984, though some observers have remarked that the government could be effectively challenged by a coalition of opposition parties. The main political parties in Panama, which cover both sides of the political spectrum, are the Liberal Party, the Christian Democratic Party, the Socialist Democratic Party, the Republican Party, and the Panamanian Popular Party; the latter follows the Soviet communist party line.

The traditional focus for opposition groups and Panamanian-US tensions has been the United States' control over the Panama Canal. The Panama Canal treaties negotiated by Carter and Torrijos resolved this issue, and, therefore, reduced the level of domestic opposition and ushered in the present conditions for economic growth and political stability.

COSTA RICA

The current Costa Rican economic situation poses the greatest challenge to President Luis Alberto Monge. In late April 1982, the government announced a 100-day emergency economic plan. The main objective of this plan is to attract international companies involved in agribusiness to invest in projects which would revive the domestic industry. However, landowners were worried that such a plan would lead to radical land reforms, and, as a result, were hesitant to commence planting. However, Monge appears to have gained support from the majority of the labor force.[50] In addition, the new plan calls for reduced government spending and a renegotiated foreign debt.

Faced with high unemployment and inflationary rates, along with declining economic growth, the Costa Rican government fears that political instability may result if these economic problems are not resolved. Under Reagan's Caribbean Basin Initiative, Costa Rica will receive $70 million in emergency aid, provided that an agreement with the International Monetary Fund is reached to renegotiate Costa Rica's foreign debt.[51]

In addition to Costa Rica's economic plan, the new administration is planning to enact strict immigration policies to prevent foreign counterrevolutionaries from using Costa Rican territory to launch terrorist activities against the Nicaraguan government. In fact, to protect its neutrality and reduce the mounting tensions with Nicaragua, Costa Rica recently deported former Sandinista leader Eden Pastora and forty other Nicaraguans from Costa Rica.[52]

The United States has expressed concern over the increased domestic terrorism in Costa Rica during the past year, and hopes that the US economic package will prevent any future insurgency from taking place. A Costa Rican investigation into an attempted kidnapping revealed the existence of 20 terrorist cells under the leadership of the

Revolutionary Party of Central American Workers.[53]

Provided that Costa Rica can improve its economic situation and maintain neutrality in the Central American region, future political development, as in the past, should be characterized by political stability.

The national security interests of the US dictate that our regional policy regarding Central America falls within our global policies. The preceding analysis and recommendations have sought to take into account those interests and policies. Of importance will be the US commitment to respect for human rights in the countries of the region. Our own values dictate that a vigorous policy of human rights should not be compromised for the purposes of expediency. To do so is tantamount to condoning the tactics of those we seek to oppose. In this regard, withdrawal of aid from those governments who continue to violate human rights should be considered and, if necessary, carried out. The policy of the Reagan administration on human rights continues to be weak and thus increasingly creates a credibility gap as to our true objectives.

Finally, the Reagan administration has been right in indicating that the ills and socioeconomic problems of the region can be dealt with effectively only by long-range development plans. The Caribbean Basin Initiative could well be part of an overall development plan, but by itself will not suffice.

THE CARIBBEAN BASIN INITIATIVE

On February 24, 1982, President Reagan unveiled an economic development plan for the Caribbean and Central America entitled the Caribbean Basin Initiative (CBI), which, through positive measures such as technical assistance, country quotas for duty-free import of sugar into the US, one-way free trade, and private investment incentives, would stimulate the severely troubled economics of this region. Yet, as Abraham Lowenthal asserts in his assessment of the CBI plan, the East-West focus of this development plan illustrates that Reagan administration concern is placed more in terms of the advantages for investment by US firms, military security, and political loyalty rather than on economic development of the Caribbean region.[54] On the other hand, the CBI does reflect the priorities of Third World leaders, namely expanded trade, investment, and credit. Regardless of US motives or the East-West emphasis of this development plan, the Reagan administration has adopted an alternative approach rather than merely another new aid program.[55] Since the CBI emphasizes stimulating the private sector, the potential for success adds no greater possibility for success than previous plans aimed at the public sector. The Reagan administration's optimism that private enterprise, given the correct infrastructure, will succeed where other development plans have not may be unrealistic in respect to the complexities of the Central American and Caribbean economies. Specifically in regard to Central America, the political turmoil in El Salvador and Guatemala hardly reflects a favorable climate that would attract foreign investment. And yet this political unrest reflects the major flaw of the CBI—namely, a development plan that seeks to stabilize a region beset by political conflict. Needless to say, Central America's economic future appears bleak at the present time, but to approach economic development, in terms of the CBI, as the solution for political stabilization ignores and oversimplifies the historical and present-day realities of the region. If in fact the Caribbean Basin Initiative has any potential for success, political stability must precede long-range economic development plans.

CONCLUSION

The preceding analysis indicates that most of the Central American countries find themselves enveloped in political violence as left and right wing groups confront established governments in contests for political power.

Legitimate grievances of a socioeconomic nature have provided fertile ground for violence in an area where democratic traditions are weak. This political violence has also provided an arena conducive to the Cuban and Soviet attempts to gain a new sphere of influence by supporting radical revolutionary movements. In the case of Nicaragua, the Sandinistas have established a Marxist government responsive to Cuba and are rapidly developing military and economic ties with the Soviet bloc. Furthermore, the Sandinistas are well underway to destroying political pluralism in Nicaragua.

Political parties or organized opposition are either non-existent or have been rendered ineffective. After having reneged on their promise to hold prompt democratic elections, the Sandinistas speak of the 1985 elections as a means of strengthening the Marxist revolution. It is possible that by then the political opposition as well as the private sector would not be capable of posing a challenge to the Sandinist junta. Already *La Prensa*, along with other major publications, has been gagged by governmental censorship. In the event that the United States has concluded that the Sandinistas have failed to negotiate issues of concern to the United States and that they continue to support the guerrillas in El Salvador, posing a threat to the government of that country, the United States should be prepared to support the democratic forces of Nicaragua and to prevent the Sandinistas from acting as a Cuban-Soviet proxy in Central America.

Although Panama, Costa Rica, and Honduras continue to have governments responsive to the needs of their peoples, the latter two have begun to experience challenges from extreme leftist groups. United States policy should be one of decisive support to the governments of these countries to meet socioeconomic needs and any threats from terrorist groups.

In El Salvador the United States should encourage a dialogue to bring about a peaceful resolution of the conflict. The alternative would lead only to a protracted war with uncertain consequences for that unfortunate nation, and one that would continue to be a source of instability in the region.

In Guatemala it is difficult to assess at this early date the commitment of General Rios Montt to reforms, and thus US policy should be one of cautious support until the new Guatemalan government has had a reasonable period of time to undertake the communal reforms that the junta has verbally supported.

With regard to Cuba, since Castro has not given any serious indication of wanting positive dialogue, and since the Cubans continue to assist revolutionaries in Central America, the United States should proceed to ignore Castro while exploring ways to make Cuban military adventurism abroad costly.

Notes

1. Pastor notes that these nations averaged an annual real rate of growth of 5.3 percent during this period, which doubled the real per capita income in spite of explosive population growth (Pastor, July 1982, pp. 28-9).
2. Barber and Ronning, 1966, p. 41.
3. Bonner, New York *Times*, May 24, 1982, p. 1.
4. US Department of State, Bureau of Public Affairs, *Communist Interference in El Salvador* (Washington, DC), Special Report, No. 80, February 23, 1981. Subsequently, *The Wall Street Journal* (June 8, 1981) and the Washington *Post* (June 9, 1982) noted inaccuracies and inconsistencies in the report. More recently the ex-envoy of the US diplomatic mission in Havana, Wayne S. Smith, stated that the evidence of Cuban shipments to El Salvador "has never been solid" (Pear, New York *Times*, Septem-

ber 5, 1982, p. 3). However, in April of 1982, a senior Cuban government official stated that Cuba had in the past supplied arms to Nicaragua and the leftists in El Salvador but that these arms shipments were no longer taking place (St. Louis *Post Dispatch*, April 20, 1982, p. 11).

5. Ungo is currently the President of the FDR—an umbrella organization of the opposition.

6. See Bonner, New York *Times*, June 7, 1982, p. 6, for an interview with Jose Napoleon Duarte concerning the dismantling of the land redistribution plan.

7. Bonner, New York *Times*, May 30, 1982, p. 3.

8. Recent reports confirm that the guerrillas have no shortage of weaponry, which includes American, Soviet, and East German and Chinese-made equipment (Weinraub, New York *Times*, September 26, 1982, p. 1).

9. Johnson, 1964, p. 143.

10. Weinraub, New York *Times*, September 26, 1982, p. 1.

11. Bonachea and Valdes, 1969.

12. Mesa-Lago, 1974, pp. 117-118.

13. The most recent example of inconsistency was Castro's offer to militarily assist the Argentinian military junta in its war against England over the Falkland Islands.

14. The State Department recently reimposed travel restrictions which effectively ban tourist and business travel to Cuba after May 15, 1982 (St. Louis *Post Dispatch*, April 20, 1982, p. 11).

15. Smith, New York *Times*, September 5, 1982, p. E17.

16. Blasier and Mesa-Lago, 1979, pp. 207-14.

17. Goodsell, 1981-82, p. 104.

18. Los Angeles *Weekly Report*, May 14, 1982, p. 10.

19. Cuzan, 1982, pp. 66-67.

20. Hoge, New York *Times*, January 4, 1982, p. 1.

21. Gorman, 1981, p. 145.

22. New York *Times*, July 4, 1982, p. 10.

23. Blair, New York *Times*, May 14, 1982, p. 4.

24. Bonner, New York *Times*, September 5, 1982, p. 12.

25. Gorman, 1981, pp. 146-149.
26. At a press conference in San Jose, Costa Rica (April 15, 1982), Pastora denounced abuses against the Miskito Indians.
27. The US severed all economic aid in January 1981 and to date has refused to resume negotiations with the Nicaraguans.
28. Hoge, New York *Times*, January 10, 1982.
29. Los Angeles *Weekly Report*, May 21, 1982, p. 1.
30. New York *Times*, May 30, 1982, p. 7.
31. New York *Times*, May 1, 1982, p. 4.
32. Washington *Post*, August 4, 1982, p. A20.
33. New York *Times*, August 29, 1982, p. 12.
34. Pisani, *World Press Review*, March 1, 1982, p. 26.
35. Oberdorfer, Washington *Post*, February 12, 1982.
36. Dillon, Miami *News Herald*, February 4, 1982.
37. The CGUP is comprised of the Guerrilla Army of the Poor, the Rebel Armed Forces, the Organization of the People in Arms, and the Communist Labor Party.
38. General Rios Montt was Chief of the Armed Forces general staff (1970-74), and after 1974 he was military attaché in Madrid.
39. Weinraub, New York *Times*, June 3, 1982, p. 4.
40. St. Louis *Post Dispatch*, April 25, 1982, p. 8A.
41. Bonner, New York *Times*, June 10, 1982, p. 12.
42. Bonner, New York *Times*, May 20, 1982, p. 4.
43. *Ibid*.
44. Simons, New York *Times*, September 12, 1982, p. E3.
45. Riding, New York *Times Magazine*, August 24, 1980, p. 18.
46. Los Angeles *Weekly Report*, December 11, 1981, pp. 9-10.
47. On April 29, 1982, the terrorist group hijacked a Honduran airliner in Tegucigalpa, demanding ransom and the release of 32 political prisoners. The Juan Rayo guerrilla group claimed responsibility for the bomb explosion in a Coca-Cola owned plant in January of 1982. This group accused Colonel Alvarez Martinez, Chief of the Armed Forces, for repression of labor movements in the province of La Ceiba, and pledged a sabotage campaign against Alvarez's appointment as Chief of the Armed

Forces. Earlier in January they claimed responsibility for the bombing of a US mining company. On September 17, 1982, the Cinchonero Popular Liberation Movement stormed the Chamber of Commerce in San Pedro, taking more than 100 officials and businessmen hostage. On the eighth day of the seige, the guerrillas were flown in a Panamanian Air Force jet to Panama and then on to Havana.

48. Rosenfeld, Washington *Post*, March 12, 1982.
49. Gugliotto, Miami *Herald*, March 20, 1982.
50. Los Angeles *Weekly Report*, May 14, 1982, pp. 5-6.
51. Riding, New York *Times*, May 9, 1982.
52. New York *Times*, June 20, 1982, p. 4.
53. Crossette, New York *Times*, March 23, 1982, p. 12.
54. Lowenthal, *Foreign Policy*, Summer 1982, p. 115.
55. Johnson, *Foreign Affairs*, Summer 1982, p. 119.

SELECTED REFERENCES

BOOKS

Adams, Richard Newbold. *Crucification by Power, Essays on Guatemalan National Social Structure, 1944-1966*. Austin: University of Texas Press, 1970.

Ashcraft, Norman. *Colonialism and Underdevelopment: Processes of Political Economic Change in British Honduras*. New York: Columbia University, Teachers College Press, 1973.

Barber, William F. and C. Neale Ronning. *Internal Security and*

Military Power, Counterinsurgency and Civic Action in Latin America. Columbus: Ohio State University Press, 1966.

Bartley, Russell H., ed. *Soviet Historians on Latin America.* Madison: University of Wisconsin Press, 1978.

Bell, Belden, ed. *Nicaragua, An Ally Under Siege.* Washington, DC: Council on American Affairs, 1978.

Betancourt, Ernesto. "Exporting the Revolution to Latin America." In *Revolutionary Change in Cuba,* ed. Carmelo Mesa-Lago. Pittsburgh, 1971.

Blasier, Cole. *The Hovering Giant: U.S. Responses to Revolutionary Change in Latin America.* Pittsburgh: University of Pittsburgh Press, 1976.

Blasier, Cole and Carmelo Mesa-Lago, eds. *Cuba in the World.* Pittsburgh: University of Pittsburgh Press, 1979.

Bonachea, Rolando E., and Nelson P. Valdes, eds. *Che: Selected Works.* Cambridge, Ma.: M.I.T. Press, 1969.

————. *Cuba in Revolution.* Garden City, N.Y., Anchor Books, 1972.

————. *Revolutionary Struggle, 1947-1958: The Selected Works of Fidel Castro.* Cambridge, Ma.: M.I.T. Press, 1972.

Crawley, Eduardo. *Dictators Never Die: A Portrait of Nicaragua and the Somoza Dynasty.* New York: St. Martin's Press, 1979.

Dorner, Peter, ed. *Land Reform in Latin America.* Publication by Land Economics for the Land Tenure Center, Number 3. Madison: University of Wisconsin, 1971.

Durham, William H. *Scarcity and Survival in Central America: Ecological Origins of the Soccer War.* Stanford: Stanford University Press, 1979.

Feder, Ernest. *The Rape of the Peasantry: Latin America's Landholding System.* Garden City, N.Y.: Doubleday and Co., 1971.

Fernandez, Julio A. "Honduras" in *Political Forces in Latin America: Dimensions of the Quest for Stability.* Ed. Ben G. Burnett and Kenneth F. Johnson. 2nd Ed. Belmont, Ca.: Wadsworth Publishing Co., 1970.

Galeano, Eduardo. *Guatemala Occupied Country.* Trans. Cedric Belfrage, New York: Monthly Review Press, 1969.

Goldrich, Daniel. "Panama" in *Political Systems of Latin America.* Ed. Martin C. Needler. Princeton, N.J.: Van Nostrand Reinhold Co., 1965.

Gott, Richard. *Guerrilla Movements in Latin America.* New York: Doubleday and Co., 1971.

Helms, Mary W. and Franklin O. Loveland, eds. *Frontier Adaptions in Lower Central America.* Philadelphia: Institute for the Study of Human Issues, Inc., 1976.

Herrera, H. Roberto Caceres. *Honduras y la Problemática del Derecho Internacional Publico del Mar.* Tegucigalpa: Publicacion de la Unah, 1975.

Herrick, Bruce, and Barclay Hudson. *Urban Poverty and Economic Development: A Case Study of Costa Rica.* New York: St. Martin's Press, 1981.

Herring, Hubert. *A History of Latin America.* New York: Alfred

Knopf Co., 1968.

Johnson, John J. *The Military and Society in Latin America*. Stanford: Stanford University Press, 1964.

Lieuwen, Edwin. *The United States and the Challenge to Security in Latin America*. Columbus: Ohio State University Press, 1966.

_____. *United States Policy in Latin America*. New York: Frederick A. Praeger, 1965.

Levinson, Jerome, and Juan de Onis. *The Alliance that Lost its Way*. Chicago: Quadrangle Books, 1970.

Malloy, James M., ed. *Authoritarianism and Corporatism in Latin America*. Pittsburgh: University of Pittsburgh Press, 1977.

Mesa-Lago, Carmelo. *Cuba in the 1970s: Pragmatism and Institutionalization*. Albuquerque: University of New Mexico Press, 1974.

Millett, Richard. *Guardians of the Dynasty*. New York: Orbis Books, 1977.

Orantos, Isaac Cohen. *Regional Integration in Central America*. Lexington, Ma: D.C. Heath and Co., 1972.

Organization of American States General Secretariat. *Situation, Principal Problems and Prospects for the Integral Development of Nicaragua*. Washington, DC: OAS, 1976.

Poppino, Rollie E. *International Communism in Latin America 1917-1963*. New York: The Free Press, 1964.

Schneider, Ronald M. *Communism in Guatemala, 1944-1954*. New York, 1958.

Segel, Aaron Lee. *Population Policies in the Caribbean*. Lexington, Ma.: D.C. Heath and Co., 1975.

Seligson, Mitchel A. *Agrarian Capitalism and the Transformation of Peasant Society: Coffee in Costa Rica*. Council on International Studies, No. 69. New York: State University of New York at Buffalo, 1975.

Suarez, Andres. *Cuba: Castroism and Communism, 1959-1966*. Trans. Joel Carmichael and Ernst Halperin. Cambridge, Ma.: The M.I.T. Press, 1967.

Szulc, Tad. *The United States and the Caribbean*. New Jersey: Prentice-Hall, Inc., 1971.

Walker, Thomas W. *Nicaragua: The Land of Sandino*. Boulder, Co.: Westview Press, 1981.

Wiarda, Howard J., ed. *The Continuing Struggle for Democracy in Latin America*. Boulder, Co: Westview Press, 1980.

Wynia, Gary W. *Politics and Planners: Economic Development Policy in Central America*. Madison: The University of Wisconsin Press, 1972.

ARTICLES

Blair, William G. "Ending of Torture Seen in Nicaragua." New York *Times,* May 14, 1982, p. 4.

Bonner, Raymond. "Duarte Says Salvadoran Land Plans Have Been Stopped and Could Die." New York *Times,* June 7, 1982, p. 6.

_____. "Guatemalan Leader Says God is Guiding Him." New York *Times*, June 10, 1982, p. 12.

_____. "Guatemalan Reports Private Aid Offer." New York *Times*, May 20, 1982, p. 4.

_____. "Salvador Blocks the Enforcement of Land Program." New York *Times*, May 24, 1982, p. 1.

_____. "Salvador Evicts Peasants from Land." New York *Times*, May 30, 1982, p. 3.

_____. "Uprooted Indians Voice Discontent in Nicaragua." New York *Times*, September 5, 1982, p. 12.

Chislett, William. "Sandinistas Economy Totters Under a State of Siege." *Financial Times of London*, February 19, 1982.

Crossette, Barbara. "Increasing Terrorism in Costa Rica is Now Causing Concern in the U.S." New York *Times*, March 23, 1982, p. 12.

Cuzan, Alfred G. and Richard Heggen. "A Micro-Political Explanation of the 1979 Nicaraguan Revolution." *Latin America Research Review*, Vol. XVII, No. 2 (1982), pp. 66-67.

Dillon, Sam. "Guatemala Elections Breed Hope, Fear." Miami *News Herald*, February 4, 1982.

Ebel, Roland H. "The Coming of the Post Agricultural Society: An Exercise in Economic and Political Futurism." *Inter-American Economic Affairs*, Vol. 35, No. 4 (Spring 1982), pp. 77-96.

_____. "Political Instability in Central America." *Current History*, Vol. 81, No. 472 (February 1982), pp. 56-59.

Gomez, Leonel, and Bruce Cameron. "El Salvador: The Current Danger." *Foreign Policy*, No. 43 (Summer 1981), pp. 70-78.

Gonalez, Heliodoro. "When is Military Aid Justified? The Case of El Salvador." *Inter-American Economic Affairs*, Vol. 35, No. 2 (Autumn 1981), pp. 71-83.

Goodsell, James Nelson. "Nicaragua: An Interim Assessment." *International Journal*, Vol. 37, No. 1 (Winter 1981/1982), pp. 91-107.

Gorman, Stephen M. "Power and Consolidation in the Nicaraguan Revolution." *Journal of Latin American Studies*, Vol. 13, Part 1. (May 1981), Cambridge Ma., pp. 133-149.

Gugliotto, Guy. "U.S. Role in Honduras Grows." Miami *Herald*, March 20, 1982.

Hoge, Warren. "Honduran Rebels on Way to Havana." New York *Times*, September 26, 1982, p. 15.

————. "Its Border Raided, Nicaragua Trains Civilians." New York *Times*, January 4, 1982, p. 1.

————. "Salvador War Also Puts Squeeze on Managua." New York *Times*, January 10, 1982.

Leiken, Robert S. "Eastern Winds in Latin America." *Foreign Policy*, No. 42 (Spring 1981), pp. 94-113.

"Liberals Face 'Economic Dunkirk.'" Los Angeles *Weekly Report*, December 11, 1981, pp. 9-10.

Lowenthal, Abraham F. *et al*. "The Caribbean Basin Initiative." *Foreign Policy*, No. 47 (Summer 1982), pp. 114-138.

"106 Miskitos are Convicted for Subversion in Nicaragua." New York *Times*, July 4, 1982, p. 10.

"40 Nicaraguan Exiles are Being Deported by the Costa Ricans." New York *Times*, June 20, 1982, p. 4.

"Nicaragua's Strange Bedfellow." Los Angeles *Weekly Report*, May 14, 1982, p. 10.

Oberdorfer, Don. "Reagan Wants Authority to Send Guatemala Aid." Washington *Post*, February 12, 1982.

"Ousted Bank Head Linked to Pastora." Los Angeles *Weekly Report*, May 21, 1982, p. 1.

Pastor, Robert A. "Our Real Interests in Central America." *The Atlantic Monthly*, (July 1982), pp. 27-39.

Pear, Robert. "Ex-Envoy Dubious Over Cuban Arms." New York *Times*, September 5, 1982, p. 3.

Pisani, Francis. "Guatemala's 'Moment of Truth' A Violence-torn Nation on the Brink of Explosion." *World Press Review*, Vol. 29, No. 3 (March 1982), p. 26.

"Promises, Promises from Monge." Los Angeles *Weekly Report*, May 14, 1982, pp. 5-6.

Rabkin, Rhoda Pearl. "U.S.-Soviet Rivalry in Central America and the Caribbean." *Journal of International Affairs*, Vol. 34, No. 2 (Fall/Winter 1980/1981), pp. 329-351.

Riding, Alan. "Civilian President Installed in Honduras After a Decade of Military Rule." New York *Times*, May 13, 1982, p. 1.

———. "Guatemala: The State of Siege." New York *Times Magazine*. August 24, 1980, pæ 16.

———. "Troubled Costa Rica Gets New Chief." New York *Times*, May 9, 1982, pæ 3.

Rosenfeld, Stephen S. "Honduras: Central American 'Sandinista'." Washington *Post*, March 12, 1982.

Seligson, Mitchell A. "Agrarian Reform in Costa Rica: The Impact of the Title Security Program." *Inter-American Economic Affairs*, Vol. 35, No. 4 (Spring 1982), pp. 31-56.

Sigmund, Paul E. "Latin America: Change or Continuity?" *Foreign Affairs* (America and World 1981), Vol. 60, No. 3, pp. 629-657.

Simons, Marlise. "Guatemalans are Adding a Few Twists to 'Pacification'." New York *Times*, September 12, 1982, p. E3.

Smith, Wayne S. "It is Not Impossible to Deal with Castro. Realism is Required." New York *Times*, September 5, 1982, p. E17.

"U.S. Considering Sending Relief Aid to Nicaragua." New York *Times*, May 30, 1982, p. 7.

"U.S. Cuts Travel to Cuba." St. Louis *Post Dispatch*, April 4, 1982, p. 11.

"U.S. Eases Guatemala Arms Freeze." St. Louis *Post Dispatch*, April 25, 1982.

"U.S. is Said to Rule Out a Plan for Sandinist Talks." New York *Times*, May 1, 1982, p. 4.

U.S. Department of State. *Communist Interference in El Salvador.*

Special Report No. 80, February 23, 1981, Washington, DC, pp. 1-8.

Weinraub, Bernard. "Panel in House Votes Arms Aid for El Salvador." New York *Times*, May 13, 1982, p. 1.

_____. "Guatemalan Exiles Urge U.S. to Halt Aid to the New Junta." New York *Times*, June 3, 1982, p. 4.

_____. "Salvadoran Rebels Said to Extend Fighting to Quiet Parts of Country." New York *Times*, September 26, 1982, p. 1.

White, Robert. "There is No Military Solution in El Salvador." *The Center Magazine* (July/August 1981), pp. 5-13.

REFLECTIONS ON
RELIGION AND
PUBLIC POLICY

By
RICHARD L. RUBENSTEIN

The bitter and divisive public debates concerning nuclear armament, nuclear energy, environmental pollution, human rights, abortion, and prayer in public school are but a few of the policy issues around which religious leaders have come to play important roles in the formation of public opinion. Nor is the involvement of religious leaders in matters of public policy confined to one segment of the political spectrum. Both right and left are represented. If fundamentalists have tended to support the current administration on a rapid build-up of America's defense establishment and have sought the reinstatement of prayer in the public schools, the leaders of mainstream Protestantism have tended to favor a nuclear freeze and have been wary of the "right to life" movement.

Although there have always been religious leaders who have sought

---

Richard L. Rubenstein is Robert O. Lawton Distinguished Professor of Religion at Florida State University and President of the Washington Institute for Values in Public Policy.

actively to influence public policy, the current wave of political activism can be seen as an outgrowth of the civil rights struggles of the nineteen-sixties and of the Vietnam War. Until the upheavals of the sixties, an American religious leader who took an active part in the political arena, or who even gave expression to strong opinions on political matters, ran the risk of incurring the disfavor of powerful elements in his community for not "sticking to religion." The idea that religion and politics were discrete realms was deeply rooted in the minds of most Americans. Yet, there was a certain naivete about it. Both religion and politics are concerned with power and the ways in which men and women come to terms with power.

In the ancient Near East, the office and person of the ruler was held to be sacred and there was no separation between religion and politics. The king was considered to be an incarnate god, or at the very least, a sacred mediator between the community and its gods. Until the end of World War II an aura of divinity was said to rest in the person of the Emperor of Japan. The idea of divine kingship, which represents the ultimate union of religion and politics, has had a long and continuing history in human civilization.

Yet, if the institution of divine kingship has proven durable over millenia, it is also true that the Judeo-Christian tradition had its beginnings in a successful revolt against that instititution and that both Judaism and Christianity have been its implacable opponents since their inception. It is the opinion of many of the best contemporary biblical scholars that the beginnings of the biblical idea of God, an idea that was originally utterly novel in the ancient Near East, as well as mankind's obligations to that God, are to be found in the decisive encounter between the Hebrew slaves and their Egyptian masters at the time of the exodus.[1] In any consideration of religion and public policy in the United States, it is important that we understand what is at stake politically and socially in the biblical idea of the ultimate source of power in human affairs. More than any other major civilization, the culture of the United States has been shaped by those religious communities, the dissenting Protestant denominations, that placed greatest stress on the authority of the Bible as a source of values in human affairs. It is possible to reflect on the problems of religion and public policy without considering biblical ideas when discussing Japan or India, for example, but not the United States. Let us, therefore, consider the ways in which biblical thought and experience are relevant to our topic.

As is well known, the ancient Egyptian state depended upon a system of corvée labor for many of its most important projects, such as the building of pyramids and temples. Because Pharaoh was considered to be a living God, he was regarded as the sole proprietor of all of the goods and services within the nation. In theory, there was no such thing as private property in the ancient Egyptian state. As was the case with most of the other rulers of the ancient Near East, one of Pharaoh's chief social functions was to redistribute the community's wealth. Since the Egyptians lacked any conception of either personal freedom or private property, they did not regard any service they rendered to Pharaoh, whether in the form of goods or labor, as a form of slavery. However, this was not true of those non-Egyptians who had been condemned to corvée labor because they were prisoners of war, hostages or had experienced a radical degradation in status, such as occurred to the "Hebrews" after the Semitic Hyksos domination of Egypt had been overthrown in the thirteenth century BC.[2] We have terse evidence of this degradation of status in Scripture:

And there arose a new King who knew not Joseph. (Ex. 1:11)

Scripture further tells us that the "Hebrews" were condemned to slavery, and, when their numbers increased beyond the labor requirements of the slavemasters, all male Hebrew infants were ordered put to death at birth (Ex. 1:16). Apparently, extermination was a method of eliminating a surplus population in ancient as well as modern times.

As the story is told in Scripture, it would appear at first glance that the "Hebrews" enslaved by the Egyptians shared a common religious and ethnic background. This is, of course, the way they are normally regarded within the Judeo-Christian tradition. In reality, Scripture offers hints that the group that escaped with Moses did not share a common inheritance. Referring to the band of Moses' followers in the wilderness, Scripture tells us:

> Now there was a mixed company of strangers who had joined the Israelites. (Num. 11:4)

For several centuries before the Exodus, people from Palestine and Syria had entered Egypt, some as prisoners of war, some who were forced to take up residence by the Egyptians after engaging in activities hostile to Egypt in their home communities, others who were merchants. Not all were slaves, but the situation of all resident aliens tended to deteriorate as time went on. It is thought today that each group within the resident aliens retained something of its own identity, particularly insofar as its religious traditions involved some elements of ancestor worship.[3] As we know, Scripture identifies the resident aliens as "Hebrews," but that name designated a number of peoples who shared a common condition and social location but were of diverse origins.[4] In some respects, the situation of the "Hebrews" had some similarities to that of members of a modern multi-ethnic metropolis, in which diverse groups share common problems in the present but remain distinct from each other because of differences in origin, religion and culture.

When the time came for the escape from Egypt, the "Hebrews" shared a common yearning for liberation and a common hatred of their overlords, but little else. This was enough to unify them so that they could escape. However, as soon as they were beyond the immediate reach of the Egyptians, a compelling basis for unity beyond shared hatred and a desire to escape had to be found if the band of fugitives and outcasts was to survive the natural and human hazards of the wilderness. Fortunately, the escape provided a further shared experience, the exodus itself.

An important function of any new religion that originates in a radical break with past tradition is to facilitate the founding of a community for those who share no community. This was later to be the case with both Christianity and Islam.[5] In any event, there could be only one basis for communal unity in the ancient Near East where the distinction between group membership and religious identity was unknown. The diverse peoples could only become a single people if they were united by a common God. Moreover, the God had to be a new God whose power was greater than that of the Egyptian god-king. It would have been difficult for any of the peoples among the escapees to assert that its particular ancestral god ought to be the God of the entire band without arousing the mistrust and hostility of the others. *The "Hebrews" shared a common historical experience rather than kinship.* Ancestral gods were an impediment to unity. Only a God who was the author of their shared experience could have unified them. Of course, *after* the new God had unified them, it was natural for the assorted peoples to read back elements of continuity between the new God and their ancestral gods. That process is visible in Scripture.[6]

We know that under Moses the new God and the new unity were found. It also appears that, within a relatively short time, the united escapees experienced an extraordinary increase in numbers and energy and that the enlarged group was able to gain control of much of the territory of Palestine and Jordan. The details of the conquest are unimportant for our purposes. What is important is that we understand something of the nature of the new God and his utterly novel relationship to his people.

From the very beginning the followers of this God were convinced that he shared his power with no other being, human or divine. All human power was thought to be subordinate and accountable to his power. Moreover, the new God was thought to exercise his power in a manner that was both rational and ethical. It was rational in that there was nothing gratuitous, arbitrary or purposeless in its exercise; it was ethical in the sense that it was fundamentally concerned with the *well-being of persons* rather than the maintenance of political, social or even religious institutions. His power was also thought to be ethical and rational in the sense that he gave his followers the assurance that there was a predictable and dependable relationship between their conduct and the way he exercised his power over them.

The structure by means of which the new God offered the followers of Moses a secure relationship was, as we have indicated, utterly novel. It resembled a form of treaty that had been used in the ancient Near East, especially among the Hittites, in international relations in order to define the relationship between a suzerain and his vassals. It had, however, never been employed by a God to define his relationship to a people whom he had adopted as his own. This treaty form was that of a *covenant*.[7]

Modern biblical scholarship has given us a relatively accurate picture of the origins of the covenant form. There were two types of covenant, one between equals, and the other the suzerainty type, which was a pact imposed by a powerful lord upon a vassal stipulating what the vassal must do to receive the lord's protection. These Hittite instruments were basically a device for securing binding agreements in international relations. The Hittite overlords were trying to cope with a problem that continues to plague nations to this day. Although there are means of enforcing agreements, once made, within a nation, there is no effective, impartial institution capable of enforcing the keeping of promises between sovereign states if one of the parties to the agreement should conclude that its interest is no longer served by so doing. In such a case, the injured party has no choice but to accept the breach of faith or to resort to military force to enforce the pact. The purpose of the Hittite covenant was to give international agreements a binding character. This was done by the lord binding the vassal by an oath to meet the obligations stipulated in the agreement. An oath is a conditional self-curse, in which the person appeals to his own gods to punish him should he break the agreement. In the ancient Near East, oaths were initially effective in guaranteeing that a promise would be kept. As we know, they lost their effectiveness later on. It could also be said that a covenant was a means of achieving unity of purpose between groups that were bound to each other neither by ties of kinship nor by common ancestral gods. It was this aspect of the covenant that was to prove so important in its use in religion.

According to George Mendenhall, perhaps the preeminent authority on the subject, the Hittite covenants had an elaborate form which was later used in the biblical covenant. Among the elements that are of interest are the following: (a) a preamble identifying the king who was the author of the covenant; (b) a review by the king, speaking in the first person of the past benefits he had bestowed upon the vassal as well as an assertion that these benefits were the basis for the vassal's future obligation to the suzerain. Both in the Hittite documents and the biblical covenant, *historical events* rather than the magic qualities of the lord were the basis of obligation. Since history is the record of the ways in which men have used power that are considered worthy of memory, it was the lord's possession of and past use of power that constituted the basis of obligation; (c) a statement of the precise nature of the obligations incumbent upon the vassal. Moreover, in the Hittite treaties the vassal was explicitly excluded from entering into relationship with any other suzerain, just as in the biblical covenant, Israel is excluded from having any God other than Yahweh.

It is impossible to reconstruct fully what happened at Sinai, but there is no reason to doubt that Moses had a revelatory experience at a sacred desert mountain and that that experience became the basis for a covenant between the new God and the escapees in which the God stipulated the conditions under which he would accept and protect the former slaves as his people. The novelty of the encounter with the new God can be expressed sociologically: Before Sinai there had been high gods, nature gods, ancestral gods and gods of the polis, but there had never been a high God of escaped slaves and declassed fugitives. Moreover, by his election of the outcasts as his people, his "peculiar treasure," he had overturned all existing social hierarchies, in principle if not yet in fact. This was something utterly novel in human history and was to have revolutionary consequences. The Bible does not confirm social hierarchies.

The escapees had witnessed the dark side of Egyptian sacral

kingship, a political system, incidentally, that was not without merits in offering its people a kind of stability and security that is unknown in the modern world. Nevertheless, the escapees had concluded that there were ethical and political values in the Egyptian system that had to be overthrown. Briefly stated, the new tradition asserted the priority of personal ethical values legitimated, as expressions of the will of the God of the covenant, over the primacy of political values. In Egypt, where the ruler was a divinity, the interests of the state had a claim that transcended the claims of any of its subjects. There was, of course, a strong note of social protest in the new values. Escaped slaves, who had been the object of abusive power, were far less likely to give priority to the state's monopoly of force than were members of the ruling class. It is not surprising that oppressed classes have frequently identified themselves with Israel in Egypt and at Sinai. Because the stories of Israel in the wilderness form such a familiar part of our inheritance, we seldom give thought to the socio-political significance of the transformation wrought at Sinai.

Like the Hittite pacts, the Sinai covenant has a prologue in which Yahweh, the divine author, identifies himself and states his past benefits to those with whom he is to enter a covenant. "I am Yahweh your God who has brought you out of Egypt out of the land of slavery" (Ex. 20:2) identifies the author of the covenant, and states the basis of obligation. Just as in the Hittite document, the memory of concrete historical events within the human world is the basis of the vassal's obligation. Similarly, just as the vassal is prohibited from fealty to more than one lord, so the Hebrews are excluded from loyalty to any other God. "You shall have no other gods to set against me . . . for I am Yahweh, your God, a jealous God" (Ex. 20:3-5). Yahweh's insistence on exclusive worship had both political as well as religious import. It united those who accepted it into a community and effectively barred them from giving their loyalty to any of the sacralized kingships of the ancient Near East.

The second set of covenantal obligations dealt not with God but with the relations between man and man. Scholars identify several very old collections in Scripture that offer slightly different accounts of these obligations but in all these collections the *ethical relations between individuals have a priority over both political and cultic values.*[8] Moreover, all accounts of the covenantal obligations are based on a *new conception of the place of power in human affairs.* The functions and the authority that had normally been ascribed to human rulers are depicted in Scripture as the prerogative of God alone.

When, as in ancient Egypt, the ruler is declared to be a god, the state and its institutions are thought of as self-legitimating, a view rejected by Scripture. Where such is the case, whether in ancient sacralized kingdoms or modern secular states, there is no effective limit to the actions that can be committed and legitimated by those who command the political institutions and control the state's monopoly of power. This does not mean that those in command will invariably abuse their power. Nevertheless, when political power is self-legitimating, in principle there is no value or institution that can serve as an effective check on those in command. Even in the United States, with its constitutional system of checks and balances, in a national emergency the normal checks on the executive branch of government can be suspended. The programs of mass enslavement, extermination and expulsion initiated by such governments as Nazi Germany, the Soviet Union, the Cambodian Pol Pot regime, Castro's Cuba and North Vietnam are among the contemporary examples of the extremes to which the exercise of power can go when the authority of the state is regarded as self-legitimating. In the contemporary world, the balance of nuclear terror is the only credible restraint upon sovereign states that recognize no value as overriding their own requirements for security and self-maintenance.

Those who truly accepted the covenant at Sinai as binding upon them rather than as mere pious rhetoric were bound unconditionally by values that transcend and sometimes contradict the state's requirements for self-maintenance. Murder, adultery, theft, false testimony and coveting are forbidden by the covenant, although such categories of behavior can at times become legitimate means of maintaining or enhancing the power of the state. This is evident in the difference between the kind of behavior a state will tolerate in its citizens in peacetime and the kind of behavior it will not only tolerate but reward when carried out by members of its intelligence agencies. Violent behavior, often carried out in stealth, is legitimated as being in the national interest, a claim that cannot easily or realistically be disputed.

The case of the double agent highlights some of the more complex dilemmas of the assertion of the primacy of the interests of the state. In order to establish his credibility, a double agent may have to act as if he were a traitor and even be responsible for the death of many of his fellow citizens. Sometimes governments may knowingly sustain attacks on their own citizens rather than permit an agent to be uncovered. Thus, when the maintenance of the power of the state is self-legitimating, there can be situations in which there is no predictable relationship between the loyalty and trust of citizens and the actions of their government. In ancient times rituals of human sacrifice were a regular part of the life of almost every community. To this day, the state's insistence on human sacrifice, at least in emergency situations, has not and probably cannot entirely be done away with. There are situations even in peace time when the state's requirements for self-maintenance may compel its leaders to endanger or imperil the lives of some of its loyal citizens. Undoubtedly, the age-old belief in the ultimacy of the state's interests provided the rationale for such questionable programs as the Army's secret introduction of dangerously infectuous micro-organisms into the ventilating systems of a number of American cities a generation ago, thereby making innocent citizens involuntary guinea pigs in biological warfare experiments. The list could be multiplied. It includes the involuntary administering of harmful doses of LSD to unknowing citizens by intelligence agents who were curious about the psychological effects of these drugs. As is well known, a number of these experiments resulted in the death of the unknowing subjects. It could be said that the government agents were "playing God" by their abuse of power. There is no doubt that whoever has control over the state's monopoly of force, especially in wartime, does "play God" by virtue of his life-and-death power over others. It is not surprising that ancient man regarded those who possessed such power as gods.

There are no viable alternatives to the idea that the state's requirements for self-maintenance ultimately override all other claims, if not in peacetime then certainly in times of national emergency. Nevertheless, Israel's ancient covenant with Yahweh was an attempt to create just such an effective alternative to the state's claim to ultimacy. By positing a God who possessed neither human image nor human incarnation as the power to whom the community owed its fundamental fidelity, the covenant had the effect of rejecting both the doctrine and the institutions that affirmed the ultimacy of the political order. Moreover, by insisting on the primacy of the ethical over the political in the new community's obligations to its God under the covenant, it set forth a standard that imposed unconditional standards on the behavior of men and nations alike. In addition, there was a harsh corollary to the idea that the community's obligations to its God were based upon the fact that he had redeemed them from Egypt and had constituted them a nation. It followed that if ever the new community failed to meet the ethical and religious obligations of the covenant, their God would withdraw his protection from them and they would be destroyed as a nation. In contrast to the sacralized kingdoms of both ancient and modern times that tend to view their religious traditions as giving assurance that the security and stability of the community is cosmically grounded, Israel's existence as a nation was tentative and conditional on her keeping the covenant.

In the Sinai covenant, many of the most significant features of Israel's later religious life can be discerned. Because of the decisive importance of the Bible for the religious life of America, the values that were embedded within the covenant have been of overwhelming importance to American religious life as well. By subordinating the political order to the obligations of the covenant, the Sinai covenant laid the foundation of the prophetic protest against the ethical and religious abuses of the period of the monarchy as well as the prophetic idea that men and nations alike stand under the judgment of the God of the covenant. Over and over again, Israel's prophets reiterated their warnings that the very survival of the nation was dependent upon its keeping the covenant.[9]

In a country such as the United States in which the Bible has played so central a role in both religious and cultural life, it is not surprising that there are many voices that proclaim that the nation's survival is dependent upon its acting in a way that is acceptable to God. Representative religious figures, such as the Rev. William Sloane Coffin on the left and the Rev. Jerry Falwell on the right, are far closer to each other in their basic theological presuppositions than is generally realized. *Both religious leaders reject the ultimacy of political values* in the life of the nation and insist that the nation must unconditionally subordinate its political interests to a standard which is said to derive its authority and legitimacy from God. Their critique of contemporary American politics has its roots in the prophets' condemnation of Israel's political leaders for their failure to keep the covenant. In Coffin's case, America has failed to keep the covenant by its exploitation of the Third World in the foreign arena and its exploitation of its minorities, largely of Third World origin, at home. For Falwell, and those who think as he does, America's failure is largely to be found in the power of "secular humanism" to destroy American moral life. Both Coffin and Falwell would, of course, insist that they have not subordinated the state's need to maintain itself to religious and ethical values. They would argue that it is in America's political interest to behave in what they regard as a religiously appropriate way, since America's survival depends upon her ability to be a Godly nation. Here again, both men echo the warnings and denunciations leveled by the prophets at Israel's political leaders. Mendenhall has expressed the prophetic message succinctly and accurately:

> . . . The rejection of those ethical controls that were identified with the rule of God and constituted the rejection of God Himself, and therefore the corporate existence brought about by that divine rule could no longer be legitimized by appeal to Yahweh. On the contrary, it must be destroyed as the enemy of Yahweh. But there is nothing in the prophetic message that would prescribe the death

penalty for all persons; rather it is the social institutions of state and temple that must go, once they have ceased to be responsible either to Yahweh or to those in society who most need protection.[10]

If we compare this message to that offered by the religious left and right today, we will notice the similarities.

There is yet another feature of covenant religion which continues to influence American religous thinking about power to this day: When the Assyrians destroyed the Northern Kingdom in 722 BC and the Babylonians destroyed Judea in 586 BC, the prophets saw the national catastrophes as evidence of the majesty and sovereignty of the God of the covenant. Although they could not help but be moved by the disaster that befell their people, they nevertheless saw the terrible events as a vindication of their value-system.[11] It is no exaggeration to say that a certain apocalyptic thread continues to manifest itself in contemporary American life because of the continuing influence of the prophetic theology of power. Sometimes, one discerns in the religious left a kind of guilt-ridden insistence that America does not deserve to survive unless it repents of its alleged past political sins and becomes a leader in the struggle for liberation of the oppressed peoples of the world. Translated into simpler language, the message becomes: A capitalist America deserves to perish. It is not surprising that the religious left has not only been a consistent opponent of mainstream American foreign policy but has had a tendency to take sides with the rivals of the United States in almost every international conflict. Instead of seeing America as seeking to maintain its security in a world in which all nations give priority to their own interests, the left sees capitalist America as rebelling against God by her selfishness. Like such prophets as Jeremiah, who regarded Babylonia's destruction of Jerusalem as God's judgment against a sinful Israel, the religious left has had a tendency to view America's recent defeats as chastisements the country richly deserves.[12] To say the least, this is a highly problematic subordination of the political imperative of national security to a religiously inspired ideology.

A catastrophic and apocalyptic note is also sounded by the religious right. Here the message in its simplest terms is that an unbelieving, unrepentant, un-Christian America is in danger of perishing. Once again, the religious takes priority over the political. There is, however, an important difference between the religious right and left: the religious right does not consistently favor the rivals and opponents of America in every international conflict. Moreover, on national defense issues, the religious right has had a far more realistic understanding of the defense requirements of the United States than has the left.

The perceptions of the religious right also seem more on target than those of their opponents in their claim that there must be a religious basis for community. Here the experience of the Hebrews at Sinai is instructive. Let us recall that the escaped fugitives did not share either common kinship or common religion before Sinai. That which gave them the unity that made their existence as a people viable was their unity in a common God and a common set of obligations. As we have suggested, without that unity they would have been an anomic horde with little possibility of long-term survival. Scripture records a second occasion when a number of previously diverse tribal groups united themselves by accepting the God of the covenant, the meeting at Shechem when Joshua demanded of the tribes that they forsake their ancestral gods and serve Yahweh alone (Joshua 24:1-28). According to contemporary biblical scholarship, on that occasion, the original community of Israel was augmented by the addition of a number of new groups from the land of Canaan.[13] Once more, diverse peoples were able to unify themselves by common service of a single God where there had been no other shared community.

We have already noted that the United States is also a country that includes a very large number of groups of diverse origins. Perhaps no other country in the world has so great a measure of diversity. Unfortunately, in addition to our diversity of origin, we are beset by an absence of any kind of value consensus. Regrettably, without some basis for unity beyond the fact that we all think of ourselves as Americans, there is the danger that the country might splinter apart, not in normal times when sheer inertia prevents national fragmentation, but in times of radical crisis. Historically, common faith or common origin have been the most viable bases for national unity. The religious right intuits that we are in danger of having neither. People who do not share common values are not likely to feel bound by shared obligation. In a time of crisis, the absence of any shared basis of value and community could constitute a national peril.

It is, however, my conviction that the religious right adds to national disunity by its insistence that political leaders be evaluated largely in terms of what the right regards as non-negotiable moral issues, such as abortion, sex education and homosexuality. The real dangers that confront the United States today require that our political leaders be men and women of uncommon ability. To judge their fitness on the basis of single issues, or even on the stand they took on issues a decade ago, as was the case in recent attacks by some members of the religious right against President Reagan's candidate for the office of Justice of the Supreme Court, is to run the risk of excluding capable and dedicated men and women from public office and diverting the attention of the nation from the overwhelmingly difficult economic, diplomatic and military problems that confront it to single issues which, no matter how important they may be, must be weighed in the balance with the other problems that confront us. Moreover, it does not follow that because America requires a non-secular basis for community, we shall find it in the foreseeable future. Although the religious right sees the roots of contemporary moral relativism in what it identifies as secular humanism, even the most elementary study of the history of western civilization will demonstrate that secularism and the religio-ethical problems that attend it have been with us with ever-increasing force since the beginning of the modern period. Events such as the Protestant Reformation, the Enlightenment, and the rise of capitalism all have contributed to the rise of modern secularism. Almost all responsible social theorists have been painfully aware of the dangers of the moral relativism that is an inevitable consequence of secularism.[14] It is, unfortunately, easier to identify a disorder than it is to find an effective cure.

Moreover, while the cure is being sought, there are urgent tasks which await the nation as a whole. Those of us who believe that the internal and external problems confronting our country have grown in severity in recent years cannot rejoice in the kind of divisive politics that has become the style of both the religious left and the religious right.

If the religious right is internally divisive, the religious left is positively myopic when weighing the relative merits of the United States and the Eastern European bloc. Recently, the Central Committee of the World Council of Churches met in Dresden, East Germany, of all places, where it was welcomed by Erich Honecker, the head of the Communist Party of the GDR. According to the liberal *New Republic*, "a practically infallible predictor of who will be singled out by the WCC . . . for condemnation is a country's ideological affinity with the US."[15] Such hostility to the US and willingness to break bread with a leader of one of the most repressive regimes in the Eastern bloc can make sense only to those who long ago committed themselves to a religiously-legitimated political ideology with an inexhaustible fund of apologies for the abuses of left-wing governments and an utter intolerance of even the smallest failings in the capitalist world. Unfortunately, the anti-Americanism of the religious left is more likely to grow stronger for the foreseeable future. Most mainstream religious organizations, including the major denominations and the WCC, are administered bureaucratically. Since bureaucracies tend to be self-perpetuating, once the religious left gains control of a denominational or an organizational bureaucracy, it is very likely to select its decision-making personnel on the basis of the compatibility of their political views with that of those in control of the apparatus.

Both within the religious left and right the conception of power implicit in the biblical covenant continues to exert a powerful influence in our own day. Perhaps, the influence of biblical ideas has never been stronger because of the ability of religious leaders to reach mass audiences through electronic communication. Nevertheless, there may be some serious limitations involved in the unreflective use of biblically-derived norms to evaluate contemporary political decision-making. As we have noted, the covenant accorded primacy to a religiously-legitimated personal ethic over the interests of the state. The covenant implied that, though the state may possess a monopoly on the legitimate use of force within its territory, there is a higher power before whom the state must render account. Unfortunately, this perspective does not allow for a sufficient distinction between the moral standards incumbent upon individuals and those incumbent on the state.

Fifty years ago, Reinhold Niebuhr set forth this distinction in his book *Moral Man and Immoral Society*. Niebuhr criticized the liberals of his day for their failure to discern the difference between "the morality of individuals and the morality of collectives, whether races, classes or nations."[16] Niebuhr held that the distinction between these two moralities often "justifies and necessitates political policies which a purely individual ethic must always find embarassing."[17] An important reason for Niebuhr's distinction is that normally conflicts between individuals can be adjudicated peacefully by an impartial arbiter. There is no impartial arbiter that can be trusted to adjudicate between conflicting nations. States, therefore, must adopt very different modes of behavior than do individuals if they are to survive. This simple distinction has not been taken seriously by either the religious left or the right. It is, of course, understandable that this should be so, since the biblical source of inspiration for their approach to politics implicitly rejects the distinction.

It has been emphasized in this paper that the covenant was functional in its original situation and that it facilitated the creation of a new community for a group of tenuously united fugitives who had been without access to the normal levers of power within an established community. Nevertheless, once the covenant community was established and in possession of its own territorial base, it found itself confronted by the same dilemmas of power and national interest as all of the other kingdoms of the ancient Near East. The Israelite kingdoms had to defend themselves, sometimes by making war, sometimes by making alliances with their neighbors. Often, these alliances were ratified by the marriage of an Israelite king and a pagan princess. The covenant's demand for rendering exclusive homage to Yahweh simply could not be maintained by Israel's rulers without dangerously offending their allies and putting at hazard the security of the state. Of course, the prophets insisted that exclusive fidelity to Yahweh consitituted the real security of the state, but which of us, had we been a ruler, would have deliberately endangered our nation's security in order to meet the prophetic demand for religious exclusivity? Similarly, the prophets accused the kings of favoring the rich over the poor, an accusation that is still heard in the land. Nevertheless, is it not possible that there are times when those who control large resources are a greater source of strength for the state than those who have no competence in the control of resources? It is not my intention to advocate that the rich be favored over the poor. My purpose is to suggest that there are times when the state must make decisions that do not always conform to our customary ideas of what is fair and equitable between individuals.

It is not surprising that, faced with similar political and social problems, the rulers of the Israelite kingdoms began to respond as did the other rulers in the area. Political values, especially the state's fundamental requirement that it maintain its monopoly of force against both internal and external opponents, took precedence over individual ethical values; the religion of the landless, escaped slaves was found to be less functional than the agrarian religion of Canaan to men who now possessed and had to defend their own turf.

We know how the prophets reacted to this development. We also know that the prophets' response formed the basis for much of the contemporary criticism of the state in countries with a strongly biblical culture such as the United States. What we regard as a natural and perhaps inevitable political and social evolution in ancient Israel was regarded by the prophets as unpardonable idolatry for which Israel deserved the worst kind of punishment. It can, however, be said in defense of Israel's rulers that *a very different set of values is necessary to create a community, where none had previously existed, than is required to maintain that community.* As soon as the problems of maintenance displaced those of creation, some means had to be found to legitimate the interests of the state. One can dethrone the old gods when one is rejecting the old order. When one seeks a psychologically effective and cost-effective means of maintaining the new order, there will almost always be the strong impulsion to resacralize political institutions, or at the very least, to ascribe primacy to the state.

It can, of course, be argued that Israel's trust in political institutions proved futile, that both the kingdoms of Israel and Judah fell to the assaults of their enemies. Much of the continuing authority of the prophets came from the fact that their prophecies of doom proved accurate. Nevertheless, it does not follow from the fact that the prophets were correct in predicting disaster that they were also correct in their analysis of its causes. This observation also applies to the contemporary would-be prophets who offer their judgments on American politics. Is it reasonable to believe that the kingdoms of Israel and Judah would have been able to withstand the assaults of the Assyrians and the Babylonians if they had scrupulously maintained the personal and religious obligations of the covenant? What destroyed the two small kingdoms was their relative military weakness. If permitted to develop, such a flaw might some day destroy the United States as well. Undoubtedly, national morale in ancient Israel would have been higher had the prophets' warnings against the exploitation of the poor been heeded, but even a perfectly just Israelite state could not have withstood the assaults that were directed against it.

There is a measure of irony in the fact that the religious values that originated in the needs of escaped slaves have perennially been the basis of so much of the religious criticism of politics in countries with a Judeo-Christian heritage. Yet on reflection, this phenomenon is not so strange. Normally, those who have turned to the prophetic critique of politics have been men and women with no realistic access to decision-making power within the political arena. A hierarchy of values originally formulated by the powerless has been more symmetrical with the condition and social location of most of the religious critics of politics than with those who possess effective means to influence the decision-making process. It is also interesting to note that, when those who use the ethic of the powerless do gain power, they invariably become just as insistent, even ruthless, in maintaining it as those whom they have displaced. They can and do claim that their exercise of power, not excluding murder on a large scale, is in the service of a higher righteousness. How often have we seen that process at work in the revolutions of our own era!

The powerless are always more likely to emphasize individual ethical values than those with power, because their lives are essentially private, whereas those with decision-making power must act in the public realm and must endure the risks and responsibilities of their station. Perhaps the problem of religion and politics in contemporary America can best be summed up by the fact that the majority of Americans have little understanding of the difference between the risks and responsibilities of the public and private realms. That distinction was clearly understood by the Greeks, but it could not have been understood by the escaped slaves at Sinai, for the slave was ever a stranger to the public realm.[18] That is perhaps the final paradox of religion and politics in America. Our religious leaders tend to evaluate the public realm in terms of values that derive from escaped slaves who had no place in the the public realm. But we are incapable of taking seriously the fact that when the descendants of the escaped slaves entered the public realm, they realized the limitations of the slaves' original values. Instead of learning from their experience, we discredit it, because the original experience of the escaped slaves has been decisive in forming our permanent image of mankind's obligations to God. Still, we in America have no choice but to take the awesome responsibilities of the public realm seriously. It is a mistake to evaluate that realm according to norms that are appropriate only between private individuals. We have power in greater measure than any other community has ever had before. Unfortunately, so too do our potential enemies. Perhaps the time has come to reexamine the foundations of the religious critique of American politics.

Notes

1. See George E. Mendenhall, *The Tenth Generation: The Origins of the Biblical Tradition* (Baltimore: 1973), pp. 1-31.
2. See Moshe Greenberg, "The Hab/Piru," *American Oriental Series,* Vol. 39 (New Haven: 1955), pp. 55-57.
3. See Gerhard von Rad, *Old Testament Theology* (London: 1973), Vol. I, pp. 8-9, 20.
4. See Greenberg, "The Hab/piru," loc. cit.
5. On Islam, see Montgomery Watt, *Muhammed at Mecca* (Oxford: 1953), p. 153 ff.
6. See, for example, Exodus 3:13. After God reveals himself to Moses as the God of the Israelites' forefathers, Moses is depicted as asking him, "If I go to the Israelites and tell them, and they ask me his name, what shall I say?" See also Exodus 6:2,3 in which God is depicted as saying to Moses, "I am the Lord. I appeared to Abraham, Isaac and Jacob as God Almighty. But I did not let myself be known to them by the name Yahweh."
7. See article, "Covenant" in *Encyclopedia Judaica* (Jerusalem: 1972), V., 1012-22; George E. Mendenhall, *Law and Covenant in Israel and the Ancient Near East* (Pittsburgh: 1955).
8. On the collections in Scripture that are said to derive from the encounter at Sinai, see von Rad, *Old Testament Theology,* Vol. I, pp. 187 ff. On the ethical character of the contents, see Mendenhall, *The Tenth Generation,* pp. 29, 30.
9. For a comprehensive discussion of the theology of covenant in the Bible, see Dennis J. McCarthy, S.J., *Old Testament Covenant* (Richmond, Va.: 1972).
10. Mendenhall, *The Tenth Generation,* p. 30.
11. See Article, "Prophecy," *The New Encyclopedia Britannica* (1981), Vol. 1, p. 645.
12. Jeremiah 26:1—24 describes Jeremiah's prophecies of doom and the reaction of his hearers.

13. See George Mendenhall, "The Hebrew Conquest of Palestine" in *The Biblical Archaeologist Reader* (Garden City, N.Y.: 1970), pp. 25-53.

14. See Anthony Giddens, *Capitalism and Modern Social Theory* (Cambridge, Ma.: 1971), pp. 178-184.

15. Charles Krauthammer, "Holy Fools" in *The New Republic*, September 9, 1981, pp. 10-13. For a discussion of the movement towards an anti-American bias on the part of the WCC, see Ernest W. Lefever, *Amsterdam to Nairobi: The World Council of Churches and the Third World* (Washington: 1979).

16. Reinhold Niebuhr, *Moral Man and Immoral Society* (New York: 1932), p. XI.

17. Niebuhr, *Moral Man,* loc. cit.

18. See Hannah Arendt, *The Human Condition* (Chicago: 1958) pp. 22 ff. and Giddens, op. cit., pp. 178-84.

INDEX